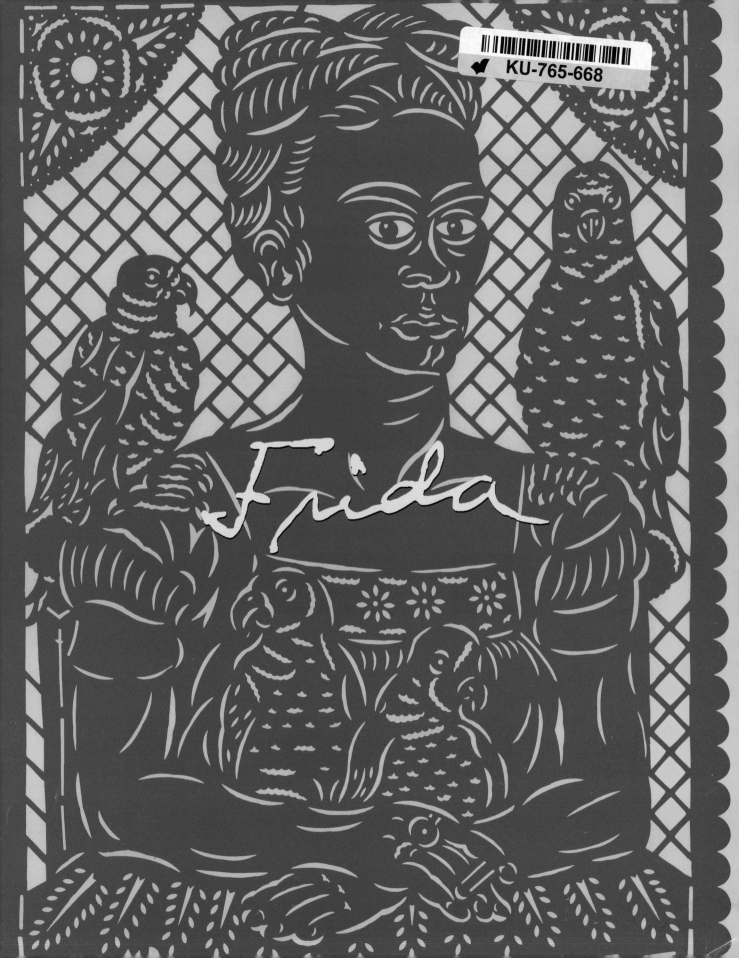

Frida

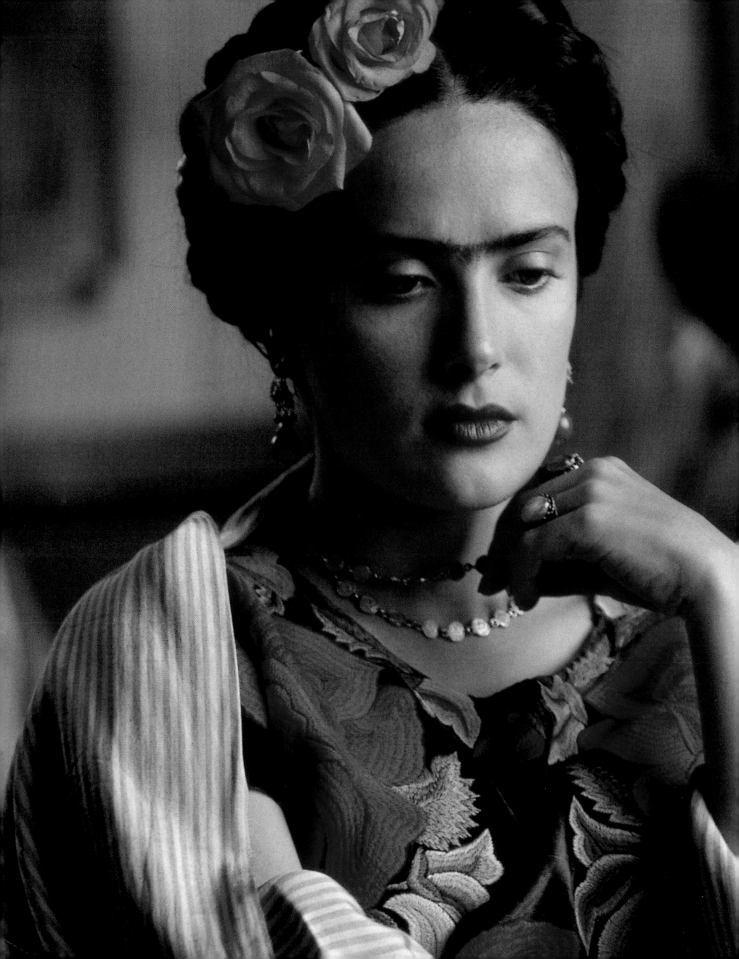

Frida

FOREWORD BY
HAYDEN HERRERA

INTRODUCTION BY
JULIE TAYMOR

INTRODUCTION BY
SALMA HAYEK

STILL PHOTOGRAPHS BY
PETER SOREL

ADDITIONAL PHOTOGRAPHS BY
RODRIGO PRIETO

BASED ON THE BOOK BY **HAYDEN HERRERA**

SCREENPLAY BY
CLANCY SIGAL AND **DIANE LAKE** AND **GREGORY NAVA** & **ANNA THOMAS**

EDITED BY
LINDA SUNSHINE

DESIGNED BY
TIMOTHY SHANER

POCKET
BOOKS

PUBLISHED BY SIMON & SCHUSTER
LONDON · SYDNEY · NEW YORK · TOKYO · SINGAPORE · TORONTO

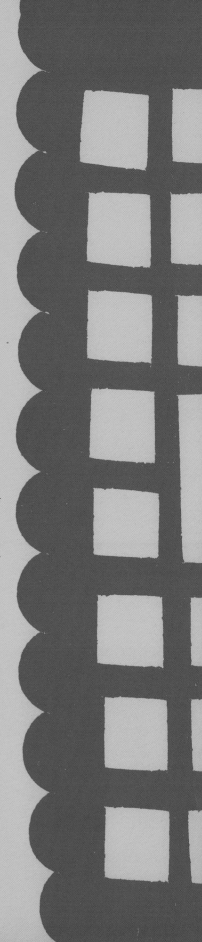

Manufactured in the United States of America.

Design by Timothy Shaner.

POCKET BOOKS
Simon & Schuster UK Ltd.
Africa House
64-78 Kingsway
London
WC2B 6AH

www.simonsays.co.uk

First Pocket Books edition 2002

A CIP catalogue record for this book is available from the British Library

ISBN 0-7434-6807-4

ACKNOWLEDGMENT OF PERMISSIONS: We are grateful to the publishers and other copyright holders named below for permission to reprint artwork and excerpts from these previously published works. Excerpts and artwork appear on the pages listed.

EXCERPTS: **Page 158:** Malka Drucker, *Frida Kahlo.* © 1991 by Malka Drucker. Used by permission of Bantam Dell Publishing Group. 58, 62, 89: Pete Hamill, *Diego Rivera.* © 1999 by Pete Hamill. Used by permission of Harry N. Abrams. 25, 41, 43, 54, 60, 68, 76, 89, 90, 96, 99, 110, 111, 121, 148, 154: Hayden Herrera, *Frida: A Biography of Frida Kahlo.* © 1983 by Hayden Herrera. Used by permission of HarperCollins Publishers, Inc. 32, 46, 86, 122, 139, 158: Hayden Herrera, *Frida Kahlo: The Paintings.* © 1991 by Hayden Herrera. Used by permission of HarperCollins Publishers, Inc. 7, 9, 14, 38, 40, 44, 57, 58, 75, 88, 92, 95, 107, 113, 114, 122, 133, 145, 151, 157: Frida Kahlo, *The Diary of Frida Kahlo.* © 2002 Banco de México Diego Rivera and Frida Kahlo Museums Trust. Av. Cinco de Mayo No. 2, Col. Centro, Del. Cuauhtémoc 06059, México, D.F. Reproduccion autorizada por el Instituto Nacional de Bellas Artes y Literatura. Used by permission of Harry N. Abrams. 62, 83: Patrick Marnham, *Dreaming with His Eyes Open: A Life of Diego Rivera.* © 2000 by Patrick Marnham. Used by permission of Knopf Publishing Group. 96, 139: Diego Rivera, *My Art, My Life.* Dover Publications, 1992.

ARTWORK: All paintings © 2002 Banco de México Diego Rivera and Frida Kahlo Museums Trust. Av. Cinco de Mayo No. 2, Col. Centro, Del. Cuauhtémoc 06059, México, D.F. Reproduccion autorizada por el Instituto Nacional de Bellas Artes y Literatura. 1, 158: Papel picado card by Fernando Sanchez. Courtesy of Gusano de Luz. 6: *Self-Portrait with Monkeys*, 1943, by F. Kahlo. Courtesy of the Vergel Foundation. 8: Photo courtesy of AP/Wide World Photos. 10-11: Photo © 2002 by Annie Leibovitz. 12: Photo courtesy of Bettmann/CORBIS. 16: Photo courtesy of Bettmann/CORBIS. 33: Photo by Guillermo Kahlo, 1926. Courtesy Isolda Kahlo. 38: *The Bus*, 1929, by F. Kahlo. Copyright Schalkwijk/Art Resource NY. Fundacion Dolores Olmedo, Mexico City, D.F, Mexico. 51: *Portrait of Christina Kahlo*, 1928, by F. Kahlo. © Christie's Images/CORBIS.

62: *Portrait of Tina Modotti*, 1926, by D. Rivera. Philadelphia Museum of Art. Purchased: Lola Downin Peck Fund from the Estate of Carl Zigrosser. Photo by Joan Broderick, 1984. 63: *Portrait of David Alfaro Siqueiros*, 1921, by D. Rivera. Museo Diego Rivera, INBA, Guanajuato. 67: Photographer unknown. 73: *Frida and Diego Rivera*, 1931, by F. Kahlo. Courtesy of San Francisco Museum of Modern Art, Albert M. Bender Collection, Gift of Albert M. Bender. Photo by Ben Blackwell. 76: Photo courtesy of Peter A. Juley & Son Collection, Smithsonian American Art Museum. 79: *Portrait of Guadalupe*, 1926, by D. Rivera. The Vassar College Gallery of Art, anonymous loan. 95: *Henry Ford Hospital*, 1932, by F. Kahlo. Copyright Schalkwijk/Art Resource, NY. Fundacion Dolores Olmedo, Mexico City, D.F, Mexico. 99: Photograph by Juan Gúzman. 105: *What the Water Gave Me*, 1938, by F. Kahlo. Copyright Schalkwijk/Art Resource, NY. Coll. Isadore Ducasse, Fine Arts, New York, NY, USA. 107: *My Dress Hangs There*, 1933, by F. Kahlo. Courtesy of Christie's Images, New York/SuperStock, Inc. 112: *Self-Portrait with Cropped Hair*, 1940. Collection of the Museum of Modern Art, New York. Gift of Edgar Kaufman, Jr. Photograph courtesy of Hayden Herrera. 115: *A Few Small Nips*, 1935, by F. Kahlo. Copyright Schalkwijk/Art Resource, NY. Fundacion Dolores Olmedo, Mexico City, D.F, Mexico. 118: Photo © Bettmann/CORBIS. 122: *Memory*, 1937, by F. Kahlo. © Christie's Images/CORBIS. 123: *The Suicide of Dorothy Hale*, 1939, by F. Kahlo. Collection of Phoenix Art Museum, gift of an anonymous donor. Photograph by Craig Smith. 141: *The Two Fridas*, 1939, by F. Kahlo. Museo Nacional de Arte Moderno, Instituto Nacional de Bellas Artes, Mexico City, D.F, Mexico. Courtesy of Schalkwijk/Art Resource, NY. 145: *The Broken Column (detail)*, 1944, by F. Kahlo. Courtesy of Schalkwijk/Art Resource, NY. 146: Photo courtesy of Isolda Kahlo. 148: Photo © Bettmann/CORBIS. 151: From Frida Kahlo's diary. Collection of the Frida Kahlo Museum Mexico City. Photograph by Bob Schalkwijk. 152: Photo © Gisele Freund/Photo Researchers. 156: *The Dream*, 1940, by F. Kahlo. Private collection, New York. Photo courtesy of Hayden Herrera.

The publisher has made every effort to contact copyright holders; any errors or omissions are inadvertent and will be corrected upon notice in future reprintings.

Contents

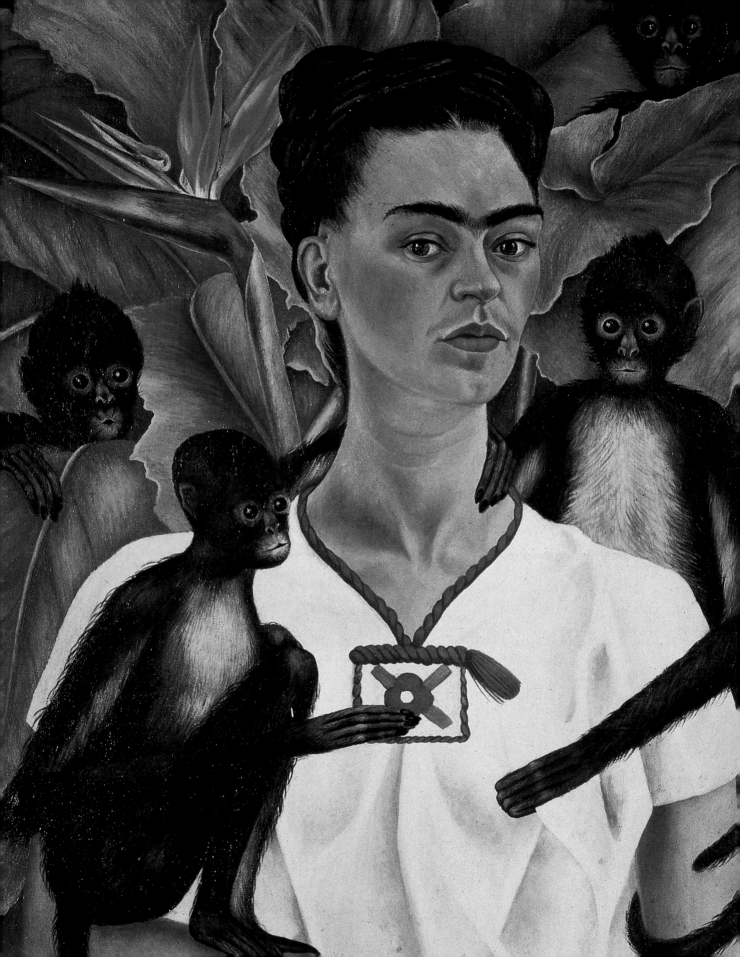

An Artist by Default
by Hayden Herrera

When a friend gave Frida Kahlo (1907–54) her first exhibition in her native Mexico, most of those who attended the opening came out of loyalty to Frida, not out of admiration for her paintings. Since that time, the originality and power of Kahlo's work have been recognized, and she has become an international cult figure. Very likely she would have both laughed at and reveled in the attention: by painting her own image again and again Kahlo tried to attach people to her and to make her reality known.

Frida Kahlo became an artist by default. She planned to be a doctor, but in 1925 the bus she was riding home from school was rammed by a streetcar, and Kahlo almost died from injuries that left her a partial cripple and unable to bear children. While convalescing at home the following year she began to paint. Her self-portraits, many of which show her encased in orthopedic corsets, undergoing a surgical operation, or even having a miscarriage, helped Kahlo to confront and to exorcise pain. Painting the image she saw in the mirror also reinforced what she felt to be her tenuous hold on life.

In 1929 Kahlo began to suffer another kind of pain when she married the renowned muralist Diego Rivera, a man nearly twice her age and size. Although he adored Frida and was a great support for her art, the anguish prompted by his constant philandering would reappear in her paintings. Usually Frida scoffed at Rivera's affairs, but when he seduced her younger sister, she left him for several months in 1935. Then in 1939 Rivera divorced Kahlo for a year before remarrying her in San Francisco. To record this kind of suffering, Frida portrayed herself weeping, cracked open, and with her heart extracted and bleeding. In one painting cupids seesaw on a ferrule that penetrates the gap left by her extracted heart. Other times

LEFT: Self-Portrait with Monkeys, *1943.*

> *Astonished she remained seeing the sun-stars and the live-dead world and being in the shade*
>
> —FRIDA KAHLO

she painted herself with a miniature portrait of Rivera on her forehead: he was the constant intruder in her thoughts. Frida Kahlo retaliated with love affairs of her own, most notably with the Russian revolutionary Leon Trotsky.

Miramax's choice of Julie Taymor to direct a film about Frida Kahlo was a brilliant stroke. Here was a director with the same fierce energy and intelligence as Kahlo herself, and Taymor also had just the right mixture of imagination and sardonic wit to keep Frida's story from turning into a melodrama. For all my confidence in Taymor, I attended a preview of *Frida* full of trepidation. What if I didn't believe in the Kahlo that Taymor and the actress Salma Hayek had invented? What if the screenplay, based on my biography of Frida, gave a false picture of Kahlo's life? As I watched the film, all my fears dissolved. The Frida who came to life on film was separate from the Frida in the pages of my book; she was a new creation, and so I was free to be deeply moved by her story. I also laughed: Taymor gave the film a light touch without losing depth and without ignoring Kahlo's dark side. Most important, she had the wisdom not to try to convey the crucial action of Kahlo's life—making paintings—by placing the artist before her easel and having her look intense as her brush slowly brought forth an image. Instead, Taymor suggested the creative process by moving imaginatively between Kahlo's paintings and the events and feelings that prompted them. Going beneath the skin of Frida's story, Taymor conveyed the meaning of Kahlo's fantastical imagery from the inside out. As a result we actually see and feel the vital link between Frida Kahlo's art and life.

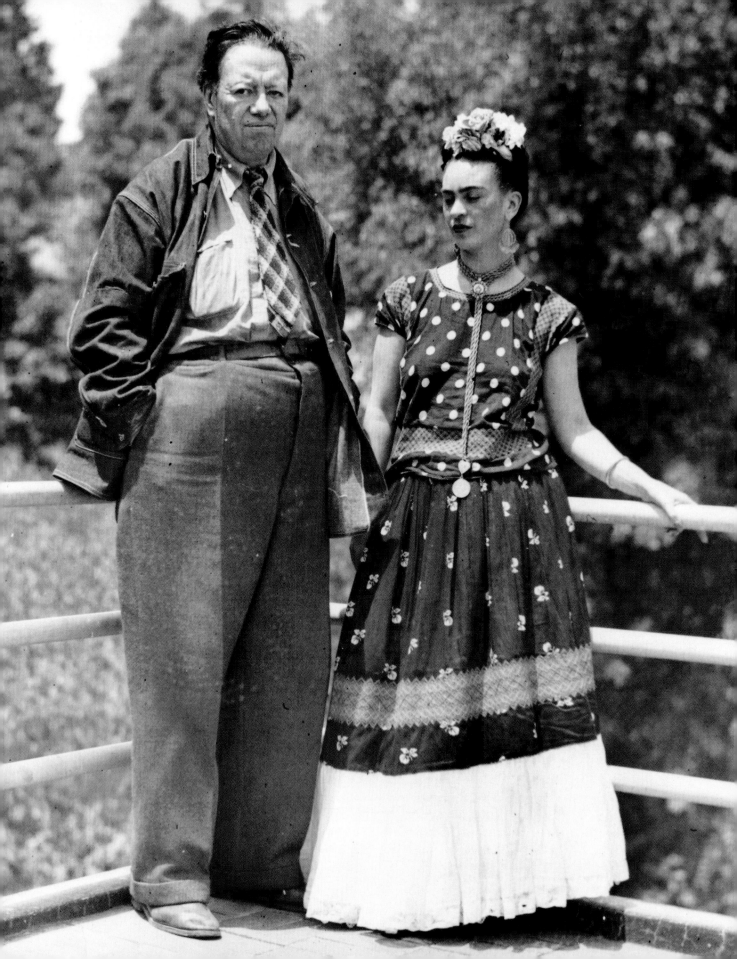

Director's Notes
by Julie Taymor

A biopic about Frida Kahlo was not a project that instantly attracted me as a director. Most films on artists' lives drown in angst, grotesque behavior and impossible suppositions on how and why the artist creates. On delving into the screenplay and the biographies of Kahlo, however, I found a different kind of story that offered unusual insight into not only the creative impulses of a truly unique woman artist, but also into one of the most passionate and complex love stories of our time. Another draw to the project was the character of Frida herself. Contrary to popular theories that chose to latch on to the icon of Frida as a victim, a St. Sebastian for the "feminist" movement, I discovered an exuberant woman: humorous, foulmouthed, erotic, tenacious, fearless and entirely feminine without sacrificing a potent sense of self-determination. Frida created herself as an icon with whatever means she had. She celebrated her lament with humor and irony as she blended her physical and emotional landscape into a way of living.

Thirty years of Frida's life are covered in the span of a two-hour film. Many choices had to be made on what to include in this epic tale of love, art and politics.

THE PAINTINGS

The question of how to show the artist creating her paintings was helped by the fact that most of Frida's work is autobiographical; you can place it to the specific events of her life; her relationship to illness, love, death

LEFT: Diego and Frida at their home in San Angel, April, 1939.
RIGHT: Salma Hayek and Julie Taymor on location during filming.

I am writing to you with my eyes.

—FRIDA KAHLO

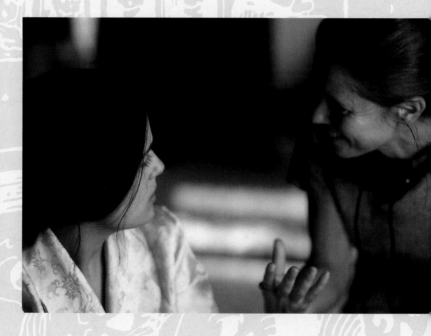

and traditional Mexican folk art. She has said that her paintings were her reality, that they tell the truth as thoroughly experienced.

In conceptualizing the film, I envisioned juxtaposing period realism with a naïve and surreal approach to what could be called 3-D live paintings. Elements of her paintings would unfold before your eyes as Frida was experiencing them in a both literal and subconscious manner. An example of this blending is evident in the New York sequence.

First, I decided to establish New York, and in fact what "America" meant to Diego and Frida, in a black-

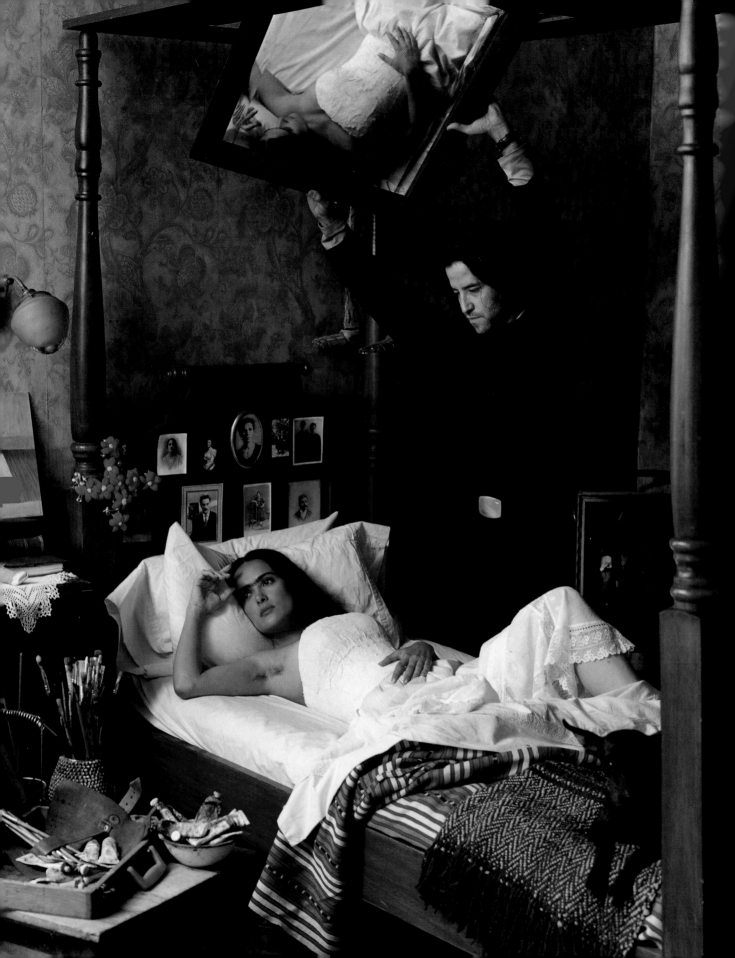

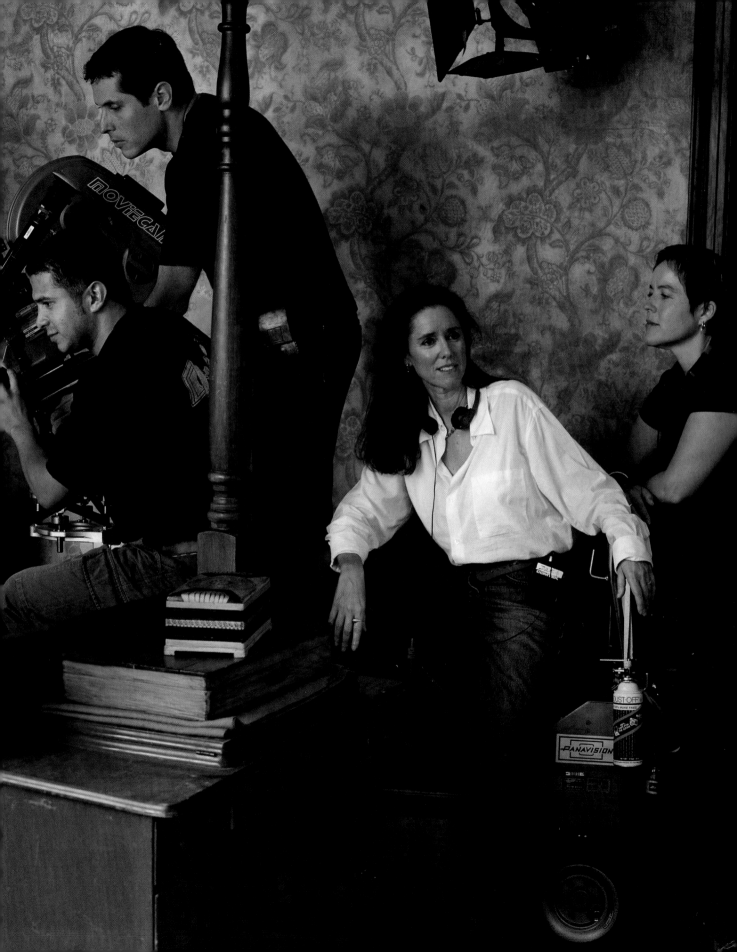

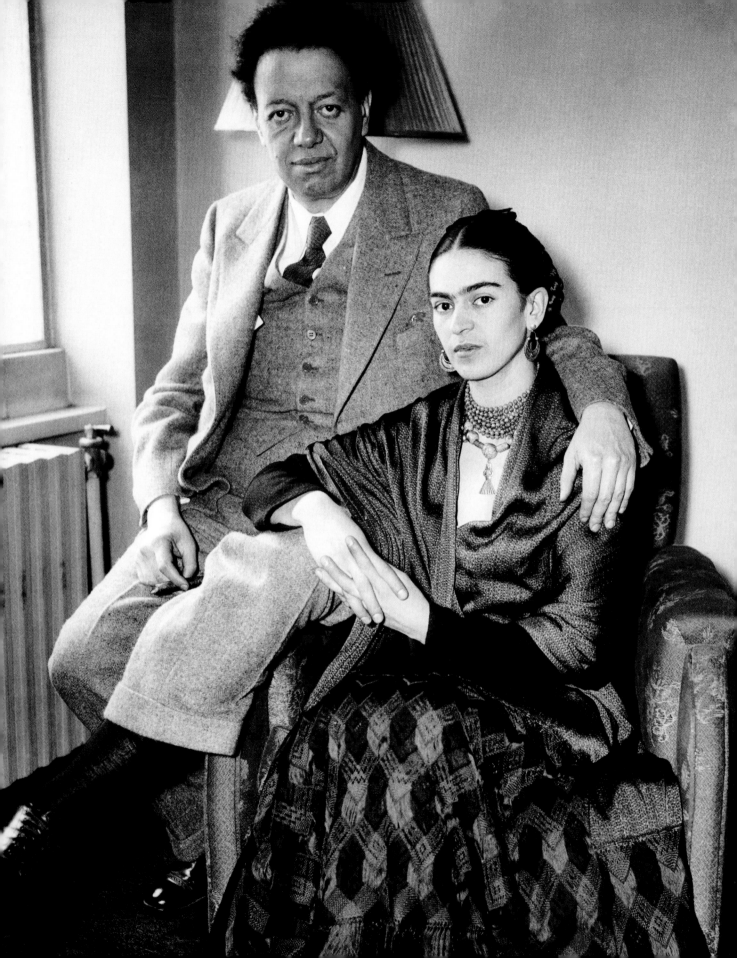

and-white photographic collage. Not having the budget to shoot in New York (the entire film was shot in Mexico) pushed us to be creative in the Frida style. With the help of Amoeba Proteus, a special effects company, we designed a scroll like Russian constructivist poster art, emblematic of the period. Frida's scribbling as she orates her letter to her sister highlights the collage in the manner of her diary doodles. We used documentary photos as well as film footage of the actual trips they took to Detroit, for example, to create the breadth of their journey with minimal means. This collage technique was used in Frida's painting, *My Dress Hangs There.*

In discovering through the biographies that Frida was attracted to the movies, especially the horror and comic genres, I decided to use a trip to the movie house to see *King Kong* as a metaphorical way of expressing her experience with Diego in New York. Diego's conquering of New York as well as his subsequent demise after the Rockefeller mural disaster is enacted first in a fantasy invasion of the actual film, *King Kong*, where, through her imagination, she plants herself as the unwitting femme in the hands of the monster. Through this device we experience, through humor and irony, Frida's ambivalence over the tremendous success and subsequent transformation of her husband in New York. Later, in Frida's daydreams that were drawn from the two paintings, *The Suicide of Dorothy Hale* and *What the Water Gave Me*, we see the outcome of that New York experience via her singular imagination. As she soaks in her tub, a primitively animated vision of King Kong falling from the top of the Empire State Building completes the tale of Diego's fall from grace. As Diego storms out the

LEFT: Diego and Frida in Mexico City, 1938. RIGHT: Salma Hayek and Alfred Molina as Frida and Diego. PREVIOUS PAGES: Annie Leibovitz photograph, shot on location in Mexico. From left: Salma Hayek as Frida, production designer Felipe Fernández del Paso, first assistant cameraman Arturo Casteñada, director of photography Rodrigo Prieto, director Julie Taymor, and producer Sarah Green.

door, after a violent argument with Frida about returning to Mexico, we follow her eyes as they take us outside of their New York tenement apartment window. Hanging from a clothesline in the midst of a snowy, bleak New York City skyline floats Frida's brightly colored tehuana dress. The surreal aspect of this vision is that the dress seems to be inhabited by an invisible but dimensional body, a reference, again, to *My Dress Hangs There.*

In essence, we have experienced aspects of three of Frida's paintings as they played themselves out in her

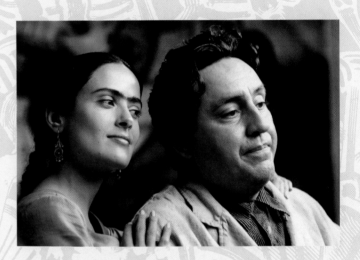

story while the actual paintings themselves will not make their appearance in the film until many scenes later, when Trotsky and Breton peruse the canvases in her studio. Hopefully, at this moment, the audience will see the paintings on a much deeper level having experienced the abstract seeds of their creation. *Frida and Diego Rivera (The Wedding Portrait), Self-Portrait with Cropped Hair, The Two Fridas, The Broken Column* and *The Dream* are some of the other works that I charted during the course of Frida's tale. Each was approached with a different style and makes its way into the film from a specific emotional event that serves as a catalyst. These events of her life's narrative are a surface reality, barely hinting at a subtext far more complex and harrowing as revealed in the paintings.

In spite of my long illness,
I feel immense joy in LIVING.

—FRIDA KAHLO, FROM HER DIARY,
FRIDAY, 30 JANUARY 1953

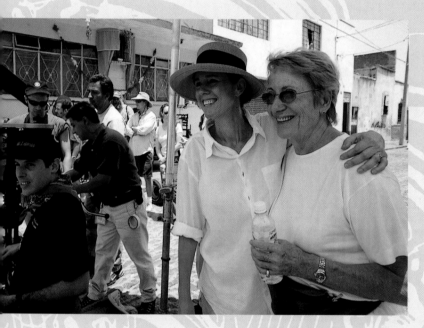

I didn't want to do another
painter-angst movie. Pain is there
but pleasure is equally there.

—JULIE TAYMOR, *Vogue*

DIEGO AND FRIDA

The love story of an "elephant and a dove," who at other times, were called "sacred monsters" is a turbulent ride through passion, abuse and dedication. Frida and Diego, on the surface, couldn't be more at odds, outrageous in their physical scale and age differences. Artistically, he was a muralist, chronicling the political and social milieu of the times, while she was a miniaturist, painting the interior landscape of her soul. They were perfect complements to one another and instead of the potential competition between artist couples, these two admired and supported each other.

The crux of the conflict, then, in this unusual love story can be summed up in the concept of "loyalty versus fidelity." Frida willingly married a man whom she knew could not be sexually faithful. She, instead, demanded "loyalty," and he promised to deliver. This subtle difference between these two principles is rarely delineated in contemporary Western society, particularly American, where a presidency practically fell to issues of infidelity. Frida managed somehow to deal with Diego's protean sexual appetite; she even took some of his lovers as her own. But the question of loyalty was breached when it came to Diego's affair with Frida's sister, Cristina. The relationship was severely damaged, almost irreparably. And yet, the power of the Frida/Diego story is that the true depth of their love managed to transcend the broken promises, the numerous infidelities on both parts, the tempests, the separations and ultimately a divorce. In the last years of Frida's life, when she was sick, bedridden and dependent on morphine—even then Diego came back to her. They truly couldn't live without one another.

ABOVE: Julie Taymor and her close friend and colleague, film editor François Bonnot, on location in Mexico. RIGHT: Cast and crew filming in the courtyard of the Blue House. The scene takes place following Frida's catastrophic accident.

THE PERIOD AND THE PLACE

Mexico in the twenties, thirties and forties is an exciting backdrop to Frida's story. The avant-garde artists were socially committed, cosmopolitan and at the forefront of international debate on the role of the artist in politics and culture. Diego and Frida bridged the European movements with a newly found appreciation for the indigenous Mexican forms of ceremony, music and art. Though communist, Frida was drawn to the reli-

center and other New York locals were built at Estudios Churubusco Azteca. San Luis Potosi doubled for old Mexico City in the bus crash sequence. The actual locations of the preparatory school, Chapingo Chapel, the pyramids of Teotihuacán, the house at San Angel, the Ministry of Education, and so on were used with the permission and tremendous support of the Mexican authorities.

We had ten six-day weeks to shoot the film, an exhausting but thoroughly exhilarating experience. The

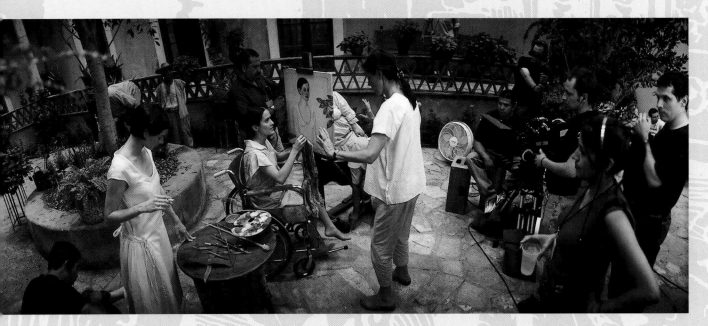

gious folk art, the retablos, for inspiration, even though her approach was irreligious. Tina Modotti, David Siqueiros, Leon Trotsky, and Nelson Rockefeller are just a few of the major figures of the time woven into the film's drama.

THE SHOOT

Though the story travels from Mexico City in 1922 to New York and Paris through the next two decades, we shot the entire film on location and constructed sets in Mexico. The Art Nouveau architecture of the city of Puebla was perfect to suggest Paris. Art Deco sets of Rockefeller

almost entirely Mexican crew was brilliant, hard working and, most importantly, fun. The actors who came from all corners of the earth were impassioned and talented. The post-production team in the editorial, sound and music departments delivered beyond my expectations. But it is Salma Hayek who made me truly want to do this film and whose performance and passion, both on and off the set so inspired me. Her grueling six-year saga of bringing Frida's story to the screen is a testament to her vision, tenacity and faith that she could make it happen. I am proud to have joined her for the ride.

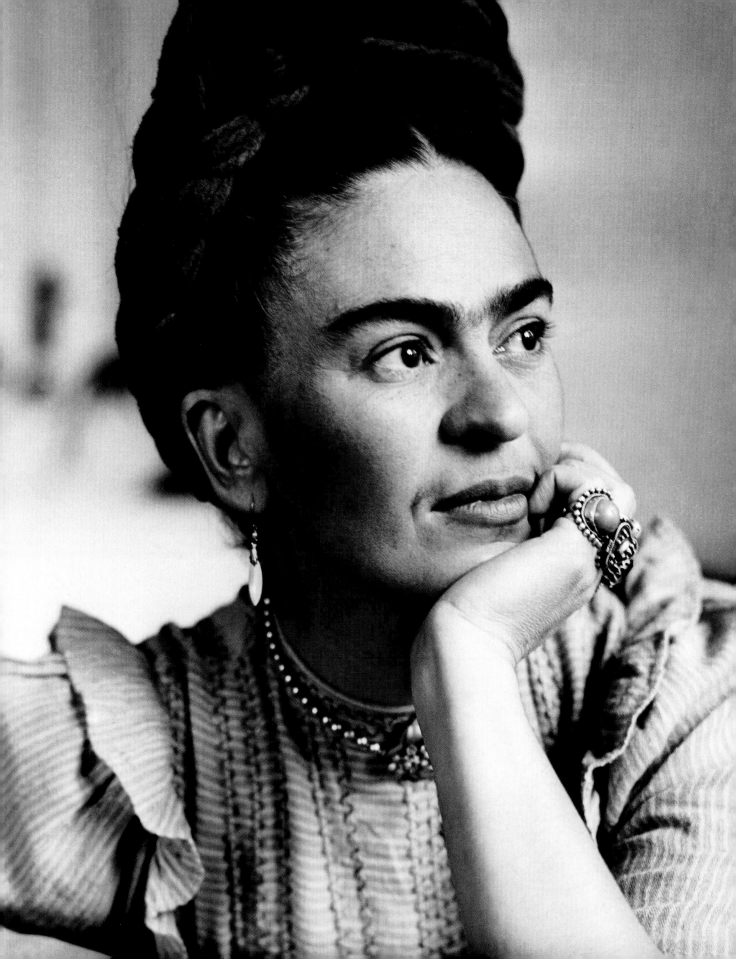

The Passion of Frida Kahlo

by Salma Hayek

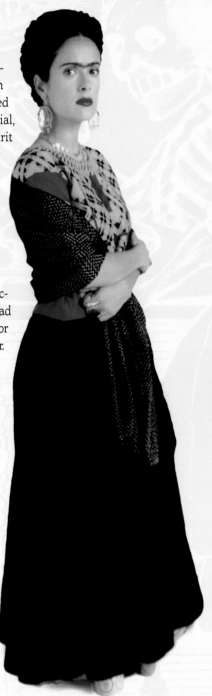

Frida tells the story about a courageous and fascinating Mexican woman who wholeheartedly lived every second of her controversial, unique and tormented life. Her colorful spirit inspired me; her passion made me passionate. Her provocative and unconditional relationship with Diego Rivera and her unusual and vibrant vision, as seen through her art, are testament that Frida Kahlo was and still is ahead of her time. Her life story is not only cinematic; it transcends time and captures the essence of her surrealistic approach to art and life.

To film this story, we needed a visionary director. Finding that person took many years. I had always hoped that we could find a female director for the film, and I was always a fan of Julie Taymor. I knew that Julie would make a beautiful and very visual film but after our first meeting, I realized that she understood Frida's vision of the world more deeply than anyone else I had met. Julie also understood Mexico. I was impressed with her knowledge of my country—our culture, music, folklore, and even our food. The more time I spent with her, the more I was convinced that Julie Taymor was the perfect director for the film I had dreamed about for so many years. Julie, like Frida, is a passionate artist with conviction, not afraid to have an unconventional vision and definitely not afraid to fight for it. I was convinced that combining Frida

LEFT: Photo of Frida Kahlo showing her elaborately braided hair, an image that appears in many of her self-portraits, 1944.

17

Kahlo's life story with the extraordinary cast that came together, the wonderful crew we assembled in Mexico, the support of Miramax and Julie's genius would result in a provocative, touching and visually stimulating film. My dream came true—a dream that started years ago, although my adoration of Frida began long before that.

The first time I saw a painting by Frida Kahlo, I was fourteen years old. A friend of mine showed me a book with these bloody paintings, which I thought were just horrendous. But the images haunted me, and I would return to my friend's house and ask, "Can

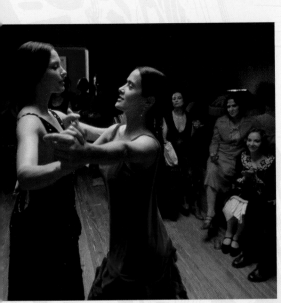

you show me those horrible pictures again? I want to see that one with the head sticking out of the vagina." And so, in the beginning, I was both horrified and intrigued; then slowly, I fell deeply in love with Frida Kahlo and her work, and she has been in my life ever since. She has also ignited the fascination of those closest to me.

When the script needed to be re-written, we were challenged to find a writer who would bring together all the disparate elements of Frida's story. It was a love story, but one that took place in a specific time and place—socially, politically and artistically. Edward Norton stepped in and delivered a brilliant screenplay. Julie and Edward had a great working relationship of mutual respect and understanding. He was clear on her vision of the film and was able to integrate her innovative visual images organically in the story. He wrote at night since he was acting in another movie during the day. He hardly ever slept. It was a very difficult task, and although he was familiar with Frida Kahlo and Diego Rivera, he undertook a great deal of new research. In addition to Edward's uncredited role as screenwriter, he also plays a cameo as Nelson Rockefeller.

I expected to make a movie that would say something fantastic about Mexico, a movie about an extraordinary woman. However, I did not know *Frida* would surround me with the love and support of artists and friends whose talent and grace touched me in ways I will never forget. In a very personal and profound way, that gift was more fulfilling than the realization of my original dream.

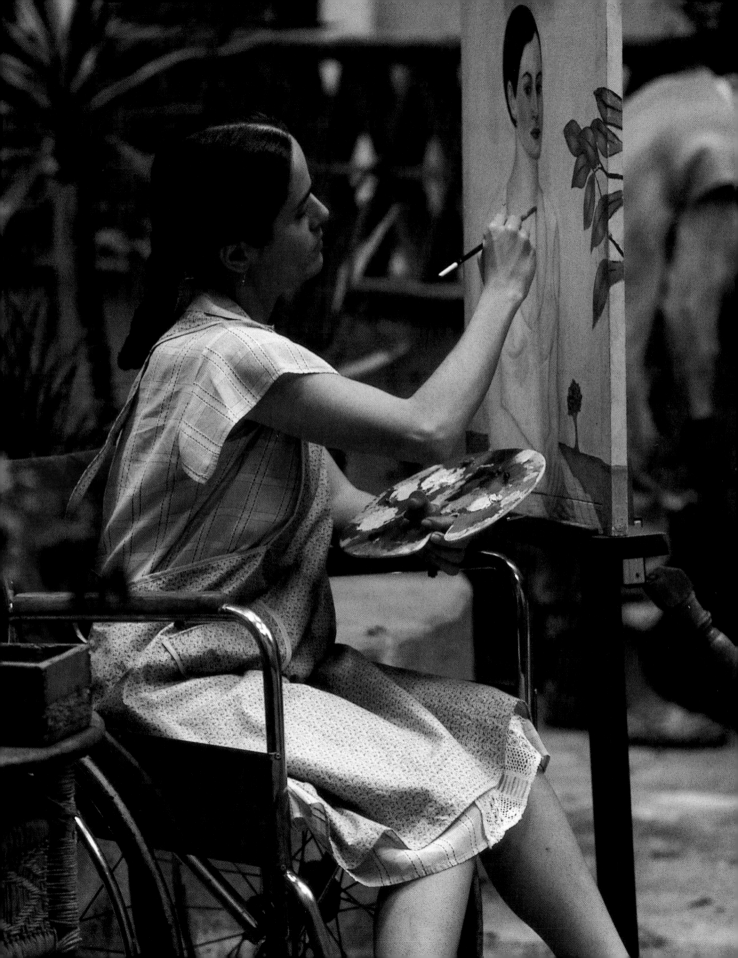

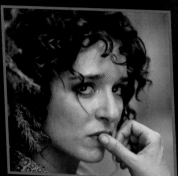

Valeria Golino
(Lupe Marín)

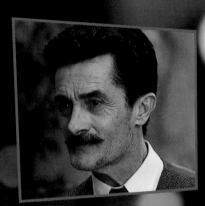

Roger Rees (Frida's father)

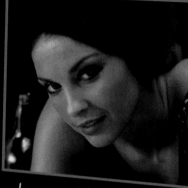

Ashley Judd (Tina Modotti)

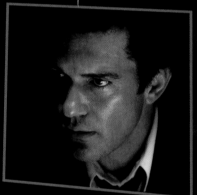

Antonio Banderas
(David Siqueiros)

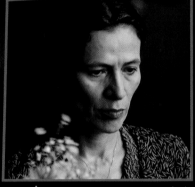

Patricia Reyes Spindola
(Frida's mother)

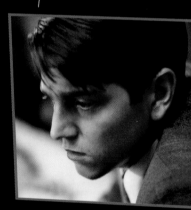

Diego Luna
(Alejandro)

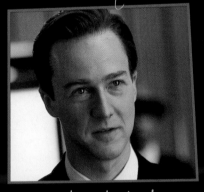

Edward Norton
(Nelson Rockefeller)

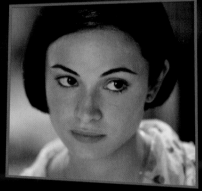

Mia Maestro
(Cristina Kahlo)

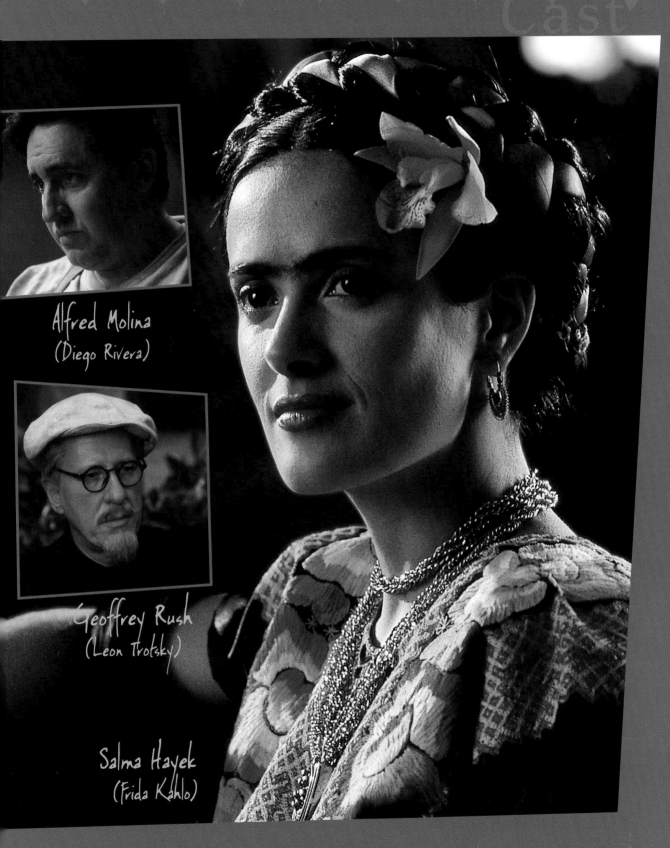

Alfred Molina
(Diego Rivera)

Geoffrey Rush
(Leon Trotsky)

Salma Hayek
(Frida Kahlo)

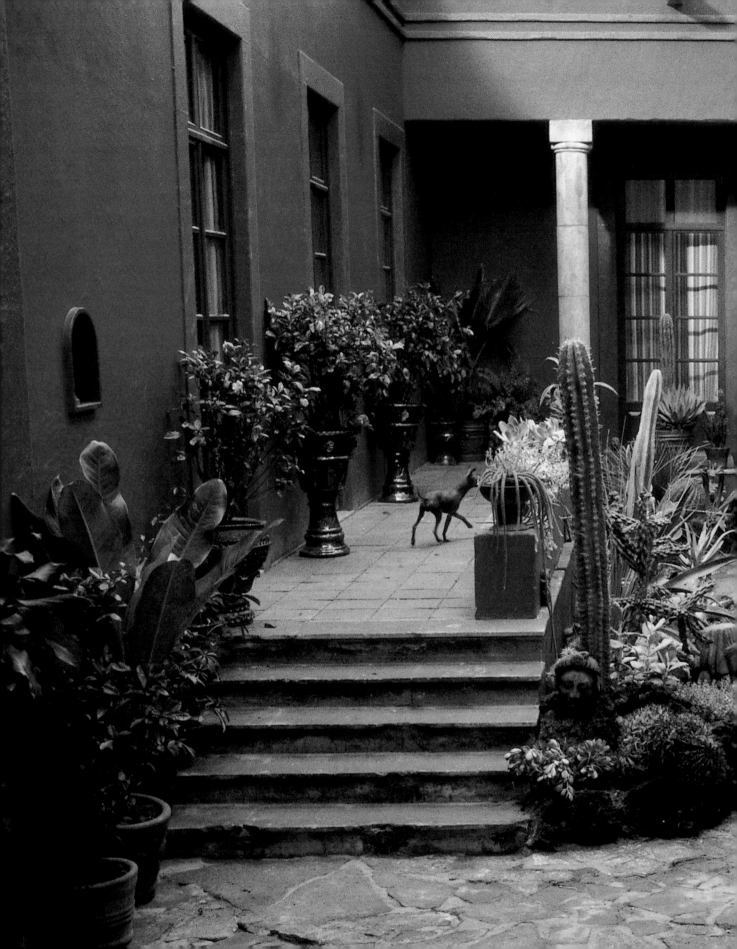

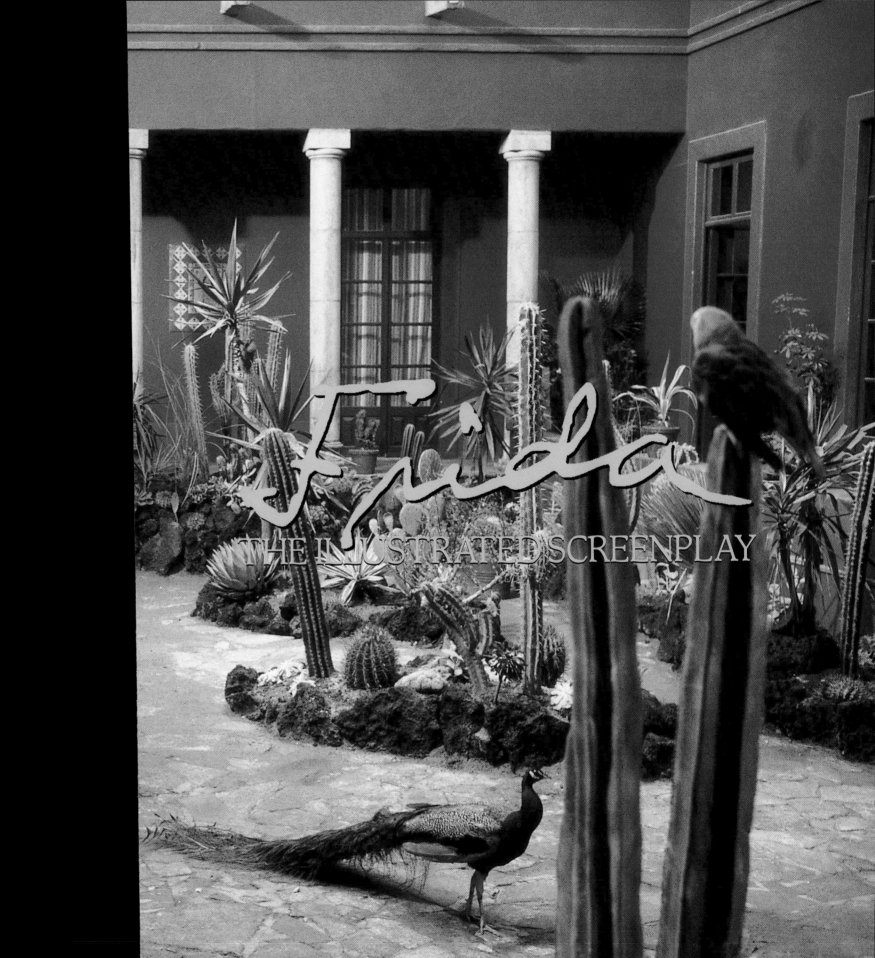

Frida
THE ILLUSTRATED SCREENPLAY

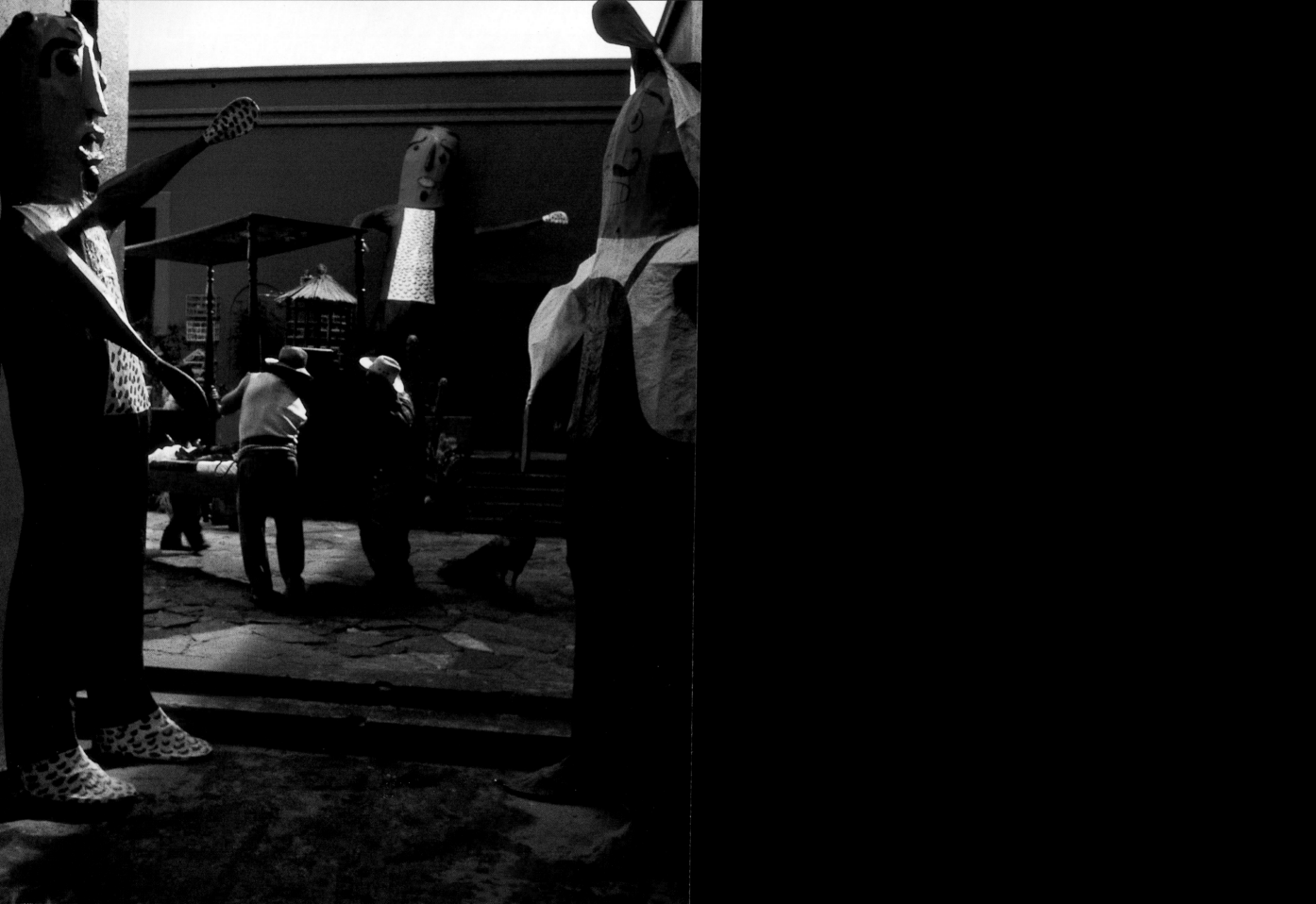

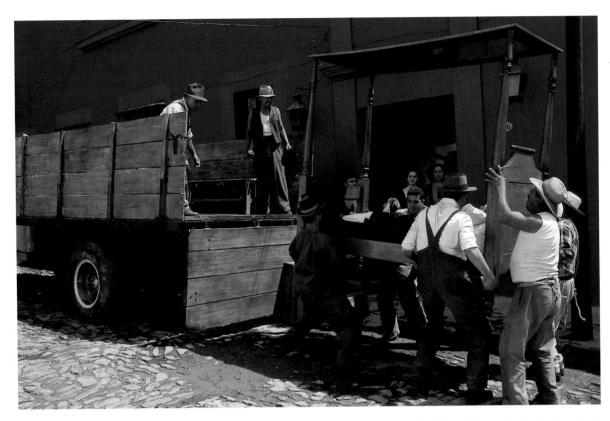

EXT. BLUE HOUSE - COURTYARD - LATE AFTERNOON

Cacti fill the courtyard, their blooms matching the brilliant blue of the walls. Two 20 foot papier-mâché Judas figures stand guard as the workmen maneuver the bed outside.

Two quivering hairless dogs watch the strange procession along with other animals: parrots, goats and a small deer.

EXT. BLUE HOUSE - STREET - CONT'D - LATE AFTERNOON

AURORA (60s), heavy set with Indian features, waits with CRISTINA (40s), vibrant and still beautiful. Both are in festive dress.

They watch, anxious, as the workmen heave the bed above their shoulders, lifting it onto a flatbed truck.

The weight of the bed overpowers the men and they stumble, knocking the bed against the side.

> FRIDA (O.S.)
> Careful, guys. This corpse is still breathing. Try to get me there in one piece.

FRIDA KAHLO (40s). She lies tucked in bed, her hair decorated with fresh flowers, wearing her traditional Tehuana dress. The beauty of her outfit is countered by her frail form and pale, drawn face, twisting with flashes of intense pain.

The workmen secure the bed. Aurora and Cristina are lifted onto the truck to sit beside Frida. The truck coughs into gear, begins to move. Aurora and Cristina

The Blue House on Londres Street

The story of Frida Kahlo begins and ends in the same place. From the outside, the house on the corner of Londres and Allende streets looks very like other houses in Coyoacán, an old residential section on the southwestern periphery of Mexico City. A one-story stucco structure with bright blue walls enlivened by tall, many-paned windows with green shutters and by the restless shadows of trees, it bears the name Museo Frida Kahlo over the portal. Inside is one of the most extraordinary places in Mexico—a woman's home with all her paintings and belongings, turned into a museum.

—HAYDEN HERRERA, *FRIDA: A BIOGRAPHY OF FRIDA KAHLO*

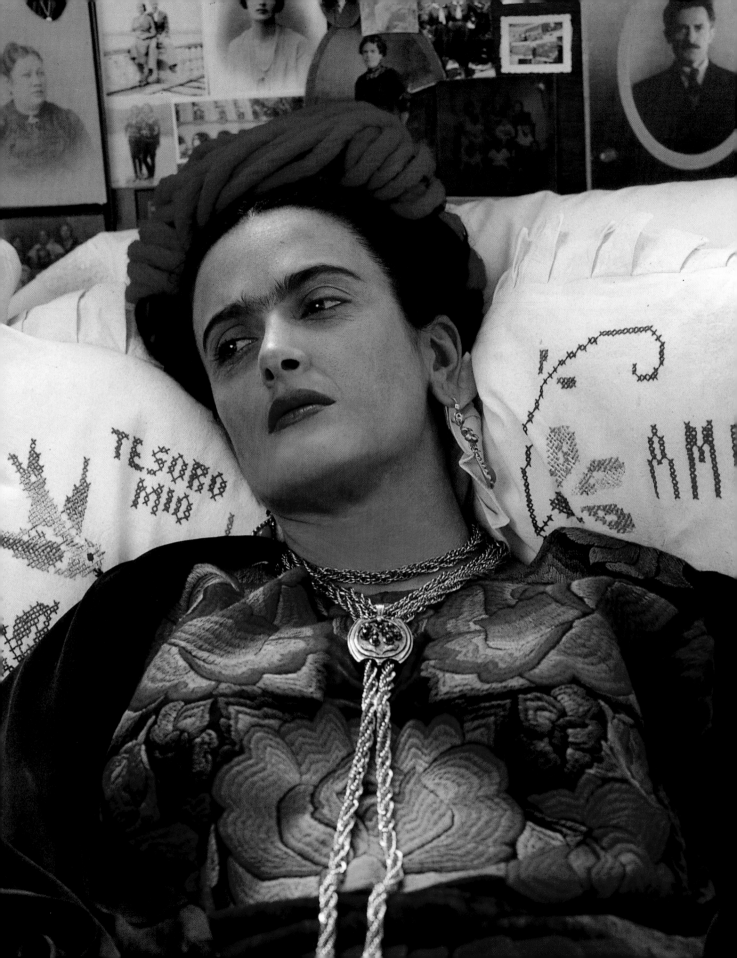

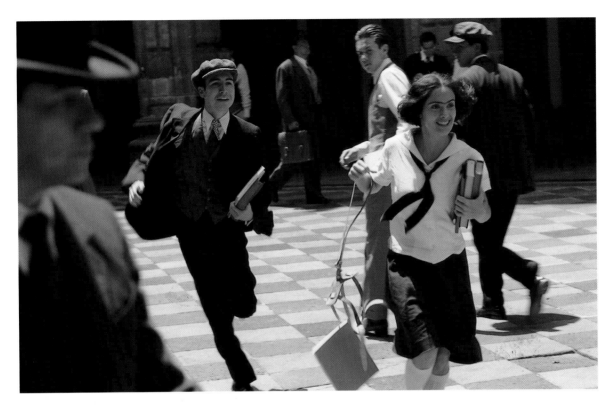

fuss over Frida but she waves them off, in too much pain to be touched.

EXT. BLUE HOUSE - STREET - LATE AFTERNOON

The truck lurches through the narrow streets.

INT. TRUCK - LATE AFTERNOON

FRIDA—staring up into a large MIRROR on the underside of the canopy. Her reflection stares back at her.

With the vibration of the truck, the mirror shudders.

Frida's reflection begins to smile and as she does...

She turns and runs away from frame... The camera follows her, pushing into the mirror as she runs away down a long hall of the...

INT. NATIONAL PREPARATORY SCHOOL CORRIDOR - DAY

...Frida is now age 14, young and full of life in her school uniform. She's running down the corridor at full speed.

Ahead, a TEACHER, prim and somber in his stiff collar and black suit, rounds the corner. Frida stops, slows to a proper walk as she passes the teacher.

> FRIDA
> Hello, Professor.

> TEACHER
> Hello, Frida.

The minute he turns his back, Frida takes off running again.

EXT. COURTYARD - NATIONAL PREPARATORY SCHOOL - DAY

ALEJANDRO, head of the student council, is talking with a group of his cronies, the Cachuchas, classroom rebels named after the red caps that they wear: MIGUEL, JOSE and CARMEN. Frida runs up to them.

> FRIDA
> Diego Rivera is back in the auditorium.

They look at her like what's the big deal. She adds calmly:

> FRIDA *(Cont'd)*
> With a naked woman.

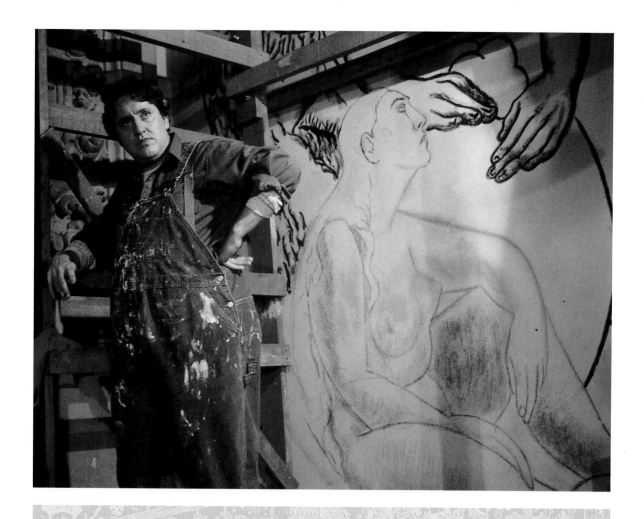

Diego Rivera

Born in Guanajuato in 1887 to a schoolteacher and his wife, Diego María de la Concepción Juan Nepomuceno Estanislao de la Rivera y Barrientos Acosta y Rodríguez was drawing and painting by the age of three. "Almost as soon as my fat baby fingers could grasp as pencil, I was marking up walls, doors and furniture," he once told a journalist.

He attended the National School of Fine Arts in Mexico City. In 1907, under government sponsorship, Rivera moved to Europe where he spent 12 years studying and painting with Picasso, Modigliani and other artists who greatly influenced him. He returned to Mexico in 1921, leaving behind an adoring Russian common-law wife, Angelina Beloff, an illegitimate daughter by another Russian woman, and a host of friends including Gertrude Stein, Guillaume Apollinaire and Diaghilev.

Enlisted by the government to create huge wall paintings, Rivera brought art to the people and reclaimed independent Mexican national culture. Eventually, his murals would cover the walls of schools, churches, hospitals, hotels and government buildings in Mexico and in major cities in the United States.

He surrounded himself with strong-willed Marxist partisans and was committed to the ideals of communism.

Throughout his life, Rivera was a passionate collector of folk and pre-Columbian art. In the 1940s, he embarked on the idea of constructing a monumental building modeled on an Aztec pyramid. Today, that building houses his collection of 60,000 items from these earlier cultures.

Diego Rivera died in his studio on November 24, 1957, two years after the death of Frida Kahlo. Although he requested that his ashes be mingled with hers in the garden of the Blue House, he was instead interred in Mexico's Rotunda of Famous Men in the Civil Pantheon of Mourning. His grave is marked with a monument that includes his face and small hands. He is considered a national treasure of his native country.

They all turn around and rush towards the auditorium.

INT. AUDITORIUM - NATIONAL PREPARATORY SCHOOL - DAY

The students huddle behind the last row of seats, hiding.

Down below in the auditorium, working on a mural high up on a scaffold, is DIEGO RIVERA, 39. Tall and fat, he wears slept-in overalls, clunky miner's boots and a gun in a holster around his waist.

Posing for him on the scaffold is a naked woman.

The door to the auditorium opens and Frida and her friends turn to see a striking woman walking in with a basket. It's LUPE MARIN, Diego's wife. Diego sees her and returns to the mural.

The model tenses up a little but holds her position. Lupe sees her:

> LUPE
> Why is this whore still here? Huh?

Diego ignores her, keeps painting.

> LUPE *(Cont'd)*
> Tell me... tell me mi amor. Are you planning to have her after lunch or have you fucked her already?

Diego talks calmly, while he paints.

> DIEGO
> Lupe, please don't start.

> LUPE
> You think I don't know what's going on? You must think I'm an idiot.

> DIEGO
> I can't work like this.

> LUPE
> Yes you can. Your food and your slut: that's all you need to paint your pinche murals.

Lupe throws the basket up at him as hard as she can but comes closer to hitting the model. Food flies out of the basket and all over the scaffold. Diego is finally angry.

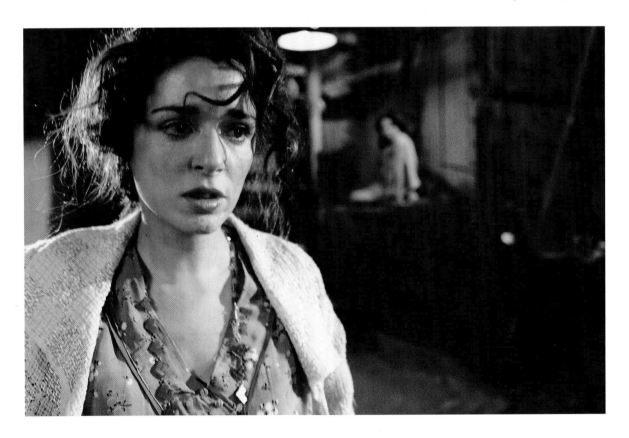

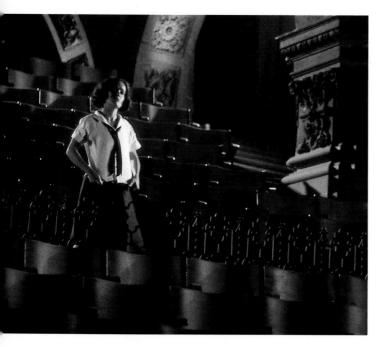

DIEGO
Hey, hey! Get out!

Lupe turns to leave. She's crying, furious.

LUPE
And don't come home. Don't come home and give me one of your speeches about the artist and the people and your fucking revolution. You only care about yourself, you piece of shit!

Lupe leaves and all is quiet again. Frida and Alejandro look at each other: this is a great opera.

DIEGO
Ah... So much for lunch. Although... I could
(turns teasingly to model)
eat you, perhaps.

The woman laughs and Diego walks over and sits next to her. He bends to reposition her and nuzzles her belly...

DIEGO *(Cont'd)*
I've eaten female flesh before...
(she laughs)
Yeah, wrapped up in tortillas. Tastes like the tenderest young pig...

ANGLE ON: The students peeking over the seats, grinning, staring, open-mouthed. Frida watches, too, but she isn't shocked. Only curious.

Diego kisses the woman's collarbone, then the cleavage of her breasts, then inches lower, lower, lower...

Suddenly a shout:

FRIDA
Watch out, Diego. Lupe's coming back!

Diego jerks his head up and untangles himself hastily...

Laughter floats up from the back of the room... He leaps up and pulls out his PISTOL...

DIEGO
Fucking punks!

He brandishes it at the kids who start to creep along the floor...

DIEGO *(Cont'd)*
Come on you little anarchists! Come and light another one of your firecrackers, if you dare!

Suddenly FRIDA stands up in the doorway, grinning, unafraid.

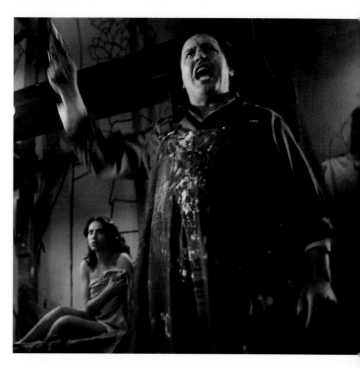

ALEJANDRO
Let's go, Frida.

FRIDA
Just keeping you honest, panzon.

They stare at each other for a beat. She turns and calmly walks out. He stares after her, amused.

DIEGO
(to the model)
Panzon!? Do I look fat to you?

INT. BLUE HOUSE - FRIDA'S BEDROOM - CLOSET - DAY

In the dark of a cramped closet, two people kissing passionately, groping furiously, trying to stay quiet...

INT. BLUE HOUSE - FRIDA'S BEDROOM - DAY

Frida emerges from the closet, half-naked, pulling up her dress. Through the window we see Matilde, Cristina and Aurora return from shopping. Frida looks around, steps out of frame and, after a beat, hisses.

The closet door opens again and Alejandro steps out, looking like he's been through a storm. He cinches his belt, tucks in his shirt, grabs his books off the bed and exits too...

INT. BLUE HOUSE - KITCHEN AND DINING ROOM - SUNSET

The kitchen bustles with activity. CRISTINA (20s), Frida's sister, puts away food from the market; MATILDE (50s), Frida's mother, a tight-lipped, stern woman, oversees AURORA (40s), the maid, as she cooks dinner. Frida slips into the room, stands in the doorway. Cristina sees her...

CRISTINA
Frida, we found the most beautiful fabric for my wedding dress today.

FRIDA
Fantastic!

Cristina's not quite sure of Frida's enthusiasm.

MATILDE
It cost a fortune.

Behind her mother's back, Frida catches Cristina's eye—looks over her shoulder, then at the door and bumps her eyes. Cristina sighs at her sister's antics, teases with a beat, then nods, understanding the silent message. Cristina picks up a large bushel of fruit, goes to Matilde.

CRISTINA
Mama?

MATILDE
Yes?

CRISTINA
Are these ripe?

Cristina has positioned herself in such a way that Matilde has to turn her back to the door to examine the fruit.

MATILDE
They should be... let me see...

Frida gestures off-screen and Alejandro slips across the patio. Aurora looks up and Frida puts a finger to her lips to signal her silence.

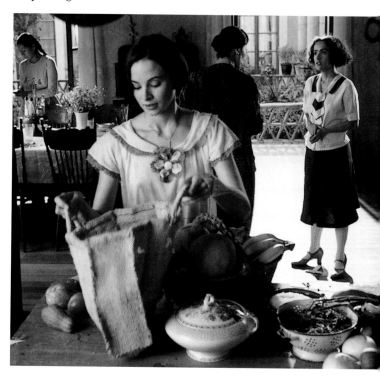

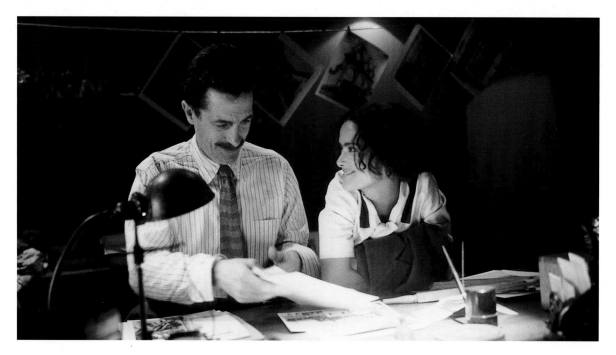

MATILDE *(Cont'd)*
These are fine...
(then to Frida)
Maybe you'll get married, too, one day.

FRIDA
One can only hope!

Matilde is not sure if she's being made fun of. Frida smiles.

MATILDE
Lunch is almost ready. Go get the artist.

EXT. GUILLERMO'S STUDIO - SUNSET

GUILLERMO KAHLO (50s), a thin, upright man with blue eyes and an elegant bearing. He is hanging photos to dry when Frida walks in. Frida looks at a picture of a dead child dressed up in crown and robes, and photographed with his mother (as is the tradition).

FRIDA
I love this one. It's beautiful.

RIGHT: Cast members recreate an archival photo of Frida (standing, left, wearing a man's suit) with members of her family. INSET: Taken by her father, Guillermo Kahlo, in 1926, the other people in this archival photo are: back row, from left: her aunt, her sister Adriana, Adriana's husband Alberto Veraza; middle row: her uncle, her mother, her cousin Carmen; front row: Carlos Veraza, Cristina.

Frida's Parents

The son of Hungarian Jews who lived in Baden-Baden, Germany, Guillermo Kahlo emigrated to Mexico in 1891 at the age of 19, and in the first decade of this century became one of Mexico's foremost photographers. For the government of the dictator Porfirio Díaz he recorded architectural monuments of the pre-Hispanic and colonial eras. His advertisement announced he was a "specialist in landscapes, buildings, interiors, factories, etc." and that he took "photographs on order, be it in the City, be it in any other point of the Republic." He also took portraits, but preferred buildings because, he said, he didn't want to improve what God had made ugly.

Soon after his first wife died giving birth to his second daughter, Kahlo married Matilde Calderón, a Mexican of mixed Indian and Spanish ancestry. "My mother was a great friend for me," Frida recalled, "but she could never make us participate in the religion thing. My mother was hysterical about religion. We had to pray before meals. While others concentrated on their inner selves, Cristi and I would look at each other, forcing ourselves not to laugh." Although she doted on her mother, Frida was critical. Matilde Calderón was, she said, "like a little bell from Oaxaca.... She did not know how to read or write; she only knew how to count money."

Frida described her taciturn, eccentric father as "very interesting, and he moved in an elegant way when he walked. Tranquil, hard working, brave, he had few friends." He did have a special love for his fifth child. "Frida is the most intelligent of my daughters," he would say, "She is the most like me."

—HAYDEN HERRERA, *FRIDA KAHLO: THE PAINTINGS*

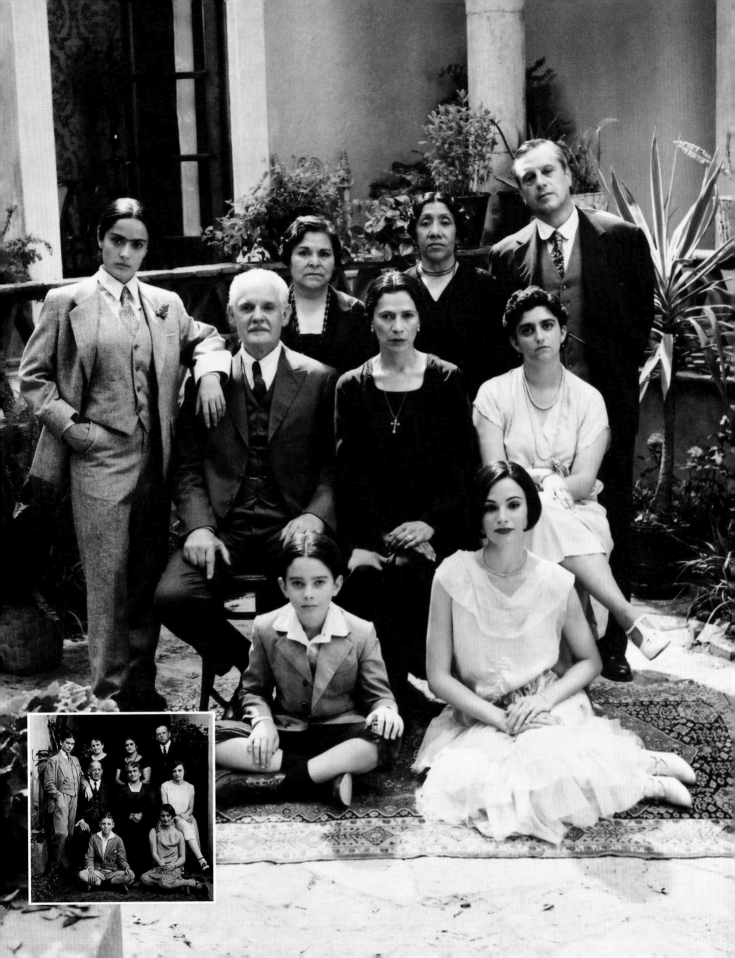

GUILLERMO
I like it too.

FRIDA
They're busy with the wedding. Cristina is so excited about her dress.

GUILLERMO
Good. Everyone should be excited when they get married.

FRIDA
I suppose... if that's what you want.

Guillermo loves his iconoclastic daughter.

GUILLERMO
Mmm, and... what do you want?

FRIDA
I don't know... I just don't think that marriage is for everyone.

GUILLERMO
You need a good reason to do it, just like with anything else.

FRIDA
What do you think matters most for a good marriage?

GUILLERMO
A short memory.

FRIDA
Why did you get married, Papa?

GUILLERMO
I can't remember. So I could have you.

She smiles and kisses him.

EXT. BLUE HOUSE - COURTYARD - DAY

The family poses for a photo: Cristina, their cousin, the other sister Adriana and her husband, their aunt and uncle and their mother, MATILDE. Guillermo is behind the camera.

GUILLERMO
Concentrate everybody...

CRISTINA
Wait. Where is Frida?

MATILDE
Adriana, go tell your sister to hurry up.

Adriana moves towards the house. Suddenly the door opens in her face and the family turns to see Frida wearing a man's three-piece suit, tie and dress shoes. Her hair is greased back and hidden behind her, under the jacket.

She takes a flower from a potted plant and puts it in her lapel. Cristina rolls her eyes. Matilde is annoyed.

GUILLERMO
I always wanted a son.

Frida joins the group, puts one hand elegantly in her pocket.

GUILLERMO (Cont'd)
Matilde, everyone, eyes to the camera, and...

Tight on the bulb of the camera and... FLASH!

EXT. BLUE HOUSE - COURTYARD - DAY

The scene becomes the famous PHOTOGRAPH.

INT. AUDITORIUM/NATIONAL PREPARATORY SCHOOL - DAY

WIDE: Behind Alex and Frida, dwarfed in front of the mural.

TIGHT ON: Alejandro and Frida's faces, staring up.

After a long beat, Alejandro looks at his watch.

ALEJANDRO
Come on. We'll miss our bus...

He exits the frame.

FRIDA stays looking up at the painting, expressionless, lost in it until...

Alejandro comes back in and pulls her out...

RIGHT: Frida standing in front of Creation, *1922-3, by Diego Rivera in the Anfiteatro Bolívar, National Preparatory School, Mexico City.*

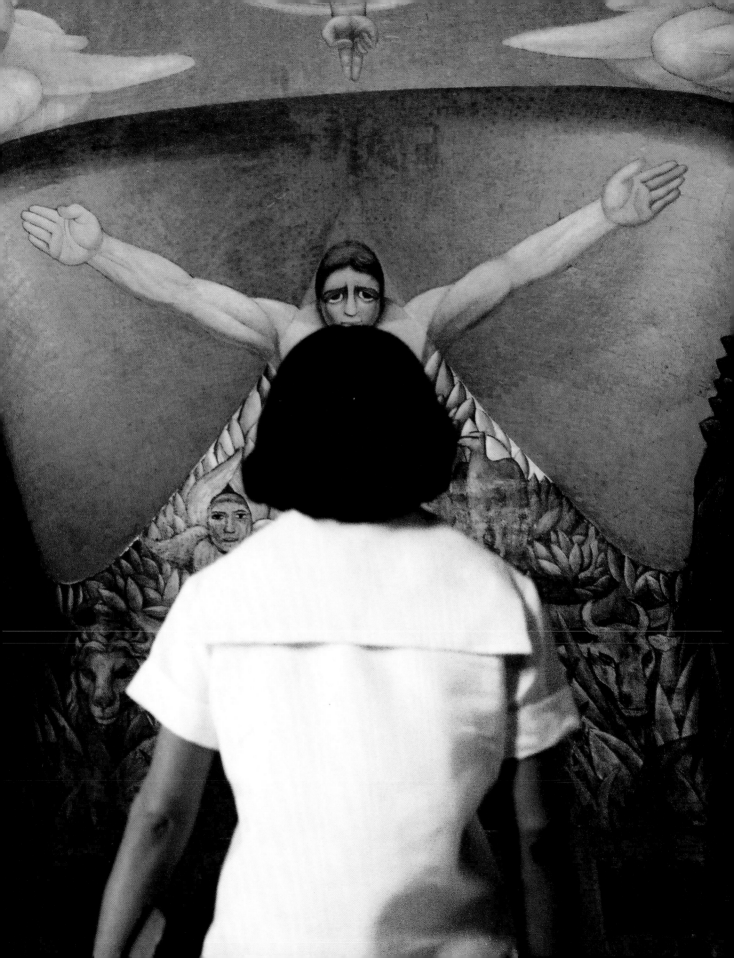

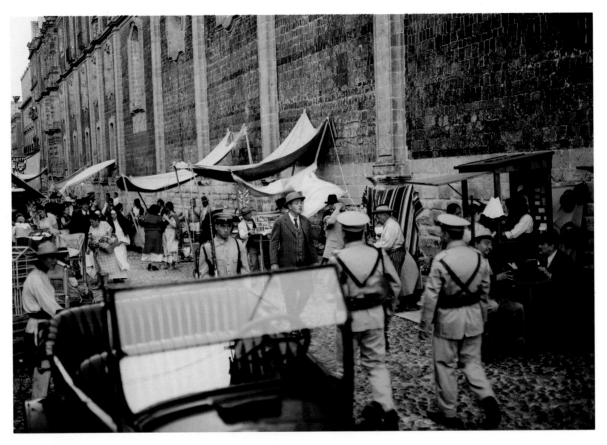

EXT. STREET BEHIND THE NATIONAL PREPARATO-RY SCHOOL - DAY

Students pour out of the building into the street scene. Peddlers, vendors, photographers, musicians, Indians, peasants, beggars, office workers, soldiers, police marching, a shouting prisoner in cuffs.

    FRIDA
    Excuse me. How much is the calaca? *(a charm in the form of a skull)*

    ALEJANDRO
    Frida, Frida, come!

EXT. ANOTHER STREET - DAY

Alejandro and Frida cross the street talking animatedly.

Frida looks up and sees their bus stopping...

    ALEJANDRO
    He's talking about how to write history...

    FRIDA
    The bus!

She runs like the wind trying to catch the bus. Alejandro laughs and runs after her.

    ALEJANDRO
    We'll take the next one!

    FRIDA
    No, no, no, come, come, come.

Frida runs down the street, catches up and runs alongside the bus, banging on the doors. The driver slows down and Frida jumps on the bus followed by Alejandro.

INT. BUS - DAY

Frida and Alejandro climb onto the bus, resuming talk...

FRIDA
Anyway... I just don't think he's completely apolitical, that's all.

ALEJANDRO
But that's because you read it after you read Marx. You always read things in the wrong order...

She laughs as they move past the camera into the back and flop into seats. Frida notices an Indian woman standing with a baby. She stands and offers her seat, nudging Alex to get up. The woman sits down, surprised by the gesture. Frida and Alejandro stand together holding the handrail as the bus lurches along somewhat wildly...

FRIDA
That's ridiculous. Why should it matter what order you read it in?

ALEJANDRO
Because if you have already read Marx then of course Hegel is going to seem political, but the truth is the idea of history as a dialectic just predicts Marx, which isn't the same as affirming him.

As Alex rambles, Frida's attention wanders to a HOUSE PAINTER in coveralls with enormous pockets, holding brushes, cans of paint. He catches her eye, smiles and pulls a packet from his coveralls. He shakes a few dry gold flakes into Frida's hand.

FRIDA
Is that gold? Real gold?

HOUSE PAINTER
For the ceiling of the opera house.

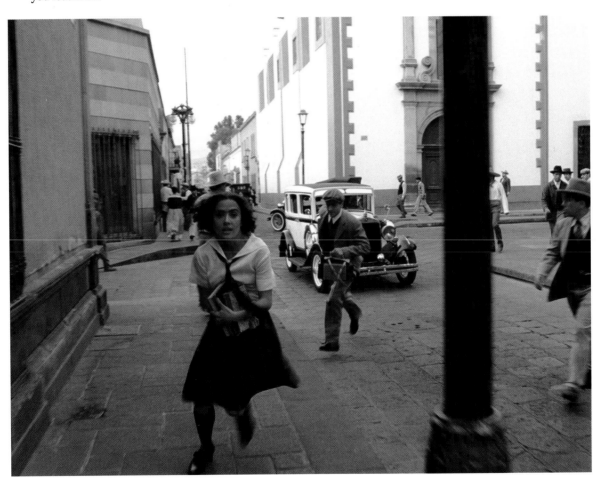

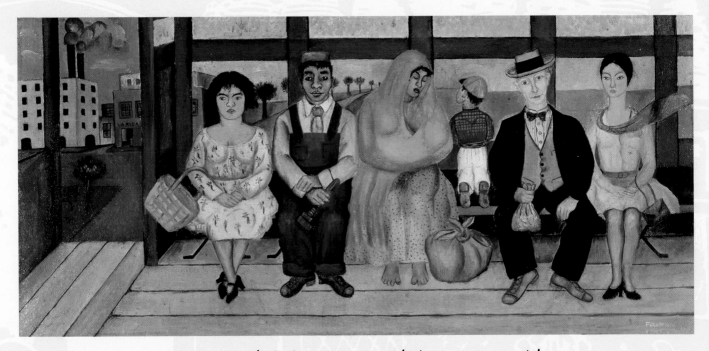

I never painted dreams. I painted my own reality.

—FRIDA KAHLO

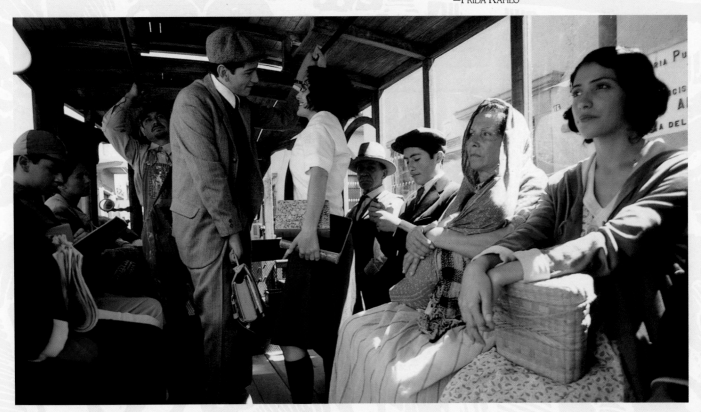

The SOUND OF A HORN starts in the distance...The bus lurches again. Frida grips the handrail, falls against Alejandro.

She sees a SCHOOLBOY catching his balance and protecting a bird, held gently in his fist...

The horn blasts, loud now and urgent.

Frida and Alex turn, looking at something out the window, someone shouts a warning

INT. BUS - DAY

CRASH! — The bus is rocked by an impact. Frida and Alex are thrown down into the laps of other yelling passengers

> BUS DRIVER
> Muevete... move idioto!

Frida looks down at herself. She is covered in gold powder...

Still inside, we don't see what has hit the bus, which seems to be getting shoved slowly sideways now. Screeching, grinding metal sounds mix with the shouts.

Alex tries to stand and pulls Frida up. Her eyes flick up and out the opposite window where a wall is rushing up to meet the bus. Someone screams, "Hang on!"

They hit the wall and we see everything explode in chaos for just a second before...

Total black filled with the horrible noise of the wreck—tearing, exploding metal, screams of agony and fear...

Silence... Then a distant noise rises, shouting.... SLAM!

INT. RED CROSS HOSPITAL - NIGHT

In the blackness, distorted sounds float in, music or voices, unclear. Low whispering sounds echo.

FADE UP SLOWLY ON FRIDA'S HALLUCINATION:

SKELETONS. Mexican Day of the Dead, POSADA skeletons, dressed like doctors and nurses, even a patient on crutches hobbling by... all in black and white

ABOVE LEFT: The Bus, 1929. Four years after her catastrophic accident, Frida Kahlo painted her memory of the bus before the collision that changed her life. BELOW LEFT: The filmmakers referred to this striking image when filming this scene.

and grey... moving and dancing and whispering... perhaps held up by ropes reaching up out of frame. A doctor skeleton holding a clipboard and chattering distorted sounds to a nurse at the foot of her bed.

Swinging to one side the POV takes in a long communal ward, a surreal vision of DANCING skeletons and mist...

POV swings back to the doctor skeleton at the foot of the bed, now talking to a skeleton in a dress praying a rosary.

> MAN'S VOICE
> The spinal column was broken as were the collarbone and two ribs. The pelvis is broken in three places. The metal rod entered the right side of the body and came out the vagina.

FRIDA'S CLOSED EYES, bruised, panicked, moving under the lids.

The SKELETONS...

> MAN'S VOICE *(Cont'd)*
> The right leg has eleven fractures and the foot was crushed...

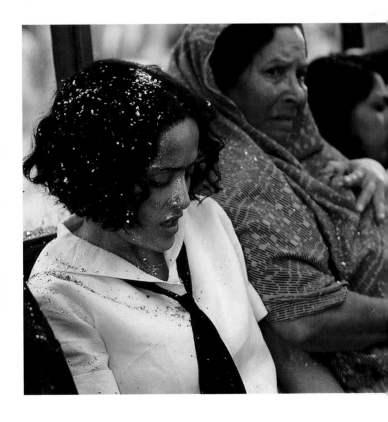

It was a strange collision. It was
not violent but rather silent,
slow, and it harmed everybody.
And me most of all.
—Frida Kahlo

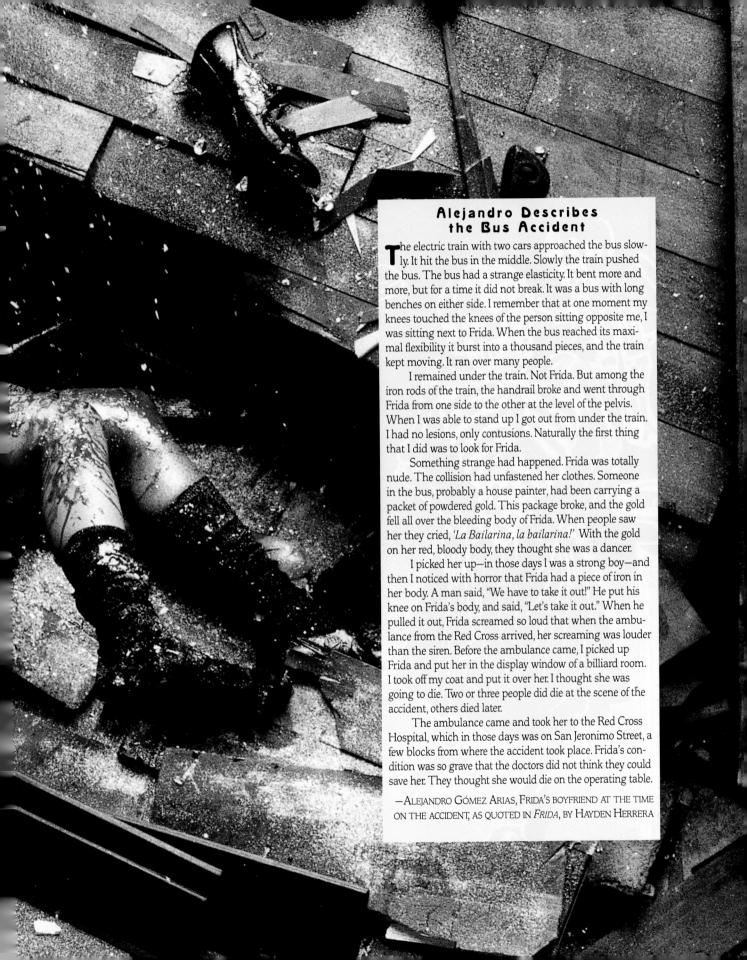

Alejandro Describes the Bus Accident

The electric train with two cars approached the bus slowly. It hit the bus in the middle. Slowly the train pushed the bus. The bus had a strange elasticity. It bent more and more, but for a time it did not break. It was a bus with long benches on either side. I remember that at one moment my knees touched the knees of the person sitting opposite me, I was sitting next to Frida. When the bus reached its maximal flexibility it burst into a thousand pieces, and the train kept moving. It ran over many people.

I remained under the train. Not Frida. But among the iron rods of the train, the handrail broke and went through Frida from one side to the other at the level of the pelvis. When I was able to stand up I got out from under the train. I had no lesions, only contusions. Naturally the first thing that I did was to look for Frida.

Something strange had happened. Frida was totally nude. The collision had unfastened her clothes. Someone in the bus, probably a house painter, had been carrying a packet of powdered gold. This package broke, and the gold fell all over the bleeding body of Frida. When people saw her they cried, *'La Bailarina, la bailarina!'* With the gold on her red, bloody body, they thought she was a dancer.

I picked her up—in those days I was a strong boy—and then I noticed with horror that Frida had a piece of iron in her body. A man said, "We have to take it out!" He put his knee on Frida's body, and said, "Let's take it out." When he pulled it out, Frida screamed so loud that when the ambulance from the Red Cross arrived, her screaming was louder than the siren. Before the ambulance came, I picked up Frida and put her in the display window of a billiard room. I took off my coat and put it over her. I thought she was going to die. Two or three people did die at the scene of the accident, others died later.

The ambulance came and took her to the Red Cross Hospital, which in those days was on San Jeronimo Street, a few blocks from where the accident took place. Frida's condition was so grave that the doctors did not think they could save her. They thought she would die on the operating table.

—ALEJANDRO GÓMEZ ARIAS, FRIDA'S BOYFRIEND AT THE TIME ON THE ACCIDENT, AS QUOTED IN *FRIDA*, BY HAYDEN HERRERA

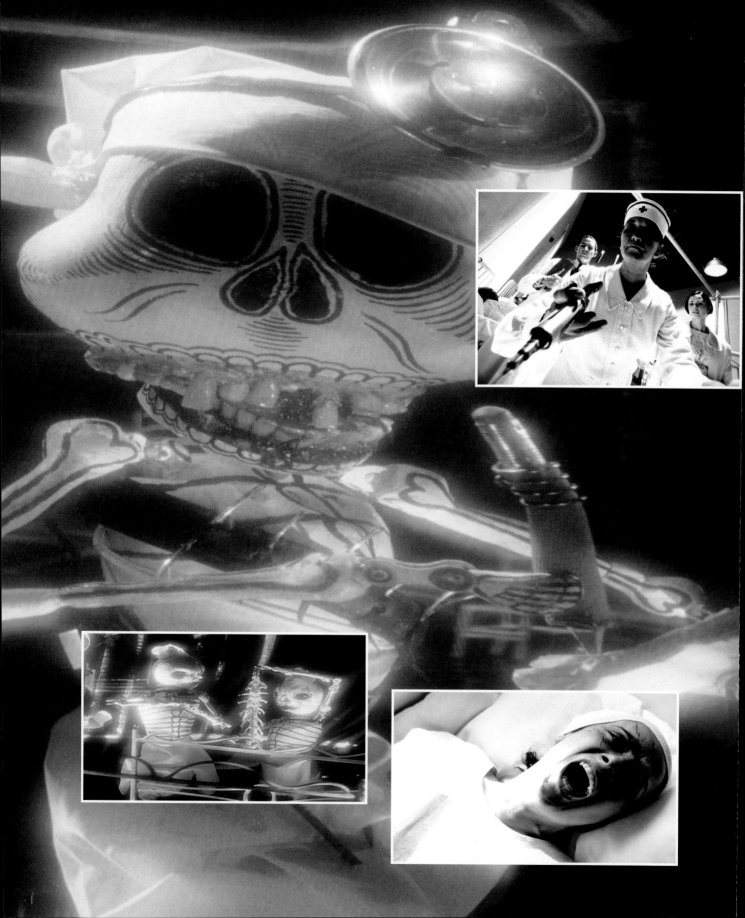

INT. RED CROSS HOSPITAL - DAY

Close on Frida. She opens her eyes slowly...

The skeletons become REAL people: A DOCTOR, a NURSE and CRISTINA, weeping...

CRISTINA
Will she ever walk again?

DOCTOR FARILL
Let's make sure she lives first.

FRIDA'S WAIL comes from O.S., cutting him off. They turn, unaware that she was awake. Cristina runs toward the camera...

FRIDA'S FACE: HOWLING IN DESPAIR

The nurse moves toward the camera with a needle...

BLACK

INT. RED CROSS HOSPITAL - DAY

WIDE and HIGH: A LARGE COMMUNAL WARD, light filtering in... Twenty-five beds with patients, one lone nurse walking the aisle.

The Hospital Nightmare

After the trolley and bus accident I wanted to create a nightmare sequence that would reflect Frida's complex relationship with death. The Mexican Day of the Dead ritual and its imagery inspired the sequence. With papier-mâché figurines like those that Frida collected all her life, I envisioned a comic, grotesque and highly theatrical scene of the hospital, replete with skeletons of beds, nurses, doctors, medical instruments and bones. I had greatly admired the 3-D-stop animation of the Brothers Quay so we commissioned them to create this sequence. We gave them research imagery, the bare outline of the concept and let them fly. After receiving the raw footage from the Quays, we cut it into an impressionistic sequence that at once disturbs and teases the audience with how the storytelling of the film will unfold. It is the first glance into the dark imagination of the artist, Frida, and how the real events of her life will dominate her art while helping her to survive. Humor was ever present with Frida as she mocked her intimate relationship with death: "La Pelona" translated as "The Bald One."

—JULIE TAYMOR, DIRECTOR

In me there were no tears

A little while after we got on the bus the collision began. Before that we had taken another bus, but since I had lost a little parasol, we got off to look for it and that was how we happened to get on the bus that destroyed me. The accident took place on a corner in front of the San Juan market, exactly in front. The streetcar went slowly, but our bus driver was a very nervous young man. When the trolley car went around the corner the bus was pushed against the wall.

I was an intelligent young girl, but impractical, in spite of all the freedom I had won. Perhaps for this reason, I did not assess the situation nor did I guess the kind of wounds I had. The first thing I thought of was a *balero* [Mexican toy] with pretty colors that I had bought that day and that I was carrying with me. I tried to look for it, thinking that what had happened would not have major consequences.

It is a lie that one is aware of the crash, a lie that one cries. In me there were no tears. The crash bounced us forward and a handrail pierced me the way a sword pierces a bull. A man saw me having a tremendous hemorrhage. He carried me and put me on a billiard table until the Red Cross came for me.

—FRIDA KAHLO

One bed toward the middle seems to have a coffin in it. A woman sits in a chair beside it, knitting.

CLOSE ON FRIDA, as she wakes up. She looks down at her body wrapped entirely in a cast and encased in a long wooden box.

She looks up at Cristina...

FRIDA
Is Alex alive?

CRISTINA
Frida!

FRIDA
Is he all right?

CRISTINA
(looks up)
He was hurt but not terribly. He was here yesterday when you were not awake.

FRIDA
And mama?

CRISTINA
It was too much for them, Friducha. They're at home. All your friends have come. They come every day. Chucho, Angel...

FRIDA
How long have I been here?

CRISTINA
Three weeks.

Frida remains emotionless, blank. She closes her eyes.

EXT. THE BLUE HOUSE

The ambulance arrives at the Blue House.

INT. COURTYARD OF THE BLUE HOUSE

Guillermo and Matilde watch with concern as Frida, on a stretcher, is carried by orderlies through the court-yard.

Cristina, her pregnancy now showing, is walking alongside the stretcher, holding her hand.

Frida moans.

CRISTINA
(stroking her head)
We're almost there...

GUILLERMO
Gently now.

INT. BLUE HOUSE - FRIDA'S BEDROOM - DAY

Dust floats in the light over Frida, lying in her full-body cast in bed. The clock ticks loudly. Move into ECU of her face. Through light and shadow time passes over her face.

From somewhere in the house, Matilde and Guillermo argue. Frida strains to hear.

MATILDE (O.S.)
...but there is nothing left to spend!

GUILLERMO (O.S.)
I will sell some of my equipment.

MATILDE (O.S.)
For another operation that probably won't work...

INT. BLUE HOUSE - KITCHEN - DAY

GUILLERMO
No. Listen, maybe this time it will work...

MATILDE
...and then how will you make money?

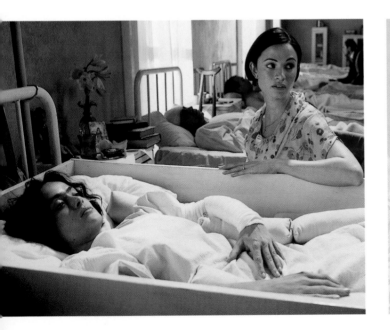

Terrible Beauty, Changed Utterly

In September of 1925 a streetcar crashed into the fragile bus she was riding, broke her spinal column, her collar-bone, her ribs, her pelvis. Her already withered leg now suffered eleven fractures. Her left shoulder was forever out of joint, one of her feet crushed. A handrail crashed into her back and came out through her vagina. At the same time, the impact of the crash left Frida naked and bloodied, but covered with gold dust. Despoiled of her clothes, showered by a broken packet of powdered gold carried by an artisan: will there ever be a more terrible and beautiful portrait of Frida than this one? Would she ever paint herself—or could she paint herself other than—as this "terrible beauty, changed utterly"?

The pain, the body, the city, the country. Kahlo. Frida, the art of Frida Kahlo.

—CARLOS FUENTES, INTRODUCTION, *THE DIARY OF FRIDA KAHLO*

44

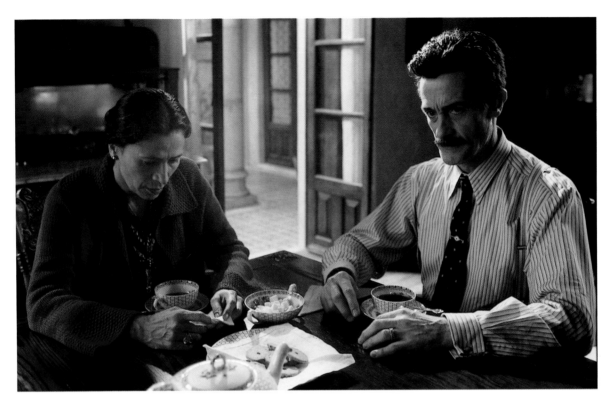

GUILLERMO
I'll paint portraits again...

MATILDE
Admit it, Guillermo. She'll never walk again.

She stops as Alex enters through the door with flowers and books...

MATILDE *(Cont'd)*
Go on in, Alex, she's waiting for you.

INT. BLUE HOUSE - FRIDA'S BEDROOM - DAY

Frida sits propped up in bed sketching her right foot. She looks much healthier. Her body cast is still imposing but one arm is free now and there is color in her cheeks.

Alex enters and stands in the doorway. She looks up and smiles.

FRIDA
Hello, ugly. They're beautiful.

ALEJANDRO
How do you feel?

FRIDA
Like I was hit by a bus.

He's not sure if she's joking.

FRIDA *(Cont'd)*
Oh come on, silly, come, come, come, sit with me.

Throughout the movie, we mixed a lot of lighting styles and took cues from Frida's writings about colors and lighting. In her diaries and letters, Frida often discussed the "mystery of darkness." Although she doesn't use a lot of light and shadow in her paintings, she was very aware of it in her life. So I tried to reproduce that mystery. Most of our interiors have dark, mysterious areas where you can't tell what's there.

Another example: After the accident we went for a very bright white look because in a letter to Alejandro, her boyfriend at the time, Frida wrote that suddenly life lost its mystery and everything became white, like ice. Very transparent. She could see everything; the mystery was gone. So we went for that look. We used a white hospital wardrobe and light that was so bright, it was even a little bothersome.

There were so many locations and scenes in the movie, it gave us a chance to explore all sorts of lighting situations.
—RODRIGO PRIETO, DIRECTOR OF PHOTOGRAPHY

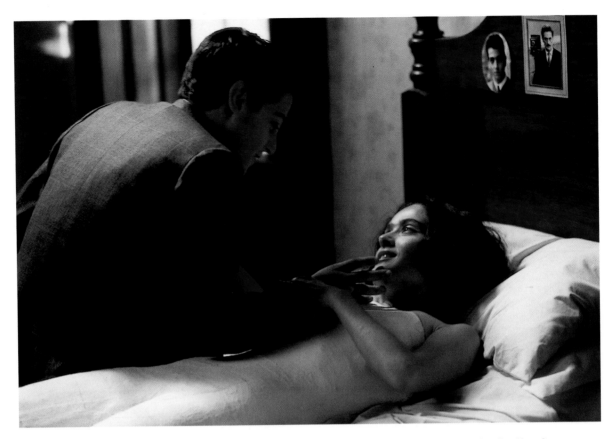

Death Dances Around My Bed

For a month Frida lay on her back encased in a plaster cast and enclosed in a structure that looked like a sarcophagus. She wrote to Alejandro: "In this hospital death dances around my bed at night." Death would continue to dance around Frida for the next twenty-nine years. Indeed, she invited it to dance, teasing and flirting with death, and keeping an eye on it so that she could hold it at bay. She dressed papier-mâché skeletons in her own clothes and hung them from her bed's canopy so that they jostled in the wind. One of her favorite possessions was a sugar skull of the type that children eat on the Day of the Dead. Frida ordered the skull to be made with her own name written in bold letters on its forehead.

Frida recovered from the accident, relapsed, and recovered again, but from 1925 on her life was a battle against slow disintegration. There were periods when she felt well and her limp was barely noticeable. And there were periods when she was either bedridden or hospitalized. She is said to have had some thirty-five operations, most of them on her spine and right foot. "She lived dying," said a friend, the writer Andrés Henestrosa.

—HAYDEN HERRERA, *FRIDA KAHLO: THE PAINTINGS*

He does. She shows him the sketch of her foot.

FRIDA (*Cont'd*)
Look, it's my only good angle at the moment.

ALEJANDRO
(*kissing her*)
No it's not... I like you this way... you're easier to keep up with.
(*gives her the books*)
Spengler because you love him and Schopenhauer because it's good for you.

FRIDA
Oh Alex... you know I adore you! I've missed you so much...
(*she kisses his hand*)
I told the doctor the handrail had taken my virginity.

ALEJANDRO
(*smiling*)
I'm sure he believed you.

FRIDA
You know, when I get out of this cast, I'm going to show you a couple things I still remember from before.

ALEJANDRO
(pulling back)
Okay...

He pauses... uncomfortable. This is going to be hard.

FRIDA
What?

ALEJANDRO
My aunt and my uncle are leaving for Europe and... they've invited me to come along.

FRIDA
But that's wonderful... when would you leave?

ALEJANDRO
Soon. Next week.

She's puzzled by his nervousness.

FRIDA
How long will you be gone?

ALEJANDRO
They're going for two months... And afterwards, I might stay on at the Sorbonne.
(A pause.)
I will be staying on.

She says nothing, crushed. She starts to draw a butterfly sitting on the foot in her sketch, not looking up.

FRIDA
Did I tell you that I'm going to walk again?

ALEJANDRO
Yes.

FRIDA
(suddenly looking up)
Do you believe it?

ALEJANDRO
Of course, I do.

FRIDA
You'd better...
(fighting tears)
Because you're going to miss it.

ALEJANDRO
Look, Friducha, I...

FRIDA
I want you to leave before I finish this butterfly.

Alex leans forward, kisses her forehead and leaves.

INT. BLUE HOUSE - VERANDAH - DAY

Guillermo sits in a chair in the hallway, waiting, agonized.

INT. BLUE HOUSE - FRIDA'S BEDROOM - DAY

Frida sits on a stool with her arms up, holding on to the bars of a traction rig while her head is pulled upward. A male nurse assists Doctor Farill as he dips new gauze in liquid and wraps it around her body. Frida bites her lip to keep from whimpering.

INT. BLUE HOUSE - FRIDA'S BEDROOM - EVENING

Frida's cast is now covered with drawings of butterflies.

Guillermo steps into the room.

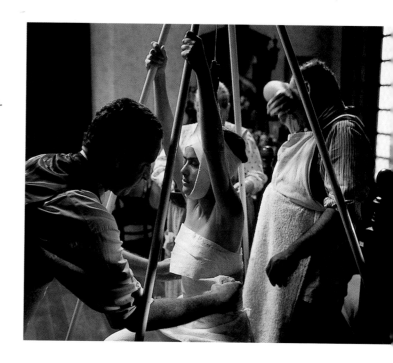

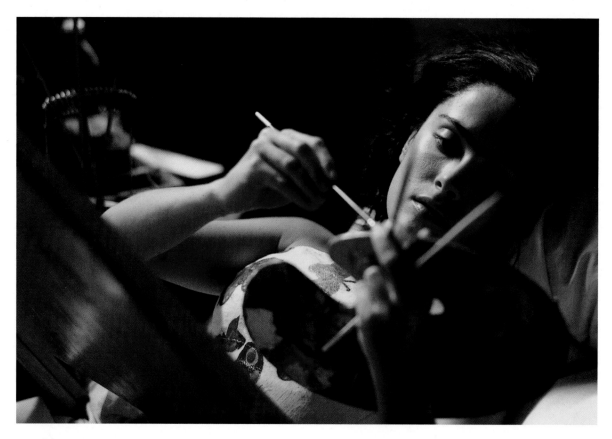

GUILLERMO
How are you feeling?

FRIDA
How am I feeling? I can't even remember what it felt like before the pain. Isn't that horrible?

GUILLERMO
Dr. Farill is coming on Monday. He's bringing a back specialist, Dr. Cervantes.

FRIDA
I feel like some rich girl with a new suitor every week. But all my suitors have turned into doctors... And I'm not a rich girl, Papa.

He pats her hand sympathetically.

FRIDA *(Cont'd)*
How come you never ask me about my plans anymore, hmm? You used to always say, "Tell me your plans, Frida..."

GUILLERMO
What are your plans, Frida?

FRIDA
Right now I'm a Burden but I hope to be a Self-Sufficient Cripple one day. After that, I don't know.

GUILLERMO
You're not a burden my love... See, here... we have something for you... Matilde!

He presents her with a small, specially constructed easel, paints, a package of various brushes. Matilde appears in the doorway, sadly observing.

GUILLERMO *(Cont'd)*
We noticed there was no more room left on your cast... So...

BRIEF MONTAGE OF FRIDA PAINTING IN HER BED:

INT. BLUE HOUSE - FRIDA'S BEDROOM - DAY

Her corset now covered with colorful painted butterflies, she paints on her easel mounted to the bed...

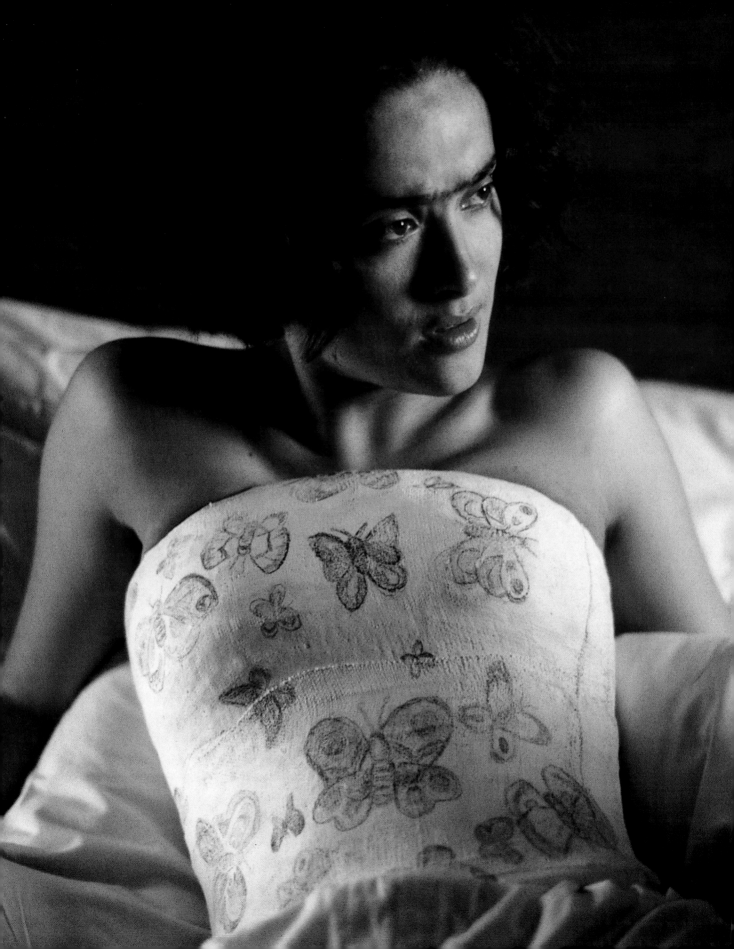

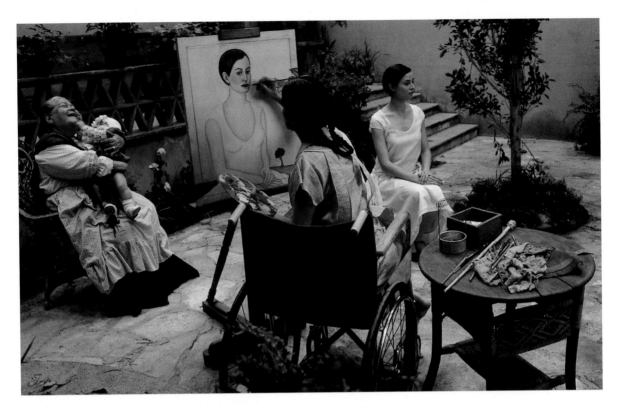

INT. BLUE HOUSE - FRIDA'S BEDROOM - DAY

Frida sits in a chair, her eyes squeezed shut, gripping Cristina's hand as Dr. Farill cuts away her cast. He splits it wide open.

Frida takes her first deep breath in months, her eyes shining with excitement and relief...

EXT. BLUE HOUSE - PATIO - DAY

Frida sits in a wheelchair in the family courtyard painting. On an unfinished PORTRAIT OF CRISTINA— Frida paints Cristina's mouth in the Kewpie-doll style of the flapper era.

> **FRIDA**
> Now you look like a gringa movie star.

> **CRISTINA**
> Let me see.

Cristina kisses Frida's head.

Guillermo and Matilde come in from the street. Frida puts down her brush...

> **MATILDA**
> It's too much money.

> **FRIDA**
> Mama, Papa, I have a surprise!

She braces herself and stands up without too much difficulty. Gingerly, she begins to take a faltering step.

Her father moves to take her hand, but Cristina stops him.

> **GUILLERMO**
> Careful now...

> **FRIDA**
> I can do it...

> **CRISTINA**
> Don't worry, it's all right.

She takes a few steps, weak, but she can do it. She triumphantly squawks like a rooster as her family laughs...

FADE OUT.

RIGHT: Portrait of Cristina Kahlo, *1928.*

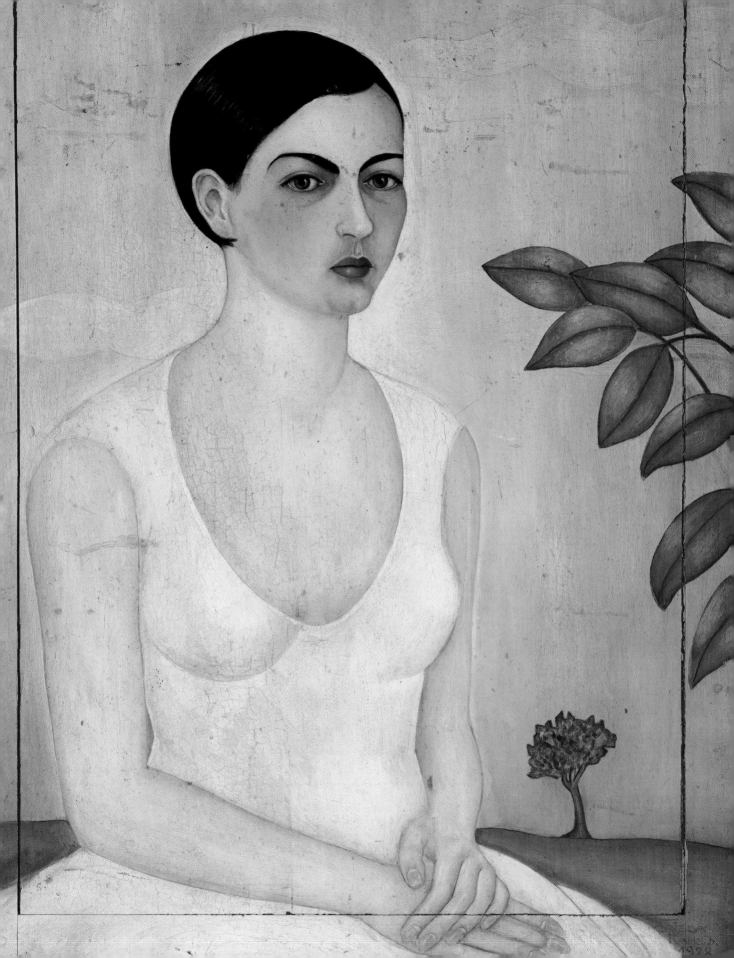

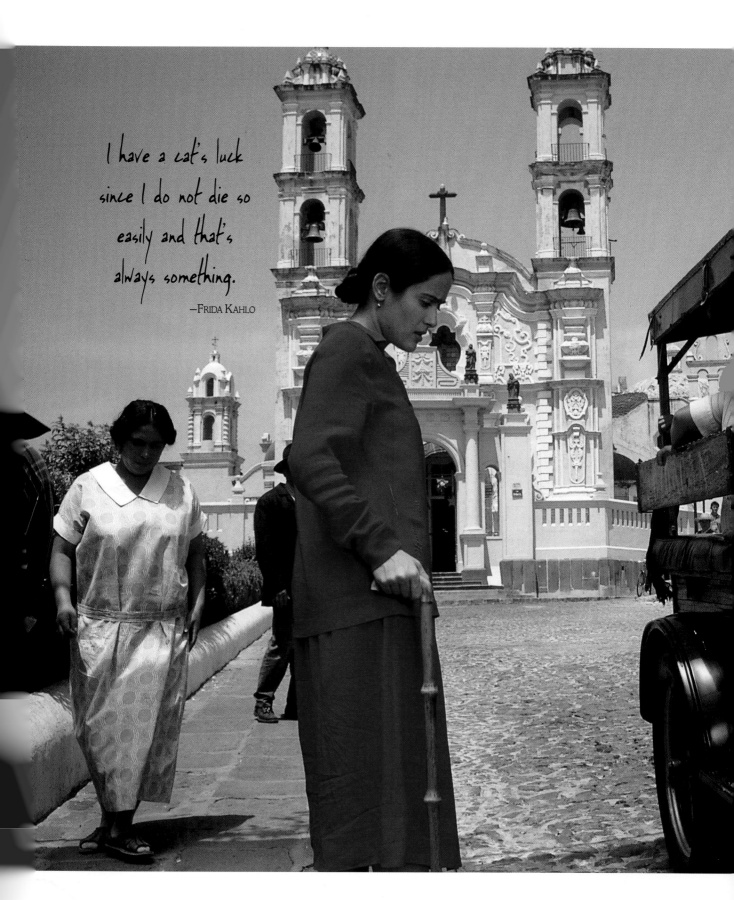

I have a cat's luck
since I do not die so
easily and that's
always something.

—FRIDA KAHLO

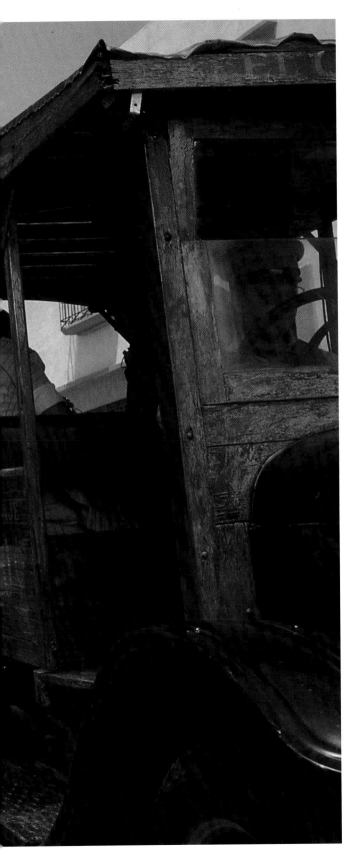

EXT. STREET - DAY

A bus moves towards us. Standing at the bus stop, leaning on a cane, Frida watches its approach with apprehension. She carries a few of her paintings under her arm.

As the bus comes to a stop, Frida waits for school children to run out of it. Then she stands there while the driver waits for her to board. She hesitates..

EXT ANOTHER STREET - DAY

As the bus rounds the corner, we see Frida sitting at a window.

EXT. MINISTRY OF EDUCATION COURTYARD - DAY

Montage of details of Diego at work, through the different stages of his mural *The Orgy*. This is the first time we've really seen him working. Painting al fresco his strokes are quick and confident, his whole body moving with a grace that contradicts his shape and size.

Frida enters the main courtyard...

A man's voice booms from above.

Frida looks up to see Diego and stops. He is on the third floor scaffold, brush in hand, painting rapidly. He never stops painting as he talks.

> **DIEGO**
> I need the ocre... Is it READY?!

> **ASSISTANT**
> Almost.

> **DIEGO**
> No. NOW! I need it NOW!

> **ASSISTANT**
> Okay.

Another assistant hands a new brush and bowl of paint to Diego.

Frida leans her cane against a column and steps forward.

> **FRIDA**
> Señor Rivera!

He doesn't reply or even turn.

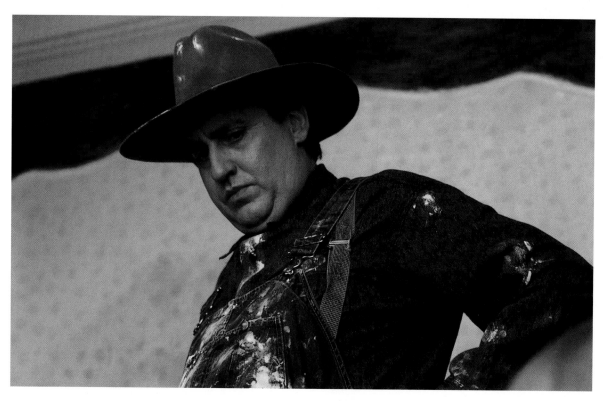

"Diego, Come Down!"

As soon as they gave me permission to walk and to go out in the street, I went, carrying my paintings, to see Diego Rivera, who at that time was painting the frescoes in the corridors of the Ministry of Education. I did not know him except by sight, but I admired him enormously. I was bold enough to call him so that he would come down from the scaffolding to see my paintings and to tell me sincerely whether or not they were worth anything... Without more ado I said: "Diego, come down." And just the way he is, so humble, so amiable, he came down. "Look, I have not come to flirt or anything even if you are a woman-chaser. I have come to show you my painting. If you are interested in it, tell me so, if not, likewise, so that I will go to work at something else to help my parents." Then he said to me: "Look, in the first place, I am very interested in your painting, above all in this portrait of you, which is the most original. The other three seem to me to be influenced by what you have seen. Go home, paint a painting, and next Sunday I will come and see it and tell you what I think." This he did and he said: "You have talent."

—FRIDA KAHLO

FRIDA *(Cont'd)*
Diego!

DIEGO
(without turning or stopping)
Who are you? What do you want?

FRIDA
I have something important to discuss with you!

Still painting, he flicks a glance back over his shoulder, probably just to see if she is beautiful. Not enough.

DIEGO
I'm working.

FRIDA
I'll wait.

DIEGO
I don't have time to chat with schoolgirls.

FRIDA
I'm not a schoolgirl, panzon.

The word rings a bell. He stops despite himself and

turns again for another look. He places the voice...

DIEGO
Give me a minute.

He puts the finishing touches on a small section and only when totally satisfied does the energy settle in him. He releases a breath, hands off the brush and turns.

DIEGO *(Cont'd)*
Okay, come on up here.

FRIDA
No, you come down.

He laughs and climbs down. The two assistants are looking at Frida. She gives them a lady's smile and a short curtsy.

Diego is on the ground now, walking toward her. He slows down expecting to meet her halfway, but she's not moving. She doesn't want him to see her walk. He

walks all the way up to her. Face to face, he towers over her.

DIEGO
What?

FRIDA
(all at once)
Look, I didn't come here for fun, or to flirt. I've done some paintings which I want you to look over professionally and I need an absolutely straightforward opinion of my work.

DIEGO
You were that girl in the auditorium.

FRIDA
...Yes, I was, but that has nothing to do with now. I just want your serious opinion.

DIEGO
What do you care about my opinion? If you're a

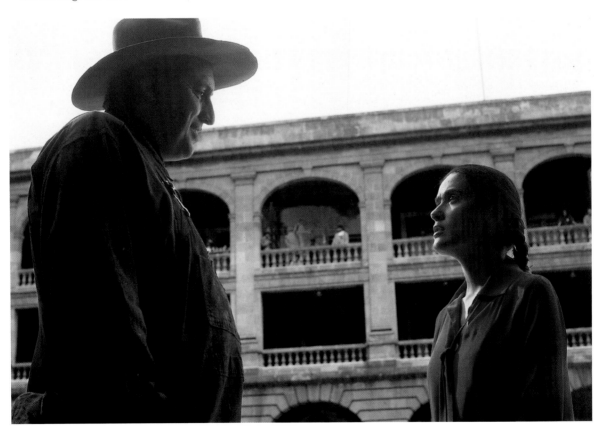

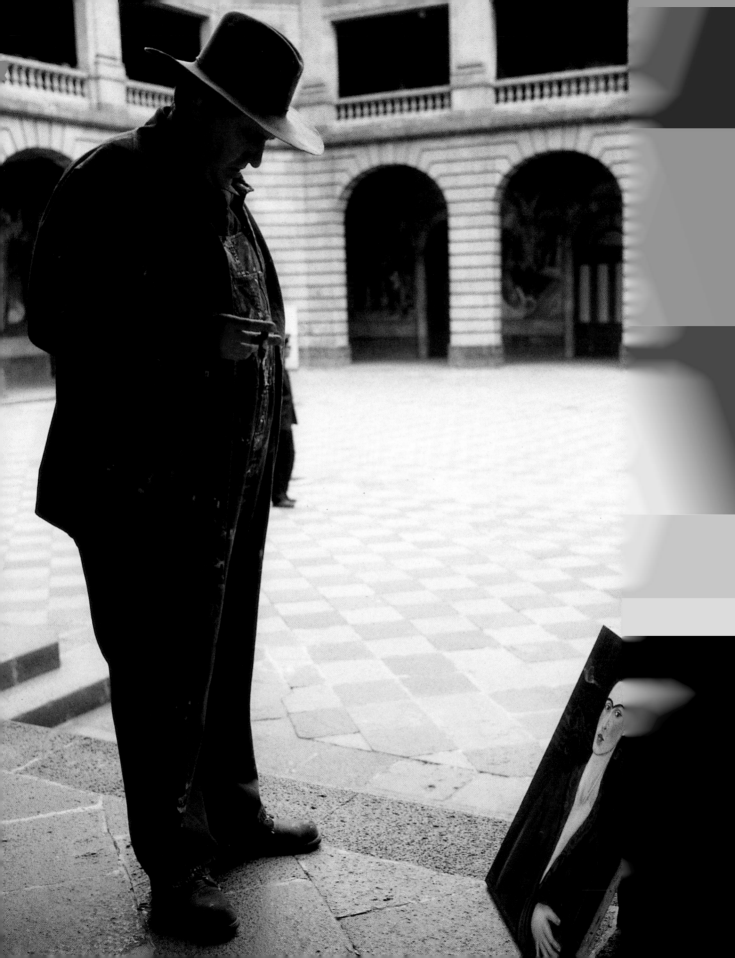

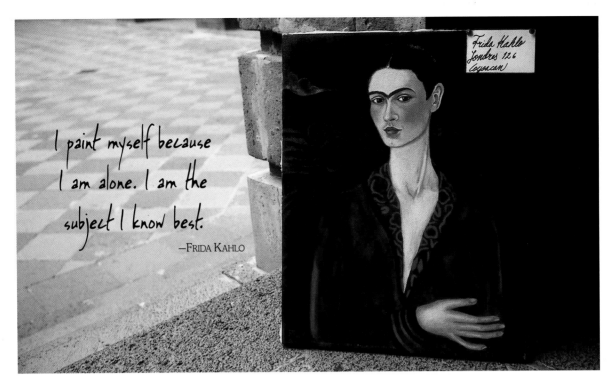

I paint myself because I am alone. I am the subject I know best.

—FRIDA KAHLO

Frida Kahlo / Londres 126 / Coyoacan

real painter you'll paint because you can't live without painting. You'll paint till you die. Okay?

FRIDA
(unfazed)
I have to work to earn a living, so I don't have time to fool around just for vanity. If I'm not good enough, I have to do something else to help my parents.

He takes her in and smiles. She's bold and serious. He turns and starts back to the scaffold... gestures at her paintings...

DIEGO
Leave the best one here. Go home and paint another one. If this one's any good I'll come and look at that one on my day off.

She stands looking after him...

EXT. MINISTRY OF EDUCATION MAIN COURTYARD - LATER - DAY

Diego, with his Stetson and coat in hand, walks away

ABOVE: Reproduction of Self-Portrait Wearing a Velvet Dress, *1926. Several key paintings were recreated for the film.*

from the scaffolding with some REPORTER in tow, scribbling quotes...

DIEGO
...Orozco is a true artist, he's tremendous...and Siqueiros could be great if he'd pull his head out of his own ass and look around...

With this, he passes a column against which is leaning FRIDA'S SELF-PORTRAIT. He glances at it as he passes and disappears, talking, around the corner. Out of view, the talking and the footsteps suddenly stop...

Diego walks back into frame and stops in front of it, staring at it, expressionless.

Through her art, Kahlo seems to come to terms with her own reality: The horrible, the painful, can lead us to the truth of self-knowledge. It then becomes beautiful simply because it identifies our very being, our innermost qualities. Kahlo's self-portraits are beautiful for the same reason as Rembrandt's: They show us the successive identities of a human being who is not yet, but who is becoming.

—CARLOS FUENTES, INTRODUCTION,
THE DIARY OF FRIDA KAHLO

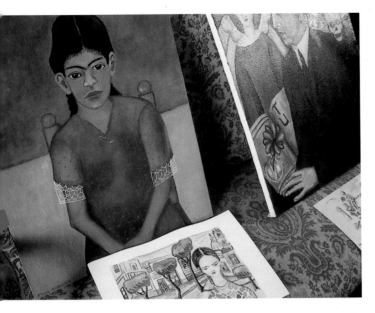

Mine was a strange world
of criminal silences
of stranger's watchful eyes
misreading the evil.

—FRIDA KAHLO

TIGHTER: A white slip of paper is pinned to the corner. In bold letters: "FRIDA KAHLO, Avenida Londres, 126, Coyoacán"

EXT. BLUE HOUSE - PATIO - LATE AFTERNOON

Frida sits up in the low branches of a tree smoking a cigarette. She hears the small sound of the gate to the street squeaking open across the courtyard. Her eyes flick up and she stops, mid-smoke...

In the archway is framed the huge silhouette of DIEGO is his Stetson with her painting under his arm. He enters out of the shadow and looks toward the house...

Frida scrambles down hastily, cigarette hanging from her lips. She walks directly to him takes a last puff, pitches it down, grinds it out and sticks out her hand.

FRIDA
Comrade Rivera. What a nice surprise.

INT. BLUE HOUSE - LIVING ROOM - LATER - LATE AFTERNOON

She sits watching him in silence as he finishes studying her work. Finally he turns and narrows his eyes.

DIEGO
What if I told you that easel painting like yours is finished... that it's headed for the trash like other elitist bourgeois pastimes...?

FRIDA
I'd say cut the propaganda.

He studies her a moment then sits.

DIEGO
This is very good work. You have real talent.

FRIDA
(exasperated)
Oh, come on... I'm not looking for your compliments. I want a serious critique.

They were made for each other

Rivera began traveling every week to the Kahlo house in Coyoacán, then a suburb of Mexico City. This was the famous Blue House that plays such a major role in the Kahlo story. He met her parents, the German-born father (whose grandparents were Hungarian Jews), her Mexican mother, her sisters.... Rivera talked to Frida for hours about her work and his own, about politics, about Mexico. He placed her in a prominent position in the Distributing Arms panel in the Ministry of Education and even found room in the composition for her younger sister Cristina. The love affair started. That year, Diego Rivera was forty-two and Frida Kahlo was twenty-one. He weighed three hundred pounds and she weighed a hundred. He was more than six feet tall and she was five foot three. Obviously, they were made for each other. They were married on August 29, 1929.

—PETE HAMILL, *DIEGO RIVERA*

Her ferocity intrigues and puzzles him.

DIEGO
But I am being sincere. These are very original paintings, none of the usual tricks.

FRIDA
But that's, that's not specific.

DIEGO
You have to trust a true compliment as much as a critique.

FRIDA
Yeah... well, some people have told me not to trust what you say. They say if a girl asks your opinion and she's not a complete fright, you'll gush all over her. I need you to tell me one thing honestly: Do you actually believe that I should continue to paint?

He looks directly at her.

DIEGO
Yes... yes.

She stares back at him without blinking.

He smiles. He admires her.

EXT. TINA MODOTTI'S APARTMENT BUILDING COURTYARD - NIGHT

An apartment building downtown. Diego and Frida enter the courtyard of the building. Up above them a party rages.

INT. TINA MODOTTI'S APARTMENT BUILDING - STAIRS - NIGHT

Diego and Frida walk in from the courtyard. She walks without a cane but slowly.

DIEGO
You'll like Tina. She's a brilliant photographer, one of the few with real taste. Do you know Alvarez Bravo?

FRIDA
I know his work... it's good.

DIEGO
I'll introduce you to him. He'll want to photograph you...

FRIDA
(smiling)
Without clothes of course.

DIEGO
Of course.

As they continue up, she notices a guard with a gun by the door... Diego nods at him, sees her concern and turns to her just outside the door..

DIEGO (Cont'd)
That's the thing about these radicals: they're a little dangerous but they definitely throw the best parties...

He throws the door open and they enter the noise of...

INT. TINA MODOTTI'S APARTMENT - NIGHT

...the party. This is the social center of Mexico's avant-garde artists, writers, photographers and journalists — leftists all with all the energy of the twenties. Couples dance the Charleston, political debate rages and everyone gets drunk.

In the center of it all, TINA MODOTTI (20s), Italian-American, beautiful and elegant photographer presides. She's sitting on the table next to her Victrola, choosing records. She looks up and sees them...

TINA
AH! At last, il mostro!

She jumps up and embraces him.

DIEGO
Tina, this is Frida Kahlo. She's a wonderful painter.

FRIDA
(slightly embarrassed)
She wants to be a wonderful painter.

Tina likes her right away.

TINA
Oh, don't be shy... nobody really thinks their own stuff is good... except Diego. He's the only one who's sure! *(to Diego)* Go find Siqueiros. He's been bad-mouthing you again. *(to Frida—smiling)* You... come with me.

FRIDA
Great party!

TINA
Everyone, I have someone for you to meet, this is Frida Kahlo. She came with Diego, another pretty girl for Diego.

Tina begins introducing Frida to the cream of Mexico's art world: Bravo, Xavier Guererro, Jose Orozco, David Siqueiros, Anita Brenner, Nahui Olin, etc.—Frida taking it all in, laughing, gossiping and becoming fast friends with Tina...

INT. HALLWAY - TINA MODOTTI'S APARTMENT - LATER - NIGHT

CLOSE-UPS: Tina's black and white photographs.

Frida stands alone to the side with a glass of wine looking at the pictures and back out at Tina draped around Diego, orchestrating her party. The pictures are striking— workers in the fields, men crowded around a newspaper, protesters...

The Frog Prince

Diego Rivera had no trouble making conquests. Although he was undeniably ugly, he drew women to him with the natural ease of a magnet attracting iron filings. Indeed, part of his appeal was his monstrous appearance—his ugliness made him a perfect foil for the type of woman who likes to play beauty to a beast—but the greater attraction was his personality. He was a frog prince, an extraordinary man full of brilliant humor, vitality and charm. He could be tender and was deeply sensuous. Most important, he was famous, and fame seems to be an irresistible lure for some women. It is said that women chased Rivera more than he chased them. He was pursued especially by certain young Americans who felt that a tryst with Diego Rivera was as much of a "must" as a trip to the pyramids of Teotihuancán.

—HAYDEN HERRERA, *FRIDA: A BIOGRAPHY OF FRIDA KAHLO*

A WOMAN'S VOICE (O.S.)
She's quite a talent... no?

Frida turns to find LUPE MARIN looking at her. A little drunk, she points at a photo of a young man.

LUPE
Julio Mella, the Cuban. Tina took the last photo of him.

Frida leans in close to examine the photos.

LUPE *(Cont'd)*
She was with him—on the street—when they gunned him down.

Laughter turns them to the party. Diego is making two women laugh hysterically.

LUPE *(Cont'd)*
Incredible. They're like clay in his hands.

FRIDA
It must be that body.

LUPE
Ha! No... it's the way he looks at you and finds beauty in all your imperfections. It's irresistible. You'd never think it to look at him but he's had half the women here... I'm sorry—did you come with him?

FRIDA
We're just friends.
(extends hand)
I'm Frida Kahlo. I'm a painter.

LUPE
A painter... no wonder. I'm Lupe Marín. I'm his wife.
(beat)
I was his wife.

They look at each other for a moment. In the main room Tina drapes her arms around Diego and kisses him. Lupe sees this.

LUPE *(Cont'd)*
(ironic)
Good luck to you.

She turns and leaves.

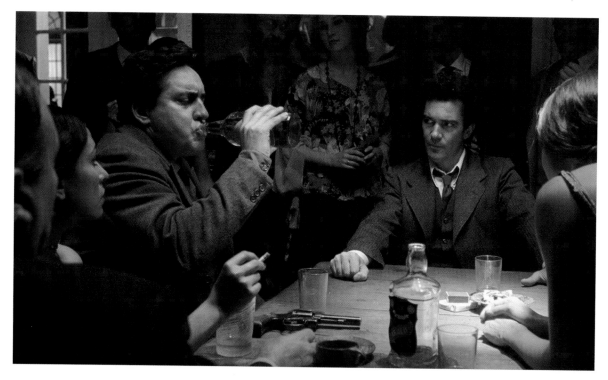

INT. TINA MODOTTI'S APARTMENT - DINING ROOM - NIGHT

Later. Diego, Frida and Tina are huddled around a table with a large group of people. Diego is arguing across the table from SIQUEIROS, a fierce, handsome man, the crowd watching and reacting to the debate like a tennis match.... They talk over the festive music still playing on the VICTROLA...

SIQUEIROS
...badmouth him all you want, Diego, but while we've been talking about Socialism over drinks at parties for ten years—Stalin's making it work! He's achieving it!

DIEGO
Achieving what? His only big idea so far is to throw out all the real thinkers in the land.

SIQUEIROS
He just threw YOU out!

Everyone laughs, even Diego.

DIEGO
No, no. Not just me...

SIQUEIROS
No, not just you—Mr. Trotsky. A man who plays the martyr when in truth he was rejected by his whole country. Good riddance!

DIEGO
He had to run for his life! Stalin would have had him shot! That's his version of socialism. Kill anyone who disagrees!

SIQUEIROS
Some people have to get shot in a revolution, Diego.

DIEGO
Well I prefer evolution. Educate the poor, mobilize the workers, rise like a slow tide. But you—you'll have your revolution and kill half the poor to save them!

SIQUEIROS
Diego, this from a Communist who's getting rich painting for the government and wealthy patrons.

DIEGO
I can't help it if the rich have good taste.

SIQUEIROS
The rich don't have good taste. They pay someone

Tina Modotti (1896-1942)

Born in Italy, Tina Modotti came to the United States in 1913 and joined her father in San Francisco. She found work as a model, then as a stage actress in the Italian-language theater, and finally landed some small parts in silent movies. But her beauty seemed to bore her and she walked away from this budding career. She married a frail young American artist who made a living as a fabric designer. Then, in Los Angeles in 1920, she met the photographer Edward Weston. He was married, too, with three children; within a year they were lovers. Modotti's husband soon left for Mexico and, after a few happy months, died of smallpox. Tina Modotti first saw Mexico when she traveled to the capital to bury him. Staying on with friends, she met Diego and Lupe for the first time. Years later, Lupe remembered her as "slim, elegant, refined and very pretty." Modotti went back to California but would return to Mexico with Weston in 1923. Months later, when he left, she stayed on. She was now an accomplished photographer and a well-known character in the bohemian and left-wing circles of Mexico City. She was also somewhat notorious. Weston had made some spectacular nude photographs of her that had been seen by many people. And she always made clear that the rigid sexual rules of the day were made to be broken.

—PETE HAMILL, *DIEGO RIVERA*

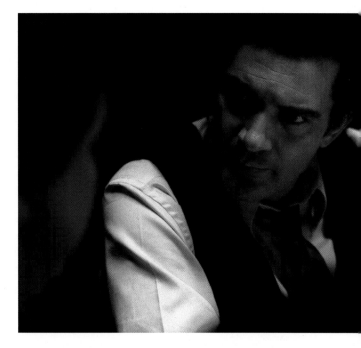

Tina Modotti died in 1942 in mysterious circumstances. She collapsed in Mexico City in a taxi, after a normal dinner with friends, aged forty-six. Questioned by police, her companion, Vittorio Vidali, who had dined with her, claimed that she had been suffering from a heart condition for some time; for this he was the only witness, and it is a mystery why anyone believed him. Vidali was growing tired of Tina by that time, and she knew far too much about his political operations both in Spain and in Mexico. Furthermore, she was showing increasing signs of disaffection with Stalinism. She had said sometime before that she hated Vidali "with all her soul," but that she was forced "to follow him till death." It seems entirely possible that Vidali "eliminated" her, although when Rivera suggested this, on hearing of how Tina had died, he was roundly abused by the Communists he was trying to rejoin.

—PATRICK MARNHAM, *DREAMING WITH HIS EYES OPEN: A LIFE OF DIEGO RIVERA*

ABOVE: Portrait of Tina Modotti, 1926, by Diego Rivera.

to have good taste for them and they don't hire you because you're good. They hire you because you assuage their sense of guilt. They use you Diego, and you're too vain to see it.

DIEGO RIPS OUT HIS PISTOL AND — BLAM! — SHOOTS THE VICTROLA. The room goes quiet. Diego and Siqueiros stare each other down. Frida is staring at Diego riveted. Tina slams a tequila bottle down on the table.

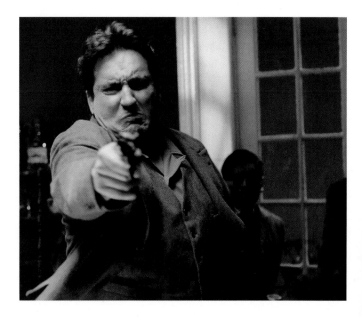

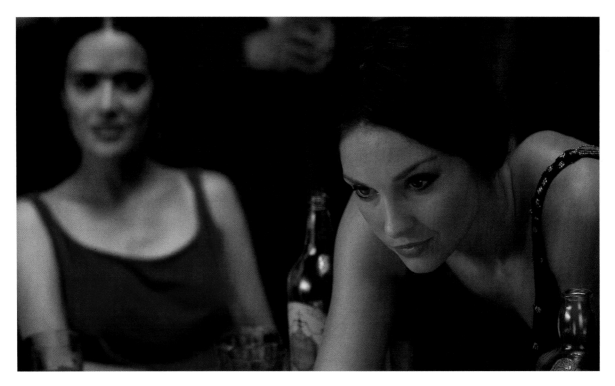

TINA *(Cont'd)*
Basta! Whoever takes the biggest swig can dance with me.

Tina shoots a look to Frida and winks. Diego sits back, letting Siqueiros go first. Siqueiros drinks deeply, sits back satisfied. Tina examines the bottle.

TINA *(Cont'd)*
Bravo.

Tina hands the bottle to Diego. As Diego drinks, Siqueiros leans close.

SIQUEIROS
I'd rather have an intelligent enemy than a stupid friend.

David Alfaro Siqueiros (1896-1974)

The controversial artist, David Alfaro Siqueiros, was born in Chihuahua on December 29, 1896. A sophisticated political ideologist and Stalinist, Siqueiros was involved in the political conflicts of the Mexican Revolution serving as a protestor, demonstrator and soldier. His radical political beliefs eventually got him expelled from Mexico. In 1932, he visited Los Angeles and painted the large-scale mural *Street Meeting* and another, still larger, titled *La América Tropical* on Olvera Street, which was so controversial at the time that it was painted over for many decades. In the late sixties, when the whitewash began to peel, the mural was rediscovered and underwent extensive conservation.

In 1934, he was named President of the National League Against War and Fascism. In 1935, he engaged in his celebrated polemics with rival muralist Diego Rivera, advocating a global, universal attitude for mural painting. In the same year, he established the Siqueiros Experimental Workshop in New York. Three works of this period are part of the collection of the Museum of Modern Art in New York.

In 1940, he took part in the bitter political struggle that resulted in the assassination of Trotsky. Legally cleared in the proceedings that followed this event, Siqueiros left for Chile and in the city of Chillán where he executed the mural *Death to the Invader*.

He spent many years in jail for his actions, which greatly influenced his art. Siqueiros often painted the sufferings of prison life. Siqueiros believed that "art must no longer be the expression of individual satisfaction, but should aim to become a fighting educative art for all." He died in 1974.

RIGHT: Portrait of David Alfaro Siqueiros, *1921, by Diego Rivera.*

Diego laughs, spits tequila everywhere. They watch as Tina checks the bottle; Frida watches Diego, eyeing Tina with appreciation.

Frida takes the bottle from Tina and guzzles it down, beating Diego and Siqueiros handily. She turns to Tina.

> FRIDA
> Shall we?

Tina laughs. Lets Frida lead her from the room.

The crowd fills the doorway as Frida whispers in the ear of a woman. As a man picks up a guitar and begins to play, the woman begins to sing a tango. Frida yanks Tina close and the two begin to dance. Frida leads. The dance is sexy and provocative. Tina loves it. Diego watches Frida, rapt, from the doorway as the crowd claps and the pace quickens.

As the music climaxes, Frida dips Tina and kisses her hard on the lips to loud cheers...

INT. WALL - DAY

Diego sits painting Frida who poses standing with a bayonet and rifle.

INT. TINA MODOTTI'S APARTMENT - DINING ROOM - DAY

The Victrola sits quiet, Diego's bullet hole in it...

A printing press has been set up in the middle of the room. Men and women, the same ones who'd been so drunk and raucous at the last party, are hard at work, intently discussing new pamphlets. Tina, sweating in the heat, works the crank on the press, spinning out new copies of *El Machete*.

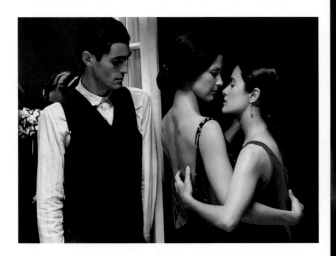
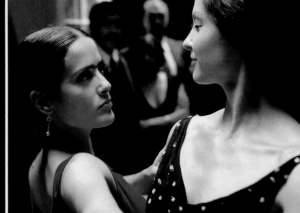
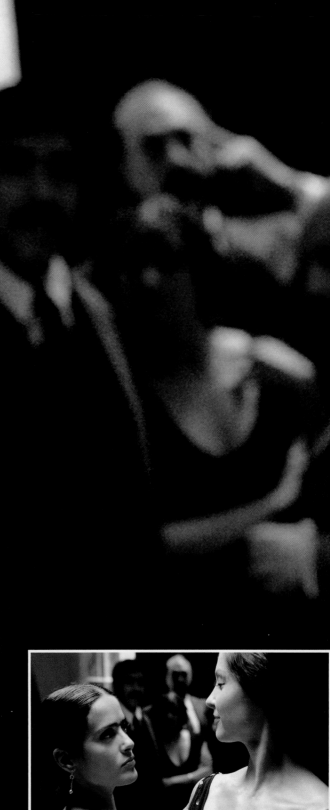

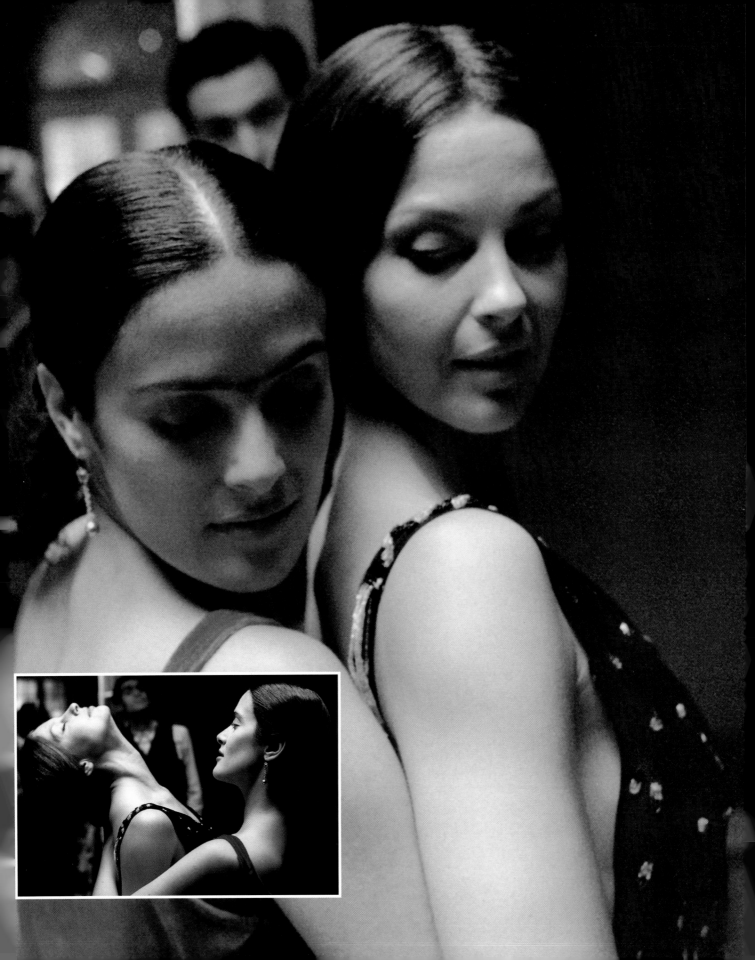

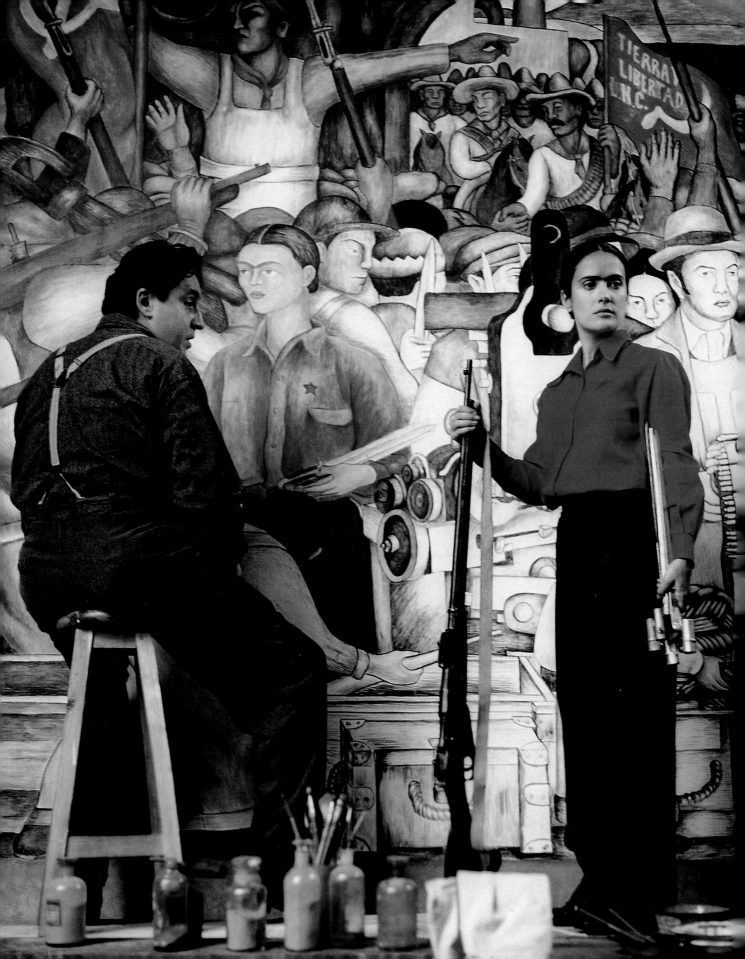

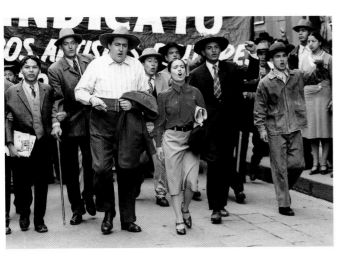

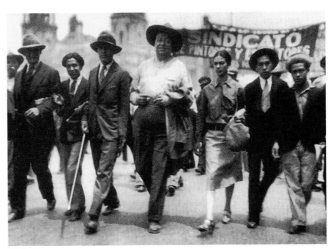

Diego sits in the corner in his shirt sleeves, a fan keeping his large body cool as he bangs out new copy on the typewriter. Frida stands behind him, dictating the content over his shoulder.

EXT. STREET - MEXICO CITY - DAY

A demonstration march moves down a street. Diego and Frida march in the front line of a group of about fifty people. Banners carried behind them read "Syndicate of Technical Workers, Painters and Sculptors."

Some government police come in from the side attempting to confiscate the banner and a scuffle breaks out, pushing some people up against Diego, who shields Frida. They both raise their fists in the air.

END OF MONTAGE.

EXT. DOWNTOWN STREET - SUNSET

Outside a little tequila cantina, Frida and Diego say goodnight to some of the other marchers.

> **MAN**
> And more women.

> **DIEGO**
> So next time I'll make sure that happens, okay? Miss Kahlo... You may have to hold me up! Ettore is a good man, but he's got to be more careful, his mouth is going to get him into trouble...

Diego and Frida walk around the corner. They stop in front of a building: his studio.

> **FRIDA**
> What is this? Your studio?

> **DIEGO**
> One of the benefits of being a party leader: you can arrange for the drinking to be done close to home.
> *(takes out a key)*
> And now that you're officially a comrade, I believe I can let you see it if you like.

> **FRIDA**
> Hey, listen, if you think I'm going to sleep with you just because you've taken me under your wing, you're wrong.

> **DIEGO**
> Me?! I was painting murals and womanizing in peace when you came along.
> *(sighs)*
> Anyway, sex is like pissing. People take it much too seriously. In Russia, oh my god, in Russia, everyone was fucking like rabbits—

> **FRIDA**
> Well, this isn't Russia.

> **DIEGO**
> No, thank Christ...

ABOVE RIGHT: Frida Kahlo and Diego Rivera photographed at a demonstration of the Syndicate of Technical Workers, Painters and Sculptors, 1929. This archival photo by an unknown photographer was recreated in the film.

She laughs, trying not to like him as much as she does.

DIEGO *(Cont'd)*
(mock serious)
I have a proposal: We will not sleep together. We will solemnly swear, right here, right now, that we will be friends only.

He waits. She considers.

FRIDA
Fine.

DIEGO
Comrades, colleagues and friends forever.

He holds out his hand. Frida takes his hand, and they shake. But she doesn't let go: she steps up to him and kisses him. As soon as their lips part again, the street lamps in the park come on. Diego smiles at her, as if it was his doing.

FRIDA
Did you arrange for that?

DIEGO
Cost me a fortune.

INT. DIEGO'S PARLOR - NIGHT

An apartment cluttered with pre-Columbian pieces and painter's tools. There is a bed in the living room among the chaos. Diego is sitting on the bed with Frida in his lap. They are kissing tenderly, patiently. Diego begins to unbutton Frida's dress. She stops him, nervous...

FRIDA
I have a scar.

How I love Diego

No one will ever know how I love Diego. I don't want anything to wound him, nothing should bother him or take away the energy that he needs to live—to live the way he wishes, to paint, see, love, eat, sleep, to feel himself alone, to feel himself accompanied—but I would like to give all to him. If I had youth he could take it all.

—FRIDA KAHLO

DIEGO
Let me see it.

She hesitates, then stands and undresses before him. It is a horrible scar: from her left buttock, around her hip and to her groin. He kneels in front of her and runs his fingers along the length of her wound, tenderly. She makes a shy gesture to stop him but he goes on. He kisses the scar.

DIEGO *(Cont'd)*
You're perfect.

He takes her in his huge arms.

DIEGO *(Cont'd)*
Perfect.

She collapses into his embrace, going down to the floor.. They kiss. Wrapping themselves around one another.

EXT. OUTDOOR MARKET - DAY

Frida and Diego browse through the market, appreciating the colorful and exotic fruits and the Indian vendors, warm to everyone. They're playful with one another; having fun. He picks up two ripe melons and weighs them judiciously, in front of his chest.

FRIDA
Mmmm... I always wanted a man with melones bigger than mine.

Diego laughs and throws her a phallic-shaped gourd.

DIEGO
You know what I've always loved?

FRIDA
What?

DIEGO
A girl with cojones!
(kisses)
Frida bursts out laughing. The vendors eye them, smiling.

INT. DIEGO'S BEDROOM - DAY

Frida and Diego lie together in bed. Diego is admiring

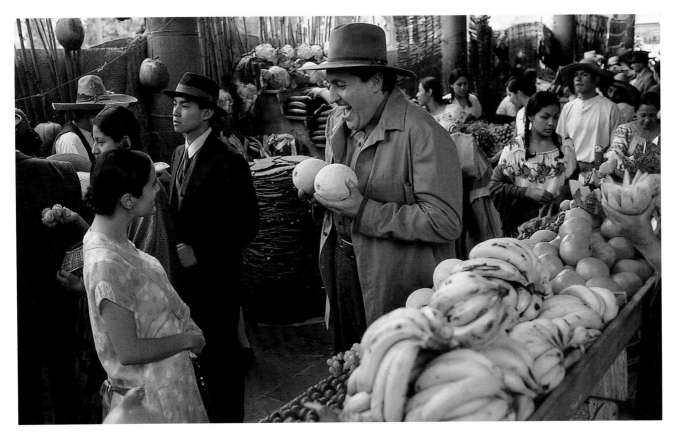

two little paintings of hers propped up near the bed: *The Bus* and *Self-Portrait, 1929.*

DIEGO
These are good, Frida, I love them.

FRIDA
You were probably painting better when you were twelve.

DIEGO
It's nonsense. I could never paint like this. I couldn't. I'm serious. I paint what I see, the world outside. But you... you paint from here... it's wonderful.

FRIDA
I can see why you're so successful with women.

Frida laughs, sits up. Diego looks up at her, quiet. His face suddenly awkward and open.

DIEGO
We'll have to get married, you know...

FRIDA
What?

She looks at him, genuinely shocked. He shrugs, casual.

DIEGO
The thing is... I think it's quite possible that we were born for each other... so we should marry.

FRIDA
But you don't believe in marriage.

DIEGO
Of course I do. I've had two wives already!

FRIDA
Exactly! You can't be true to only one woman.

DIEGO
"True," yes. "Faithful," no. Unfortunately, I'm physiologically incapable of fidelity.

FRIDA
Oh, really?

DIEGO
Yes. A doctor acquaintance of mine confirmed this.

FRIDA
What a convenient diagnosis.

DIEGO
Is fidelity that important to you?

FRIDA
Loyalty is important to me. Can you be loyal?

DIEGO
To you, always.

FRIDA
Good because I love you, panzon.

DIEGO
Friducha...

FRIDA
I accept.

They laugh at the simple matter-of-factness of it and then kiss tenderly and begin to make love.

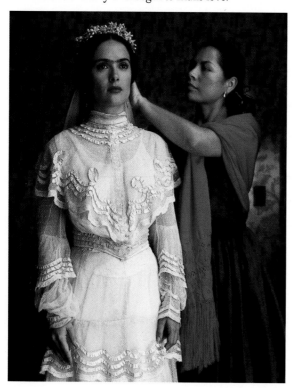

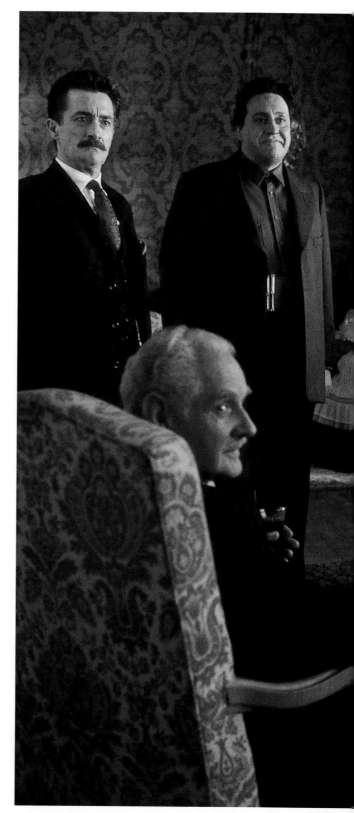

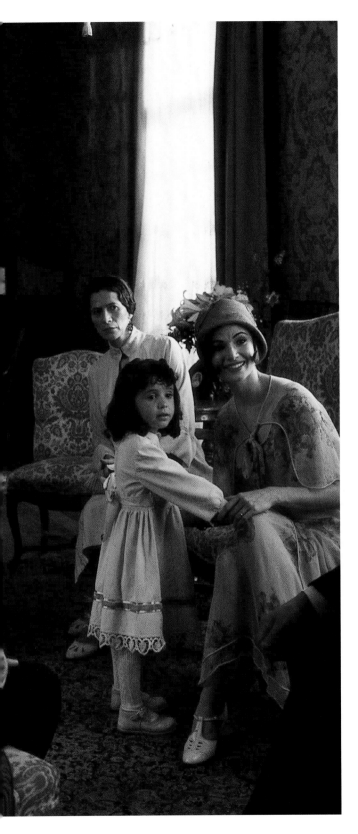

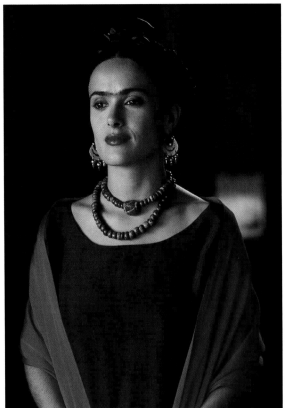

INT. BLUE HOUSE - PARENT'S BEDROOM - DAY

Frida stands at the mirror wearing a traditional wedding dress. Aurora stands behind her, pinning on Frida's veil.

> **AURORA**
> What a beautiful bride you are.

They make an odd tableau—Frida in her European wedding dress and Aurora in her green Tehuana dress and red shawl. Frida stares at their reflection, thoughtful.

EXT. BLUE HOUSE - VERANDAH - DAY

Dressed in their best, Guillermo and Matilde wait for Frida. Diego, and the rest of the family, remain in the livingroom, waiting to escort the bride to the wedding.

> **MATILDE**
> Don't touch me.

> **GUILLERMO**
> Oh, you think I'm going to hit you?

71

MATILDE
But he's divorced twice. He's had God knows how many children. And he's an atheist, Guillermo.

GUILLERMO
Perhaps you have forgotten this, and forgive me for reminding you, but I'm a German Jew, and you married me, remember?

MATILDE
Yes, well, he's also a communist.

GUILLERMO
A communist who's generous enough to pay off our mortgage.

MATILDE
Like the marriage of an elephant and a dove.

The door opens and everyone turns to see...

FRIDA—dressed in Aurora's Tehuana costume. She looks radiant. Diego is delighted.

Blue wall.

Close on the painting THE WEDDING PORTRAIT, 1931, which hangs on a wall. Move in as the painting transforms into 3-D. Fade into action as dancing couples surround the Frozen Wedding pair and we're into...

INT. TINA MODOTTI'S PARLOR - DAY

The wedding party. A sea of people dancing and drinking. Guillermo dances with Tina enjoying himself.

GUILLERMO
Your toe. It's been a long time.

MATILDE looks uncomfortably at a Soviet flag on the wall. CRISTINA holds her child and argues quietly with her husband.

MAN
Cristina! Stay here!

CRISTINA
Back!

Below: In the film, Frida's famous wedding portrait (entitled Frida and Diego Rivera (left) and painted in 1931, six years after her wedding) morphs into live action as the figures become real and walk out of the painting. Diego's palette was baked into a large cookie that the actors break and then eat as they dance out of the scene.

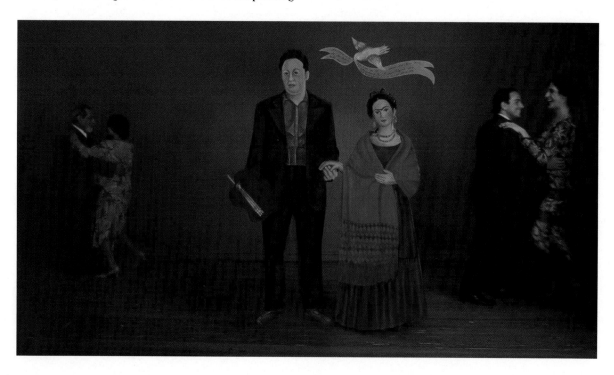

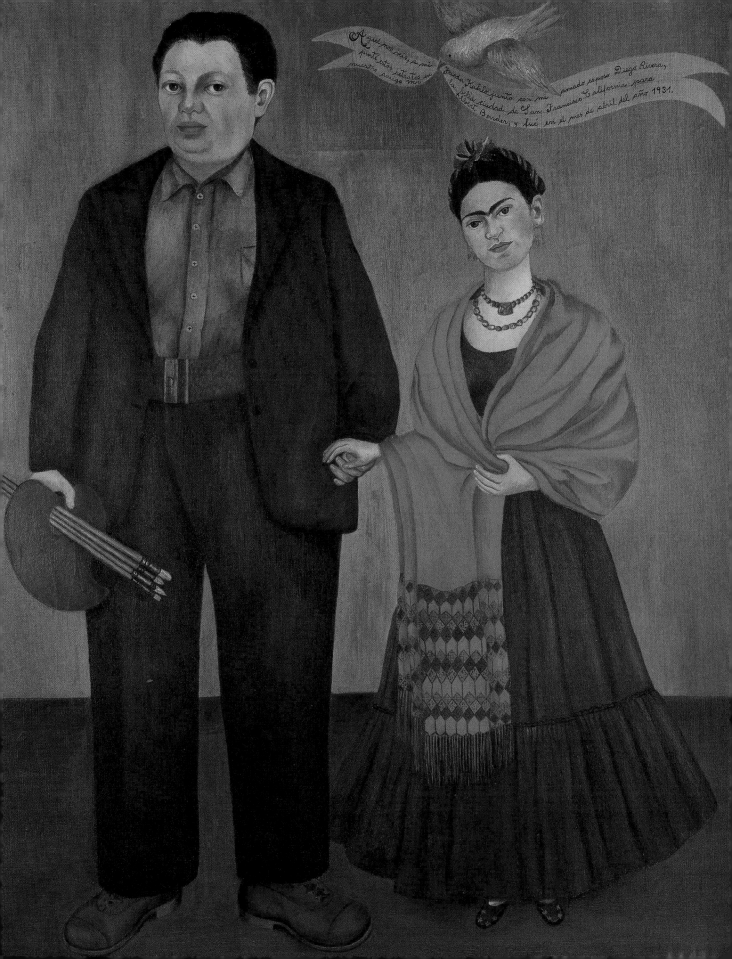

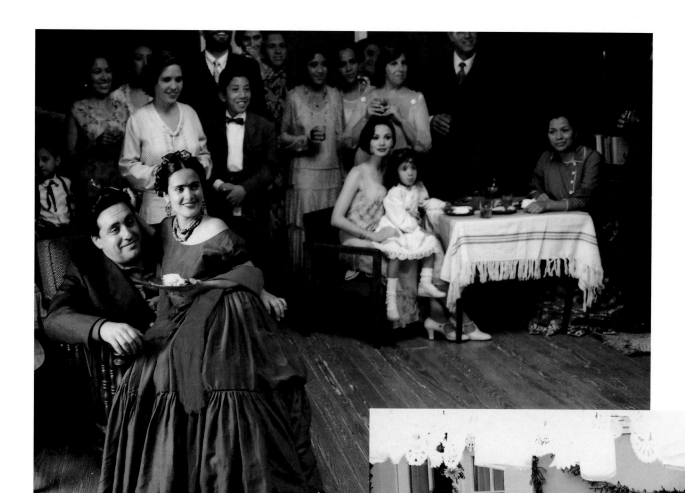

MAN
Please!

Lupe stands, drinking and talking distractedly to a man while shooting glances to.... Frida, who sits on Diego's lap, smoking a cigarette and feeding him cake. Affectionately intimate. They kiss. Across the room, a small group of women watch them, catty.

ADRIANA
I give them six months.

WOMAN #2
Six? I give them two.

The other women nod, jealous as Diego beams at his bride.

A GLASS CLINKS for a toast... TINA steps center.

TINA
I don't believe in marriage.....

Everyone laughs...

TINA *(Cont'd)*
No, I really don't! Let me be clear about that! I think at worst it's a hostile political act... a way for small-minded men to keep women in the house and out of the way, wrapped up in the guise of tradition and conservative, religious nonsense...

Matilde rolls her eyes...

TINA *(Cont'd)*
At best, it's a happy delusion... it's two people who truly love each other and have no idea how truly miserable they're about to make each other. *(pause)*

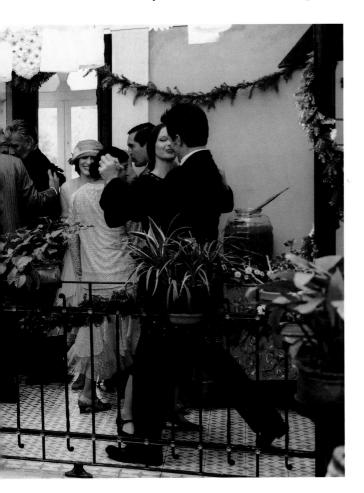

But, but when two people know that and they decide, with eyes wide open, to face each other and get married anyway... then I don't think it's conservative or delusional. I think it's radical. And courageous.... And very romantic.
(lifts her glass) To Diego and Frida.

Everyone toasts and cheers. DIEGO and FRIDA kiss.

EVERYONE
Diego and Frida.

DISSOLVE TO:

INT. TINA MODOTTI'S PARLOR - LATER - NIGHT

Frida's family has long since gone home... A circle of drunk singing, shouting people has formed around Diego and Frida. They dance in the center of the crowd—an odd pair, this giant man and this tiny woman with a limp.

Diego pauses to slam back a shot of tequila, howls, and then heaves the bottle in his hand against the wall. The bottle smashes and Frida rolls her eyes as the crowd laughs. Then over the noise of the laughter... low at first.

LUPE'S VOICE
You're crazy, you know that... YOU'RE CRAZY!!!
You son of a bitch.

TINA
Lupe. Ah.

The crowd quiets, turning as Lupe rises from a chair,

The Bull and the Butterfly

Rivera and Kahlo: has it been sufficiently stressed that they were two sides of the same Mexican coin, almost comical in their Mutt and Jeff disparity? The elephant and the dove, yes, but also the blind bull, in so many ways insensitive, rampaging, immensely energetic, poured towards the outside world, and married to the fragile, sensitive, crushed butterfly who forever repeated the cycle from larva to chrysalis to obsidian fairy, spreading her brilliant wings only to be pinned down, over and over, astoundingly resistant to her pain, until the name of both the suffering and the end of the suffering becomes death.

—CARLOS FUENTES, INTRODUCTION, *THE DIARY OF FRIDA KAHLO*

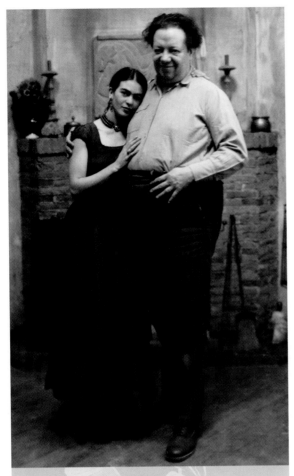

The Riveras

The Riveras had much in common: humor, intelligence, Mexicanism, social conscience, a bohemian approach to life. But the greatest bond may have been their enormous respect for each other's art. Rivera took pride in his wife's professional successes and he admired her growing artistic mastery. He would tell people that before he or any of his colleagues had had a painting hung in the Louvre, Frida had had that honor, and he loved to show her off to friends. One visitor recalls that the first thing Rivera did when she met him was to say that she must meet Frida. "There is no artist in Mexico that can compare with her!" Rivera said, beaming. "He immediately told me that when he was in Paris, Picasso had taken a drawing by Frida, looked at it for a long time, and then said: 'Look at those eyes: neither you nor I are capable of anything like it.' I noticed that in telling me this his own bulging eyes were shining with tears."

—HAYDEN HERRERA, *FRIDA: A BIOGRAPHY OF FRIDA KAHLO*

ABOVE: Frida Kahlo and Diego Rivera, shortly after their first marriage, ca. 1930–31.

very drunk. She zeroes in on Diego, then pulls up her skirt showing off her fantastic legs...

> LUPE
> You left these legs...

> DIEGO
> Oh, Lupe, Lupe. Nah.

> LUPE
> ...You left those legs, Diego.

Frida looks to see how he'll respond. Diego, amused, moves toward Lupe with his arms open to calm her... She keeps away, circling toward Frida, almost crying, drunk...

> LUPE *(Cont'd)*
> You'd give up these beauties... for these match sticks? This peg leg! Mira, mira.

She tries to yank up Frida's skirts. Frida knocks her hand away. Lupe, drunk and furious, turns and stomps out of the apartment. Frida looks to Diego for support, but he is laughing at the whole thing.

Humiliated, Frida glares at him and storms out too... Diego raises his arms, exasperated... Tina raises her glass.

> TINA
> Viva la revolution!

INT. DIEGO'S BEDROOM - NIGHT

Diego's bed: Frida sits on the edge in candlelight, taking down her hair and sulking...

Off-screen we can hear Diego enter. He crawls into frame across the bed behind her and bites her ass... She slaps him away, but he slides in to lie behind her stroking her back...

> FRIDA
> Ay. My mother was wrong about you, you know... she said you were an elephant but you're not—elephants are strong and courageous and they defend their mates. You're a toad. You even look like a toad.

> DIEGO
> And you look like a dog.

She turns to slap him again, not in the mood to be teased. He laughs and stutters defensively...

DIEGO *(Cont'd)*
DOVE! DOVE! Did I say "dog?" No I meant dove! You're my little paloma...

He grabs a sketchpad and a piece of charcoal pen off the bedside table next to her... He sketches quickly and we see that in a few simple strokes he has created a lovely little picture of a huge toad with a dove sitting on its head...

She looks at it and starts to melt...

FRIDA
What will people say about such a pair?

DIEGO
They'll have never seen a better match.

He kisses her on the shoulder and back.

DIEGO *(Cont'd)*
Thank you.

FRIDA
For what?

DIEGO
For making a fat old crazy communist a happy man.

Frida puts her head on his chest, snuggling him...

INT. DIEGO'S BEDROOM - MORNING

Late morning sun streaming in... Frida awakes alone and stretches... happy.

INT. DIEGO'S PARLOR - DAY

Diego sits at the table, eating a big lunch. He has set a place for Frida who wanders in, rubbing sleep from her eyes. He hops up and pulls her chair out for her. They kiss.

DIEGO
Sit. Eat.

Frida sits down, impressed, and begins to eat. She moans with pleasure... it's delicious.

FRIDA
Mi amore...!

DIEGO
Good, eh...?

FRIDA
What a wonderful mole!

DIEGO
It's Lupe's special recipe...

FRIDA
Well, you've mastered it!

DIEGO
I can't cook to save my life!

Frida stops and stares at him suspiciously...

DIEGO *(Cont'd)*
She brought it down for us while you were sleeping...

Frida is suddenly wide awake.

FRIDA
Brought it down...?

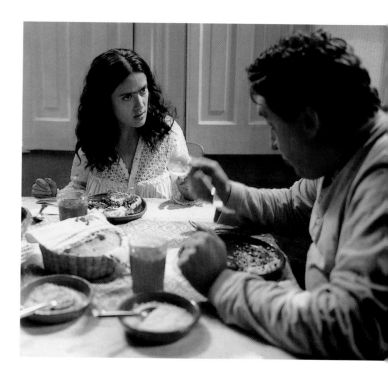

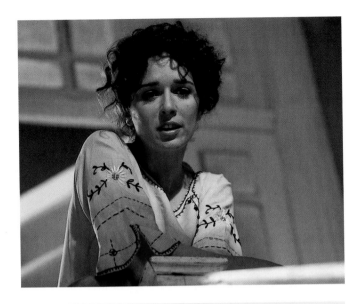

DIEGO
She's in the apartment upstairs with my kids. I let her have it until she finds a place in town—

Frida grabs his plate from him, picks up her own, marches over, dumps the plates in the trash and slams out the door.

EXT. DIEGO'S APARTMENT BUILDING - STAIRCASE - LATE AFTERNOON

Frida bangs on the door. Lupe opens it and stares at her.

FRIDA
I'm not just passing through, you know. I'm here to stay.

LUPE
Is that what you came to tell me?

She turns to walk back downstairs, mumbling...

FRIDA
I'm here to stay. So stay out of my damn kitchen.

Lupe calls after her...

LUPE
You like that mole?

FRIDA
So-so.

The Essence of Lupe

There's a story about my character, Lupe Marín, that I wish could be in the movie. Of course, it has no place in the story, but it tells you who she was. After her divorce from Diego, Lupe married a poet who was very much in love with her. Their marriage didn't last long. After she left him, and right before the desperate man killed himself, he cut off his testicles and sent them in a box to Lupe.

She opened the package while she was cooking in her kitchen and threw the testicles to the dogs. Whether that's true or not—it's probably an exaggeration—it makes you understand the essence of that lady.

—VALERIA GOLINO, ACTRESS

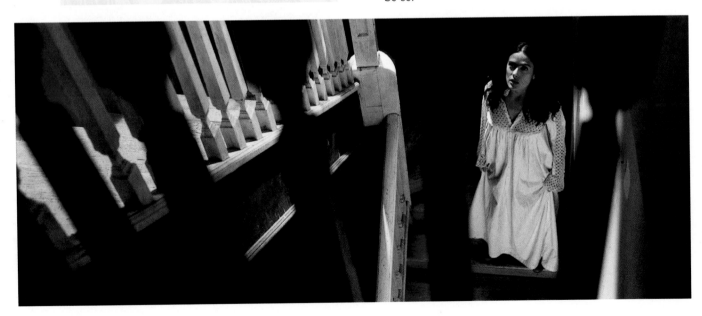

Lupe Marín

Guadalupe Marín modeled for many of Diego Rivera's murals. She became his mistress and then, in 1922, his wife. She gave birth to two daughters. Lupe and Diego had a tumultuous marriage that was both passionate and physically abusive. Their relationship ended when Rivera began having an affair with Tina Modotti who also modeled for Rivera. Despite her jealousy and temper, Lupe managed to become friends with Frida; she taught her how to cook Diego's favorite meals and, in exchange, Frida painted Lupe's portrait. Frida also remained close to Lupe's daughters.

RIGHT: Portrait of Guadalupe, *1926, by Diego Rivera.*

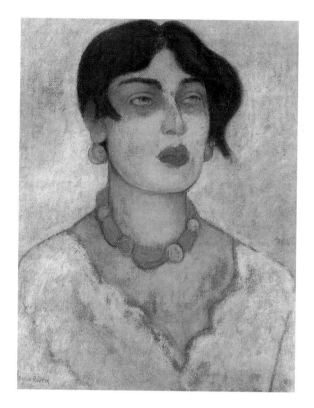

LUPE

Well, he lives for it. So if you're here to stay, you'd better learn how to make it.

INT. LUPE'S KITCHEN - LATER - DAY

Lupe's daughters play with their dog. The counters are covered with the remnants of cooking—flour, bits of onion, empty bowls. Pots bubble on the stove. Wearing aprons, Frida and Lupe sit, their feet up on the table. They're moist with the heat of the oven, passing a cold bottle of wine between them.

LUPE

I was so angry, he didn't come home for three days. Pass me the cilantro. So I took two of his damn Aztec idols that he adores, you know? And I smashed the pieces of clay in the boiling pot of beef stock and told him it was "Sopa Azteca."

FRIDA

Medea! Did he eat it?

LUPE

He did!

FRIDA

Did he like it?

LUPE

He loved it! Of course, until he found out, then he got sick, he got furious, oof, and it didn't make me feel any better, and it definitely didn't stop him from cheating. But what the hell.

A small child drops a pot on the floor and begins wailing.

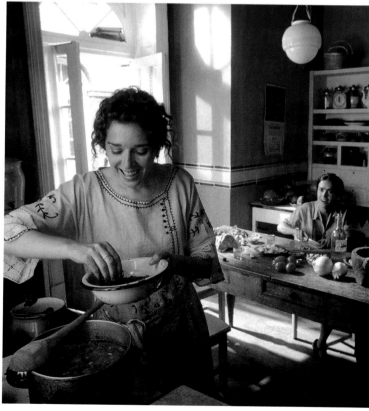

LUPE
Root, get out, come on.

Lupe takes her two children and escorts them to the door out of the kitchen.

LUPE *(Cont'd)*
Marie! Let's go. Time for a nap.

Lupe stares off for a beat... comes back to the table.

LUPE *(Cont'd)*
The other night... I was very drunk.

FRIDA
I know... it's all right.

LUPE
Oye nina, Diego has never belonged to anybody. He belongs only to himself, and that of course is what makes him so desirable. He's the best of friends and the worst of husbands.

Lupe is quiet, examining Frida. Then...

LUPE *(Cont'd)*
Diego will never be anyone's husband. Not really.

FRIDA
We'll see.

LUPE
You'll know it's over when he gets the next commission out of town. He'll say he'll send for you. But he never does.

They both fall silent thinking.

The apartment door OPENS... A maid enters...

MAID
Señora Rivera...?

FRIDA/LUPE
(both turning)
Yes...?

They turn back to each other, Lupe with a slight, sad smile...

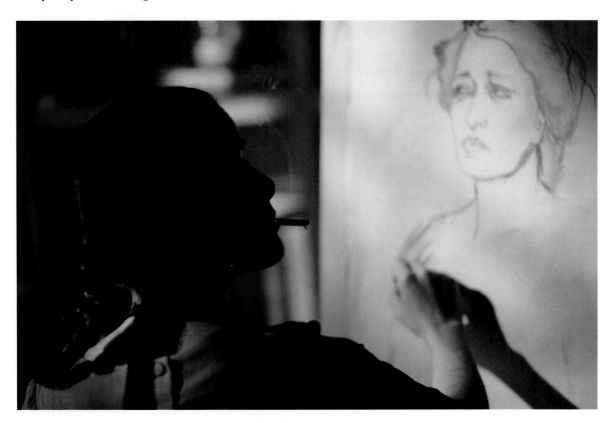

INT. DIEGO APARTMENT - PARLOR - DAY

Frida sitting, working on her sketch of Lupe, smoking...

Lost in thought, she glances up at the clock, puts her pencil down and stands up... Moving toward us, she picks up a cloth-wrapped basket of food...TIGHT ON THE BASKET, the camera swings as she passes and, without cutting, walks out into...

INT. CHAPINGO CHAPEL - DAY

Frida enters, places the basket on the table. She approaches Diego who is busily at work sketching. A voluptuous NUDE MODEL poses for him. Frida kisses him, checks out the drawing.

> **DIEGO**
> What do you think?

> **FRIDA**
> The tits lack gravity.

> **DIEGO**
> *(not enjoying the critique)*
> Ah, come on.

Frida shrugs "what can I say?" and turns to go.

Chapingo Chapel

Diego Rivera agreed to paint a major cycle of frescoes in the new National School of Agriculture in the town of Chapingo in the fall of 1924. Between the entrance to the main building, the stairway and the adjoining chapel, Rivera's work covers more than fifteen hundred square feet of wall space.

The murals he painted in Chapingo were among the first of his large-scale endeavors. "I was compelled to communicate the architectural style of the chapel—Spanish Renaissance—with a genuine Mexican aesthetic," Rivera would later explain. "The Chapingo frescoes were essentially a song of the land, its profundity, beauty, richness, and sadness."

Here Rivera sets forth his idea that an organized peasantry had the power to generate social change and that, through political action, they could bring nature into harmony with the best interests of Mexico.

His work in the chapel is considered among his foremost masterpieces.

> **FRIDA**
> Eat your pozole while it's hot.

Diego watches her leave, returns to his sketch, and starts to redraw the breasts.

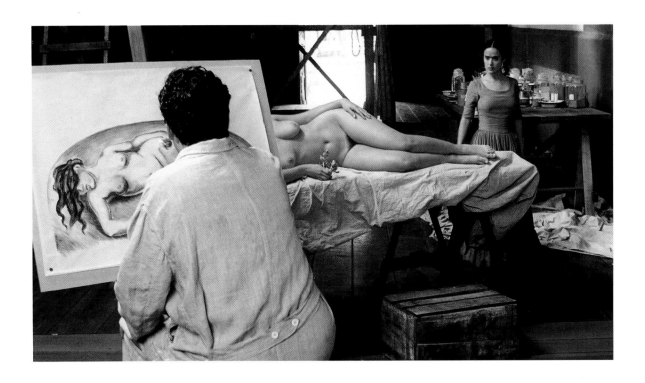

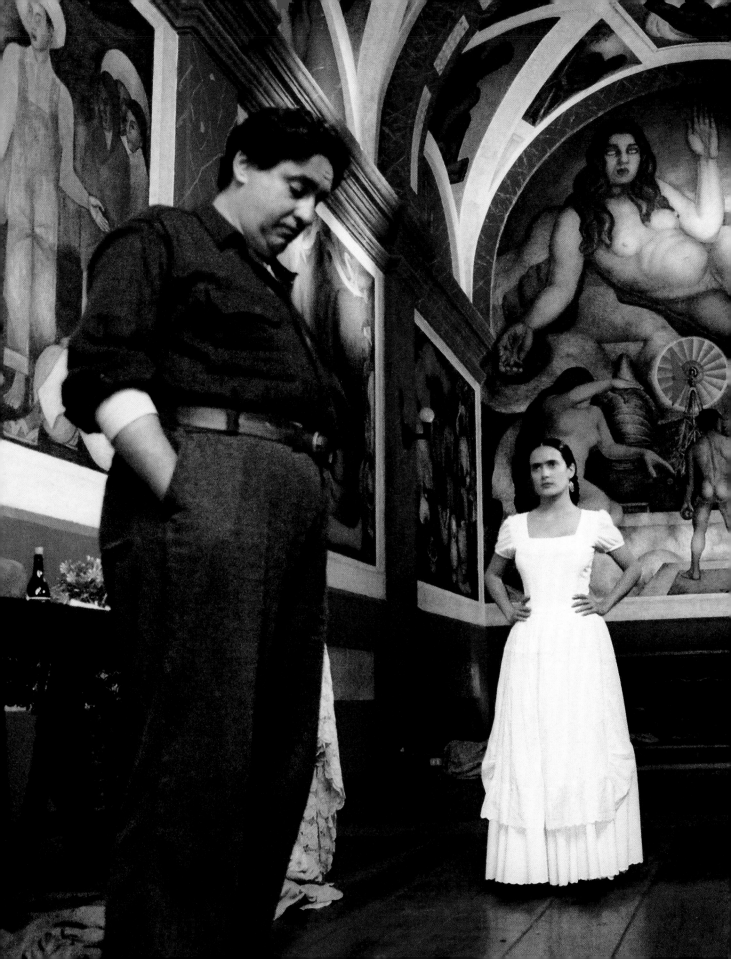

INT. DIEGO'S AND FRIDA'S BEDROOM - NIGHT

Frida sits before the mirror in a Tehuana dress. Diego sneaks up behind her and places an antique Indian necklace around her neck. They kiss.

INT. CHAPINGO CHAPEL - DAY

Frida stands in the middle of the almost completed chapel, surrounded by Diego's enormous murals of nudes. On the table by the scaffold is the beautiful lunch she has laid out for him. She has been waiting for some time. Diego enters through the door, clearly late.

FRIDA
It's not like you to be late for lunch, Diego...

DIEGO
I was at the Ministry explaining why a history of the Mexican people is an appropriate subject for the Mexican National Palace...

FRIDA
Again...?

DIEGO
When I work, they scream about my politics....
When I don't work, they scream about the delays...
It's a farce...

He kisses her and she leans into his chest... and freezes.

She puts her nose straight into his shirt and steps back like a shot, her eyes flashing...

FRIDA
Hijo de puta...
(beat—she stares at him)
That model, huh?

DIEGO
Yes.

And here it is... Right in the middle of their happiness, she faces the challenge of marriage to Diego. Unapologetic, he stares back at her...

DIEGO *(Cont'd)*
It was just a fuck... That's all. I've given more affection in a handshake...

She controls her breath...then as much as possible...

FRIDA
Well, that makes me feel so much better. Was she good at least?

DIEGO
Not very.

FRIDA
Too bad... she had such a great ass.

She turns and heads for the exit.

FRIDA *(Cont'd)*
When you get home, take a good bath. We're going out tonight.

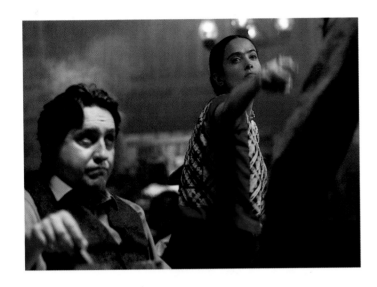

INT. PULQUERIA (BAR) - NIGHT

LOUD MUSIC—The bar is packed with people: students, artists, Socialists, etc... One large table seems to be the vortex of all the energy in the place where...

Frida is holding court, standing between two handsome young men, their arms around each others' shoulders, all raising tequila glasses and singing corridos.

DIEGO is at the head of the table watching Frida, entranced by her as ever... FRIDA and the GUYS finish the song, and shoot the tequila to loud applause. Her eyes meet Diego's. He smiles at her and puts his hand over his heart. She looks away.

FRIDA
More tequila!

YOUNG MAN
RIVERA!!... HEY!!!

They look up. A drunk young man has approached the table.

YOUNG MAN (Cont'd)
Yeah, you! You know what I think of you and your stinking murals...?

He spits...

YOUNG MAN (Cont'd)
Why don't you get the fuck out of here, huh? This is a bar for workers, not for government whores...

FRIDA quickly steps up to the KID, and tosses her tequila in his face. As the KID goes for Frida, Diego explodes out of his chair and tackles the kid, starting a general brawl...

INT. DIEGO'S STUDIO - NIGHT

Dark inside... The door bangs open and Frida and Diego enter, Diego in mid-rant. Frida sets about turning on lights.

DIEGO
I tell you that kid was one of Siqueiros' boys. Siqueiros is a hero to these punks, but what's he actually done? Nothing! I've put socialism on the government walls, I've got the fascists calling me the most dangerous subversive in the country and I'm the traitor to the Party?!

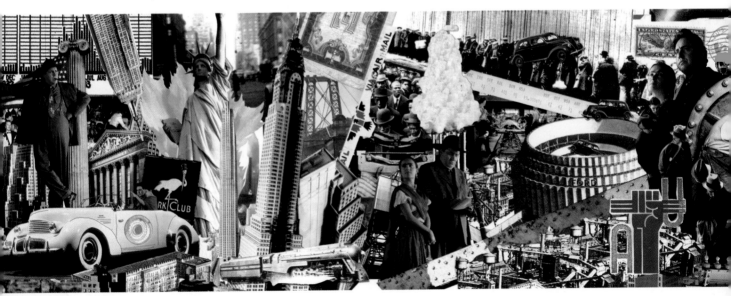

FRIDA
Soon we'll have no one left to drink with.

DIEGO
It's not funny...

FRIDA
I'm not kidding...Tina says they'll kick you out of the Party for the Palace mural.

DIEGO
They won't have to... I quit.

FRIDA
So you quit... and keep on working. That's all that matters to you anyway.

He looks at her a beat. She turns, sensing something...

DIEGO
I've been offered a show in New York. A solo exhibition at the new modern museum... It would be a wonderful entree... I could get commissions out of it...

On the word "commissions," she glances at her finished portrait of Lupe... She looks at him.

DIEGO (*Cont'd*)
I thought you'd be excited.

FRIDA
They don't care that you are a communist pig?

DIEGO
They can't afford to: all the greatest painters are communist pigs.

She softens and smiles slightly.

FRIDA
That's wonderful, Diego. When do you leave?

DIEGO
As soon as you decide to come with me.

Overcome, she leaps to hug him.

FRIDA
Ah, Mi Monstrito... we'll take Gringolandia by storm...

Begin New York MONTAGE:

EXT. NEW YORK - 1930s - DAY

The New York sequence is a long collage of still photos, real historic stock footage, recreated documentary-style footage and parodies of old films—all played under Frida's Voice Over, Diego's Interviews, etc... ALL IN BLACK & WHITE.

THEY ARRIVE: Stock footage of a steamship in New York Harbor, B&W postcard stills, punching in on 1930s New York; a picture of a boat at the dock with the tiny passengers up on the deck waving down. Frida has drawn arrows on the photo pointing out where they were in the crowd...

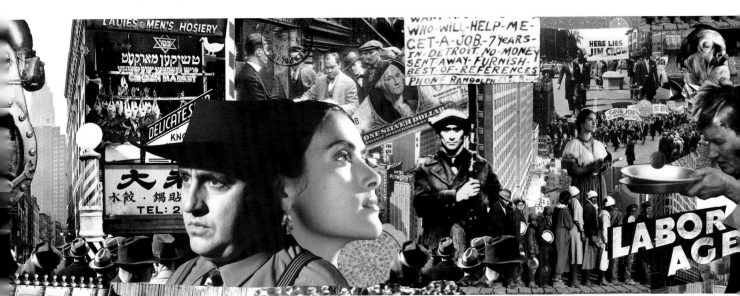

EXT. NEW YORK - 1930s - DAY

A posed photo of Diego and Frida in their travel clothes with their luggage—he with his hat and seven-inch cigar, she in Mexican garb...

> **FRIDA** (V.O.)
> Dear Cristi, the invasion of Gringolandia has begun. They are never gonna know what hit them. New York has Diego on fire...

EXT. NEW YORK - 1930s - DAY

THEY EXPLORE: Stock period shots of the bustling city: cars rushing, crowds of people, the great skyscrapers being thrown up, the factories...

> **REPORTER'S VOICE** (V.O.)
> What's your impression of New York, Mr. Rivera?

> **DIEGO** (V.O.)
> Magnificent. There is no reason why any artist born in our two continents should go to Europe for inspiration. It is all here—the might, the power, the energy, the sadness, the glory and the youthfulness of our American lands.

EXT. NEW YORK STOREFRONT - DAY

Frida and Diego wave at the camera and then turn and start walking along a "sidewalk set" that is actually a treadmill in front of a New York storefront window. As they walk, images of different areas of the city roll by in the window... In the window, we see scenes of Depression conditions, too...

> **FRIDA**
> I see the majesty that Diego sees, but all that American comfort is a myth. While the rich drink their cocktailitos, thousands are starving...

Since we couldn't afford to actually shoot in New York or Paris, we had to come up with ways of representing those trips at locations in Mexico. We wanted a subjective experience, as seen through Frida's eyes. For the New York montage, for example, we shot Diego and Frida against a green screen and inserted them into a collage of photographs and stock footage.

—RODRIGO PRIETO, DIRECTOR OF PHOTOGRAPHY

Her Thwarted Wish

Frida Kahlo miscarried the child she was carrying at the time of her wedding. In a drawing of herself holding hands with Diego, dated December 1939, she conveyed her loss by drawing a baby on her stomach and then erasing it. "We could not have a child, and I cried inconsolably but I distracted myself by cooking, dusting the house, sometimes by painting, and every day going to accompany Diego on the scaffold. It gave him great pleasure when I arrived with the midday meal in a basket covered with flowers." Her thwarted wish to bear a child became an underlying theme in many of her paintings.

—HAYDEN HERRERA, *FRIDA KAHLO: THE PAINTINGS*

INT. BARBIZON HOTEL SUITE - NEW YORK - DAY

Frida and Diego's first NY apartment, filled with flowers from Abbie Rockefeller...

> **FRIDA** (V.O.)
> Diego is working almost constantly to prepare for his show, so I have to find ways to entertain myself.

Frida sits alone by the window, smoking and thinking, looking out over the strange city...

INT. MOVIE THEATER - NEW YORK - DAY

A snippet of the old KING KONG, where Kong climbs the Empire State Building, is on the screen.

ANGLE ON: FRIDA, the light flickering on her face, happily munching popcorn...

> **NEWSREEL ANNOUNCER** (V.O.)
> Breaking all records, over 50,000 people have lined up outside New York's new Museum of Modern Art to see the paintings of Mexico's greatest artist Diego Rivera, the most talked about man this side of the Rio Grande.

FRIDA watches smiling... BACK TO THE SCREEN:

EXT. EMPIRE STATE BUILDING - KING KONG - DAY

King Kong has become DIEGO, huge, apelike, climbing the building to the top where FRIDA is Fay Wray, recoiling in terror. DIEGO swats model planes on strings, beats his chest and roars triumphantly, and as we close in on him it becomes...

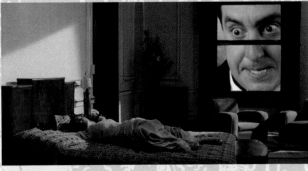
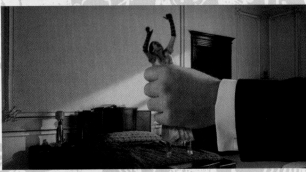
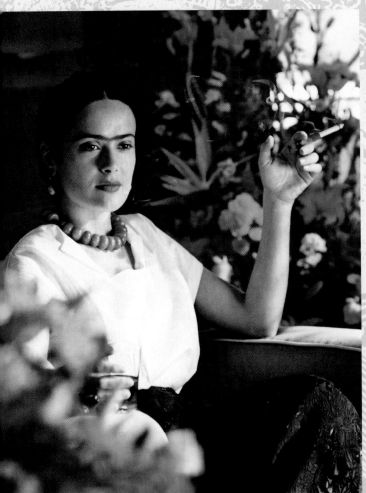
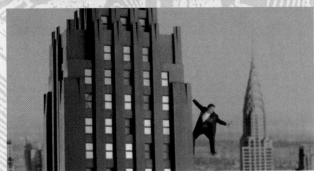
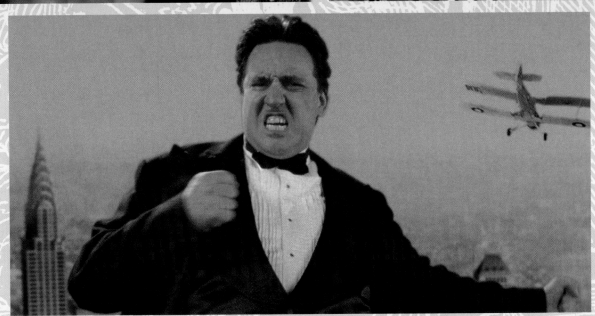

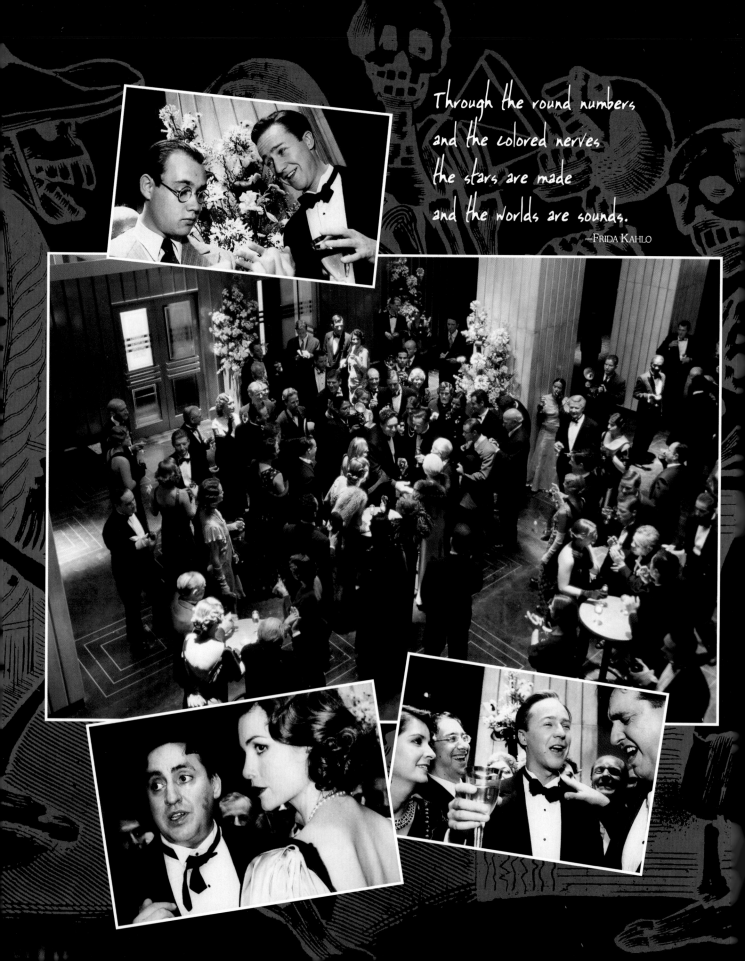

Through the round numbers
and the colored nerves
the stars are made
and the worlds are sounds.

—Frida Kahlo

INT. FANCY HOTEL RESTAURANT - NEW YORK - NIGHT

MUSEUM'S CELEBRATION PARTY FOR DIEGO

THE REAL DIEGO, howling, drunk, arms raised triumphantly with a glass of wine in each hand...

We pull back and we're in the middle of a truly upscale party... The crème de la crème of New York society and celebrity is there in all it's glory...

> ROCKEFELLER
> Señor Diego Rivera.

> FRIDA
> The gringos are friendly enough, but the most important thing in Gringolandia is to have ambi-

tion, to succeed in becoming somebody. And the "somebodies" are the only ones that interest them. I despise this pretension. Being the gran caca interests me not at all.

The crowd swarms around DIEGO, WOMEN paw at him, REPORTERS shout, "Diego! Over here!" In the black and white mob, ONLY FRIDA IS IN COLOR, trying to stay near Diego but getting shoved aside...

> FRIDA *(Cont'd)*
> Of course, Diego loves it. He's like a big Mexican piñata with enough candy for everyone...

POP! POP! FLASHBULBS firing all over send us into a series of:

STILL PHOTOS

in the society pages capturing the event... A few of them capture FRIDA, at a table with friends, we ZOOM IN on her unsmiling face and from her eyes...

> FRIDA
> Everything about this country inspires him...

WHIP OVER to a close-up of another photo revealing DIEGO'S HAND firmly planted on a YOUNG WOMAN'S ASS in the crush...

EXT. REVOLVING DOOR - DAY

A REVOLVING DOOR SPINS, and out comes

MOMA, 1932

Shyness and her dislike of gringo society made Frida stick close by Rivera's side at his Museum of Modern Art opening on December 22, 1932....

The guests merrily drank and chattered against the backdrop of Rivera's painted pageant of Mexico, their social glitter and sartorial swank in sharp contrast with the exhibition's pièce de résistance, the group of newly completed fresco panels showing Rivera's Marxist view of Mexico: Agrarian Leader Zapata, Liberation of the Peon, and Sugar Cane, which depicts workers oppressed by landowners.... In equally sharp contrast with the assembled art patrons and patronesses, decked out in black tie and pale, floor-length evening gowns, was Frida Kahlo—olive-skinned, almost swarthy, and strikingly exotic in her bright Tehuana finery—standing quietly next to the protective bulk of her garrulous husband.

Rivera's show not only received critical acclaim, it also drew the highest attendance of any exhibition at the Museum of Modern Art to that time. By January 27, 1932, when it closed, 56,575 people had paid admission to see it, and the dean of New York art critics, Henry McBride, had described the artist in the New York Sun (December 26, 1931) as "the most talked about man on this side of the Atlantic."

—HAYDEN HERRERA, *FRIDA: A BIOGRAPHY OF FRIDA KAHLO*

Diego Rivera's MOMA show

The show... was an even bigger draw than the museum's first one-man show, which was dedicated to the work of Henri Matisse. The reviews were almost all positive. Young artists looked at the work and were inspired. Diego Rivera was now a major artist on the world stage.

—PETE HAMILL, *DIEGO RIVERA*

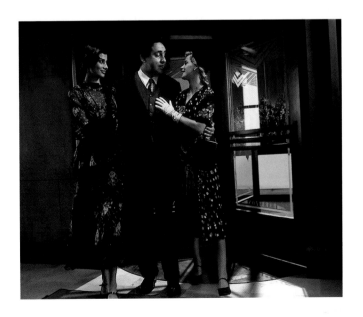

DIEGO with YOUNG WOMAN. He kisses her good-bye and goes back in the door, spinning out with another woman. Kiss, bye, back in again... out again with a third. As the door revolves faster and faster Diego keeps emerging with a different woman on his arm—sometimes two or three... and as it spins, it changes from B&W to color.

EXT. STREET - OUTSIDE BARBIZON - NEW YORK - EARLY MORNING

The door spins and Frida emerges (at normal speed) with the YOUNG WOMAN whose ass Diego had grabbed at the Museum party. They exit laughing...

INT. DINER - NEW YORK - DAY

Frida sits in a round booth with the woman (maybe Georgia O'Keefe?)...They have clearly just been lovers... The woman grins...

WAITRESS
Two loose eggs, hot cinnamon bun, two black coffees, anything else?

YOUNG WOMAN
That's fine.

FRIDA
Thank you.

WAITRESS
(at the next booth)
You guys ready? Huh?

YOUNG WOMAN
Well, I never thought I'd hear myself say this, but... you were better than your husband.

She giggles, but Frida only smiles a little...

YOUNG WOMAN *(Cont'd)*
You weren't upset about that were you? I mean he, he said... you wouldn't be.

FRIDA
Oh he did, did he? Well you weren't the first, and you won't be the last.

YOUNG WOMAN
Why do you put up with it?

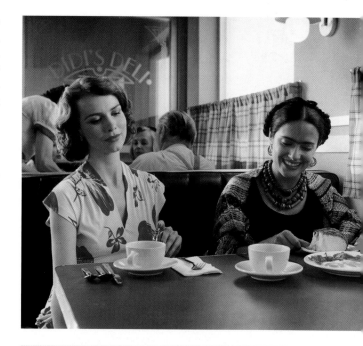

A Natural Compensation

I will not speak of Diego as "my husband" because it would be ridiculous, Diego never has been and never will be anyone's "husband." Nor will I speak of him as a lover, because to me he transcends the domain of sex, and if I speak of him as a son I will have done nothing but describe or paint my own emotions, almost my self-portrait, not the portrait of Diego... Probably some people expect of me a very personal, "feminine," anecdotal, diverting portrait, full of complaints and even a certain amount of gossip, the type of gossip that is "decent," interpretable or usable, according to the morbidity of the reader. Perhaps they hope to hear from me laments about "how much one suffers," living with a man like Diego. But I do not believe that the banks of a river suffer for letting the water run, or that the earth suffers because it rains, or the atom suffers discharging its energy... for me everything has a natural compensation. Within my difficult and obscure role of ally of an extraordinary being, I have the same reward as a green dot within a quality of red: I have the reward of "equilibrium." The pains or joys that regularize life in this society, rotten with lies, in which I live are not mine. If I have prejudices and if the actions of others, even the actions of Diego Rivera, wound me, I make myself responsible for my inability to see with clarity, and if I do not have such prejudices, I should admit that it is natural for the red corpuscles to fight against the white ones without the slightest prejudice, and that this phenomenon only signifies health.

—FRIDA KAHLO

I play this woman who appears fleetingly in the film during the New York scenes. During this time Diego and Frida seem to have had a rather unorthodox arrangement. As a couple, they shared several lovers. My character is, I guess, a fictional version of many of those women.

What I find interesting about my generation now is that we assume we are the most radical and bohemian generation that ever existed in the last hundred years. Actually I think that the time period represented in the film, the 20s, 30s, and 40s, was just as radical, if not moreso. Here was a network of artists, revolutionaries, and intellectuals across the world who were involved in and passionate about each other's work.

Diego and Frida as a couple were clearly dynamite. They were both incredible artists, but there was something about the fusion of the two of them that made them larger than the sum of two people. I've admired Frida since I was a kid in school. The fact that she was disabled and extraordinarily talented, and had such a free mind, all of those things seemed to suggest she was an amazing human being.

—Saffron Burrows, actress

FRIDA
Look, Diego is how he is, and that's how I love him. I cannot love him for what he's not.
(beat, smiling)
Anyway, my sweet Gracie, I get along just fine...

Under the table Frida slides her hand up under the girl's dress. She blushes and grips the table as Frida works her hand and smiles.

INT ROCKEFELLER CENTER - OFFICE

NELSON ROCKEFELLER AND DIEGO stand in front of a huge white wall, surrounded be photographers.

ROCKEFELLER
Congratulations. It's a lot of wall.

DIEGO
It always is.

Rockefeller and Diego shake hands and smile.

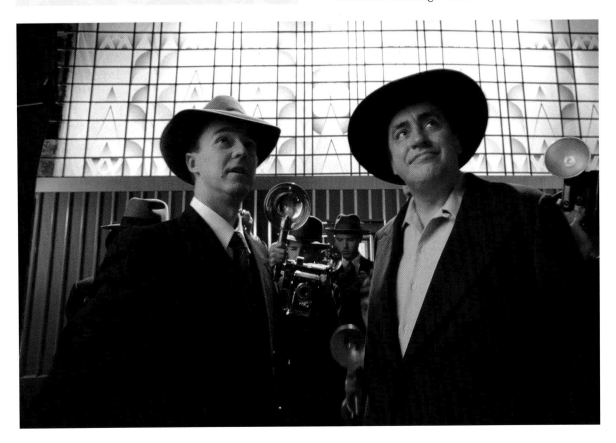

The only thing I know is that I paint because I need to, and I paint what passes through my head without any other consideration.

—FRIDA KAHLO

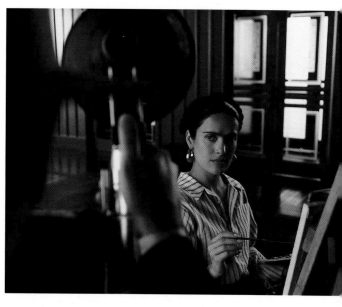

FLASH!! The image becomes a spinning newspaper photo under the headline: RIVERA TO PAINT ROCKEFELLER LOBBY

TIGHT ON: SUB HEADLINE Mural to express "A NEW AND BETTER FUTURE."

THE PAPER BLEEDS TO WHITE.

INT. ROCKEFELLER CENTER - LOBBY

Diego's mural, magnificent even half-finished and surrounded by scaffolding. Diego is a whirlwind of energy, shouting orders to his assistants while answering questions from reporters...

> DIEGO
> Gentlemen, please, please. I have to get back to work, I'm sorry.

Frida sits quietly against a wall, painting on a small easel.

One reporter peels off and comes toward Frida and smiles when he sees her painting...

> REPORTER
> Are you a painter, too, Mrs. Rivera?

> FRIDA
> Nah, just killing time.

Heads turn to listen... She grins...

> DIEGO
> She's much better than me. You'll see.

The photographer snaps a photo. She looks up, annoyed.

INT. BARBIZON HOTEL - BATHROOM - NEW YORK - NIGHT

Frida bathes Diego, sweeping the water back and forth with her hand and scrubbing him. It's a pleasant ritual.

> DIEGO
> What did the doctor say?

> FRIDA
> He might be able to improve the pain but the bones would have to be reset... blah, blah... the usual speech. You know it by heart.
> *(beat)*
> I'm pregnant.

He is surprised and worried.

> DIEGO
> Can your body take it?

> FRIDA
> If it can take you, it can take a little Dieguito.

> DIEGO
> No, no, Frida.

FRIDA
He's not very optimistic.

He turns back around, shaking his head.

DIEGO
This is not.... I can't bear to think of you in pain.

FRIDA
I'm used to pain.

DIEGO
This is not... I'm not a good example of... It's not a good time, there is the Rockefeller commission, Detroit, Chicago, all that traveling, no, it's, it's, it's too much.

He turns... She is silent.

DIEGO *(Cont'd)*
You really want this baby, Frida?

FRIDA
I do.

DIEGO
All right.

FRIDA
All right.

She nods, weeping and hugs him.

DIEGO
All right... let's try and have this baby. Shhh... shhh... listen.... listen.

He puts his ear to her belly.

DIEGO *(Cont'd)*
He's reciting the Communist Manifesto.

She laughs.

INT. BARBIZON HOTEL SUITE - NIGHT

Diego enters in the middle of the night, exhausted from working late. He moves into the dark of the bedroom where Frida's sleeping form lies on the bed. He turns on the light to find...

FRIDA LYING CURLED UP IN A HUGE POOL OF BLOOD, SOAKED IN SWEAT AND MOANING... HE RUSHES TO HER.

INT. HOSPITAL HALLWAY - NIGHT

Diego rushes along with the orderlies next to Frida's gurney through the corridors.

INT. HOSPITAL HALLWAY - SUNRISE

Shafts of sunlight cut through the hall. Diego sits with his arms on his knees and his head down on a bench against the wall opposite a doctor who is standing.

DOCTOR
She's lost a lot of blood.

DIEGO
I want to see her.

DOCTOR
She needs to sleep, you should go home and try and get some rest.

The door to one of the rooms opens and Frida steps out. She's moving slowly, in great pain. But frighteningly calm.

DIEGO
Frida!

DOCTOR
You should be in bed, Mrs. Rivera.

Frida clutches Diego's arm.

FRIDA
The baby came out in pieces.

DIEGO
Come on, niña. Let's go back to bed.

FRIDA
It never formed properly.

DIEGO
We can try again. But you must rest.

The doctor signals and a nurse comes over, puts an arm around Frida. Frida shakes her off, clutching at Diego.

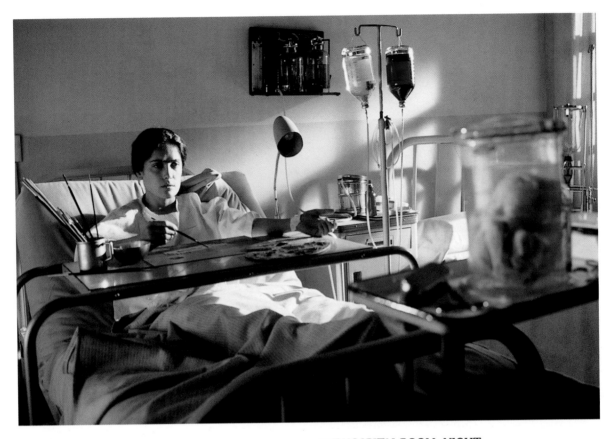

FRIDA
What did you do with him?!

Diego holds up his hand to silence the doctor.

DIEGO
All right, chiquitita. I'll take care of it. Come on. O.K.

FRIDA
Please, Diego.

DIEGO
I promise. I promise.

Frida releases Diego, walks past the nurses back into her room. The doctor turns to Diego, apologetic.

INT. HOSPITAL ROOM - DAY

Frida sits up in bed, alone, painting on a small sheet of metal. She works feverishly with sweat on her brow.

On the table next to her is a lab jar full of liquid and in the dim light we can make out the form of a fetus...

INT. HOSPITAL ROOM - NIGHT

Frida lies asleep with the UNSEEN PAINTING resting on her belly...

OFFSCREEN THE DOOR OPENS, throwing light on her, and DIEGO enters. He checks her, lifts the painting off her and exits leaving Frida lying on the bed...

INT. HOSPITAL HALLWAY - SAME NIGHT

Diego sits alone on the bench in the night hallway staring at the painting, HENRY FORD HOSPITAL. His head drops and his body begins to shake with silent weeping. His grief overtakes him, and he has to press his hand to his mouth to keep from sobbing out loud.

Frida is the only person I know who, by their own will, created their own life. She is the only person who gave birth to herself.

—LOLA ALVAREZ BRAVO, PHOTOGRAPHER
AND CLOSE FRIEND OF FRIDA KAHLO

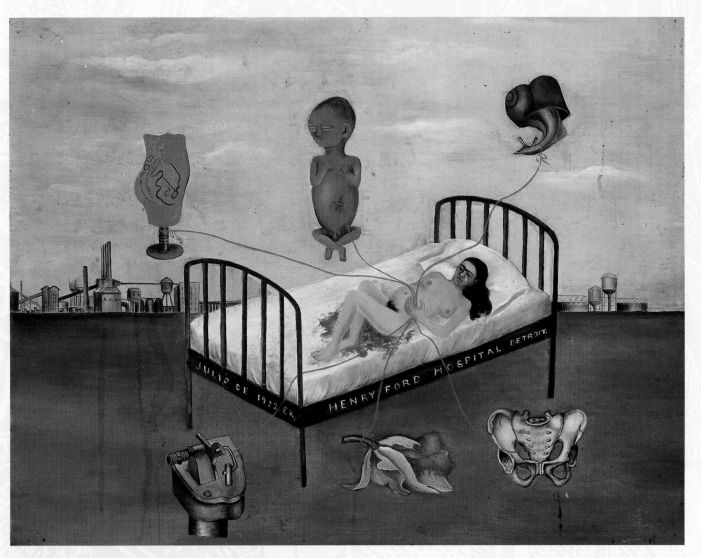

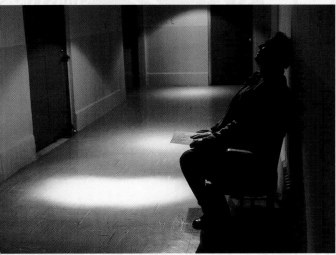

I would not wish to harbor
the slightest hope,
everything moves to the beat
of what's enclosed in the belly.

—FRIDA KAHLO

ABOVE: Henry Ford Hospital, 1932.

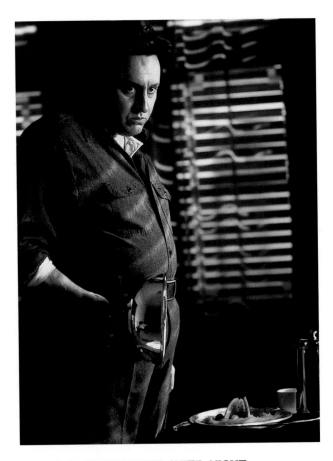

FRIDA
Breakfast.

DIEGO
You trying to kill me? I need fuel to work.

FRIDA
Listen, panzon, if you get any fatter, its going to be you in the hospital next time...

He comes over behind her and kisses her on the head.

DIEGO
You know, I don't believe in God, but I still thank him every day that he kept you safe for me.

FRIDA
Really? I tell him he's got a lot of explaining to do.

She opens a telegram reads it and goes still... He has turned back to shove some fruit in his mouth and tie his tie...

DIEGO
From now on I'm going to get Abbie Rockefeller to bring my breakfast over from 21....

He turns... She is staring at the telegram with a tear running down her cheek...

DIEGO *(Cont'd)*
Frida...?

INT. BLUE HOUSE - PARENT'S BEDROOM - DAY

MATILDE lies in the bed, thin and ashen. Next to her are TWO ELDERLY WOMEN praying a rosary in tandem. They are Matilde's sisters. Frida goes to the bed and takes her mother's hand. Matilde opens her eyes and recognizes her daughter... She sighs...

INT. BARBIZON HOTEL SUITE - NIGHT

Frida and Diego lie in bed, entwined in each other's arms.
FADE TO BLACK

INT. BARBIZON HOTEL SUITE - DAY

Frida sits in the living room at a desk facing the window, going through the mail. Diego enters from the bedroom, buttoning his shirt and vest... He goes straight for a room service tray on the dining table and lifts the silver cover.

DIEGO
What the hell is this?

MATILDE
Frida... You're here.

She kisses Matilde and lays down next to her...

Cristina enters and Frida sees that her face is bruised.

INT. BLUE HOUSE - KITCHEN - DAY

    CRISTINA
    I left him.

    FRIDA
    And that was his parting gift. I should have been
    there for you.

    CRISTINA
    You're here now.

Frida sees Guillermo in the garden outside the window.

EXT. BLUE HOUSE - COURTYARD - DAY

Guillermo is plucking dead buds off plants. He's aged considerably. FRIDA comes out of the house and goes to him.

    GUILLERMO
    She'll throw a fit if I let her damned plants die.

They are quiet for a long beat.

Sisters

Cristina and Frida were very, very close. They spent their lives together. After Frida had the accident, Cristina took care of her; she was her nurse and driver. Sometimes Frida couldn't be alone so Cristina was always there for her either cooking or cleaning or taking care of Diego's papers and problems. It was a beautiful relationship and very difficult as well. It's always hard when one person is very successful and the other one is normal like Cristina. I think that Cristina was a very typical woman of her time. She did exactly what a woman was supposed to do; she got married at the age of seventeen to a much older man. She had children when she was very young. She lived a life of excitement through her sister. And, in a way Frida lived a more down-to-earth life of family through Cristina. They complimented each other very, very well.

—MIA MAESTRO, ACTRESS

    GUILLERMO *(Cont'd)*
    We fought so much. Sometimes I... sometimes I
    would regret that I ever married her. I would think
    how I hated her. You do enough damage to one
    another, you begin to think that way. But then she
    gets sick and I tend her garden.

He opens his hands and shows her the plucked flower buds. She takes one and looks at it, then pulls him into an embrace.

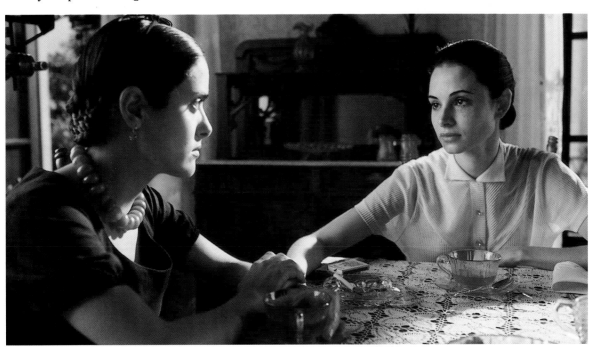

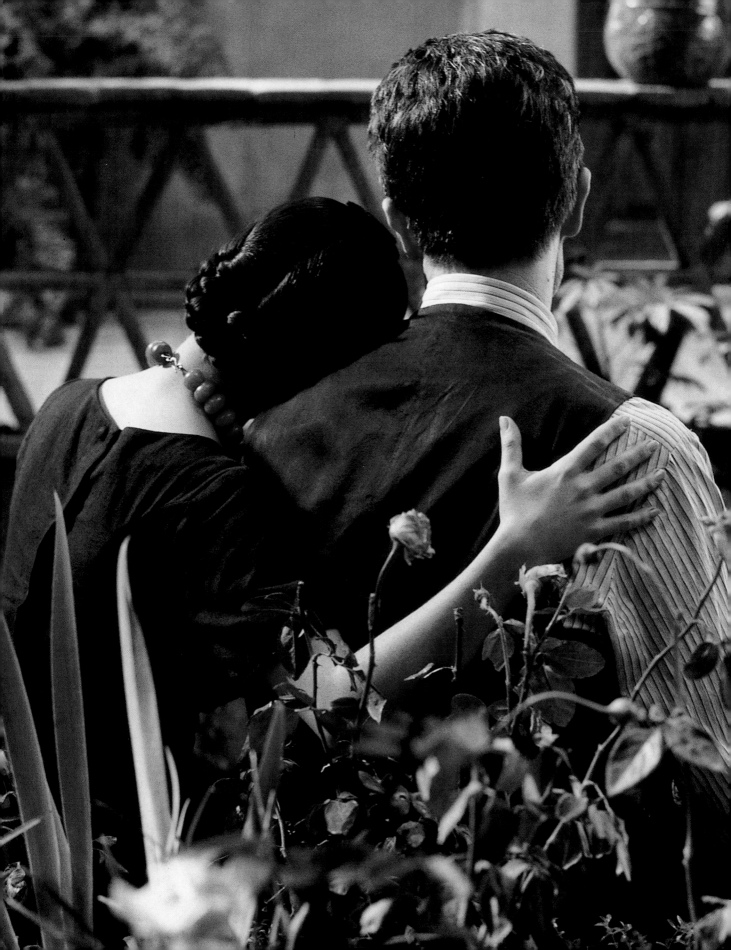

EXT. CEMETERY - DAY

WIDE: A funeral ceremony around the grave. A small gathering.

INT. ROCKEFELLER CENTER - OFFICE - DAY

NEWSPAPER HEADLINE:

RIVERA PAINTS SCENES OF COMMUNIST ACTIVITY AND JOHN D. JR. FOOTS THE BILL!

A copy of the *World Telegram* with this headline slams onto the desk of Nelson Rockefeller. Rockefeller and Diego face each other across the desk. Diego is raging...

DIEGO
You'd seen my work—you knew my politics when you hired me!

ROCKEFELLER
Yes.

DIEGO
Yeah, I showed you sketches, I discussed them with you and your father!

ROCKEFELLER
Yes.

DIEGO
So what the hell were you expecting from me? A line of dancing girls?!

ROCKEFELLER
No. But, nor was I expecting a portrait of Lenin. Now let's be honest, in the sketches that you showed me originally, it was just some anonymous worker.

DIEGO
He transformed into Lenin of his own accord!

ROCKEFELLER
No, you transformed him into Lenin because they took shots at us in the paper. Do you really think that my family is influenced by newspaper hacks? We would have defended you. I will defend you against any attack because the work is thrilling, as always. But a portrait of Vladimir Lenin will offend many people, in particular, my father. See, you're putting me in an impossible position, so I am asking you to change this one detail.

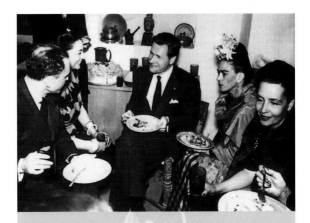

Rivera and Rockefeller

By the first of May 1933, Diego had transformed a sketch of a "labor leader" into an unmistakable portrait of Lenin. On May 4, Nelson Rockefeller wrote to him asking him to substitute the face of an unknown man for that of Lenin. Lenin's portrait, he argued, would "seriously offend a great many people." Rivera declared that to remove the head of Lenin would be to destroy the entire concept of the mural. He offered a compromise: he would balance the head of Lenin with the head of Abraham Lincoln. The answer came on May 9, at a time when most of Diego's assistants were having lunch in a nearby restaurant. Rockefeller's rental manager, followed by twelve uniformed security guards, stalked into the RCA Building and ordered the artist to stop working. Slowly Rivera laid down his big brushes and the kitchen plate he used as a palette, and climbed down from the scaffold. He was handed a check for the full amount owed to him (the remaining $14,000 due on a $21,000 contract) and a letter that told him he was fired.

Rivera was stunned. He, who usually moved with a fat man's liquid grace, walked woodenly to the work shack and changed out of his overalls. More guards appeared and pushed the movable scaffold away from the wall. Within half an hour Radio City personnel had covered the mural with tar paper and a wooden screen...

It turned out to be Rockefeller's wall in the end. Nine months later, after the Riveras had left New York, the mural was chipped off and thrown away. (Perhaps Rivera had the last word after all. When he repainted the Rockefeller Center mural in Mexico City's Palace of Fine Arts in 1934, he placed John D. Rockefeller, Sr., among the revelers on the capitalist side of the mural, in close proximity to the syphilis spirochetes that swarm on the propeller.)

—HAYDEN HERRERA, *FRIDA: A BIOGRAPHY OF FRIDA KAHLO*

ABOVE: Archival photo of Nelson A. Rockefeller (center) with Frida (on his left) and Rosa Covarrubias (on his right).

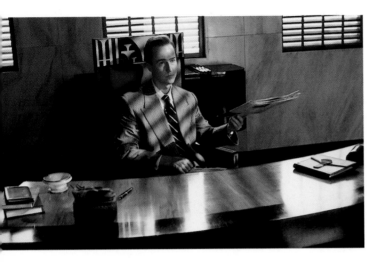

DIEGO
It's against my principles.

ROCKEFELLER
Yes, well, you've adjusted your principles to come to our parties and eat at our table. So I hope you'll reconsider.

They stare at each other.

INT. ROCKEFELLER CENTER - LOBBY - DAY

FRIDA ENTERS from the street. Diego kisses her.

FRIDA
You've got quite a crowd out there. Half of them think you're the devil, half of them think you're a hero.

She smiles at him.

INT. ROCKEFELLER CENTER - LOBBY - NIGHT

LATER: Late at night. He has finally quit for the day. They sit in the cavernous lobby eating dinner, Frida wrapped in a blanket. They eat in silence for a beat...

DIEGO
Tell me honestly what you think.

FRIDA
If you lie down with dogs, you should expect fleas.

He smiles, but he's really having doubts.

DIEGO
No, seriously, this is really frightening me.

FRIDA
Why?

DIEGO
Because I'm actually wondering if he's right! Perhaps I am being foolish, risking too much.

FRIDA
Diego, you can't lose. Forget about artistic integrity. You've done better ones than this, and you'll do more. But whatever happens, you have aroused people. You've made them get passionate about their ideals. There is not another painter in the world who could say that. He could walk in here tomorrow and tear it down. You'd still have won.

DIEGO
Maybe. *(pauses—thinking)* He doesn't have the balls.

INT. ROCKEFELLER BUILDING - LOBBY - DAY

Nelson Rockefeller strides in, followed by a phalanx of associates, all dressed in suits. Frida sees him first.

FRIDA
Diego.

ROCKEFELLER
Señor Rivera. I must ask you one last time to reconsider your position.

Diego glances at Frida then says, firmly...

DIEGO
I will not compromise my vision.

Rockefeller shakes his head, turns to the lawyer next to him who hands him a check. He turns and hands it to Diego.

ROCKEFELLER
In that case, this is your fee, paid in full, as agreed, but your services are no longer required.

DIEGO
It's my painting!

ROCKEFELLER
On my wall.

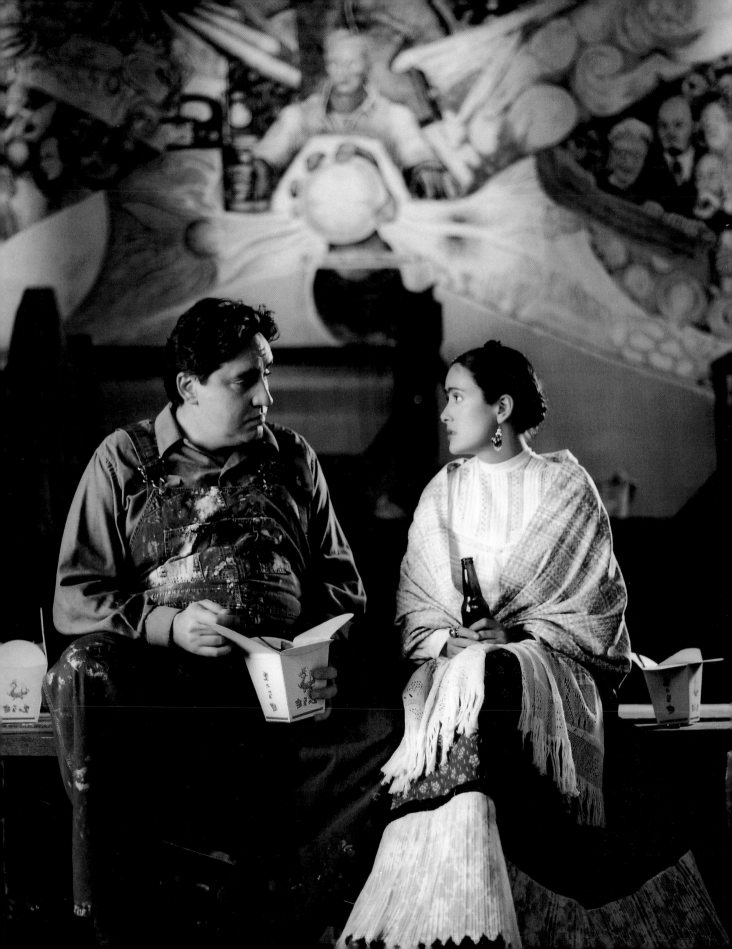

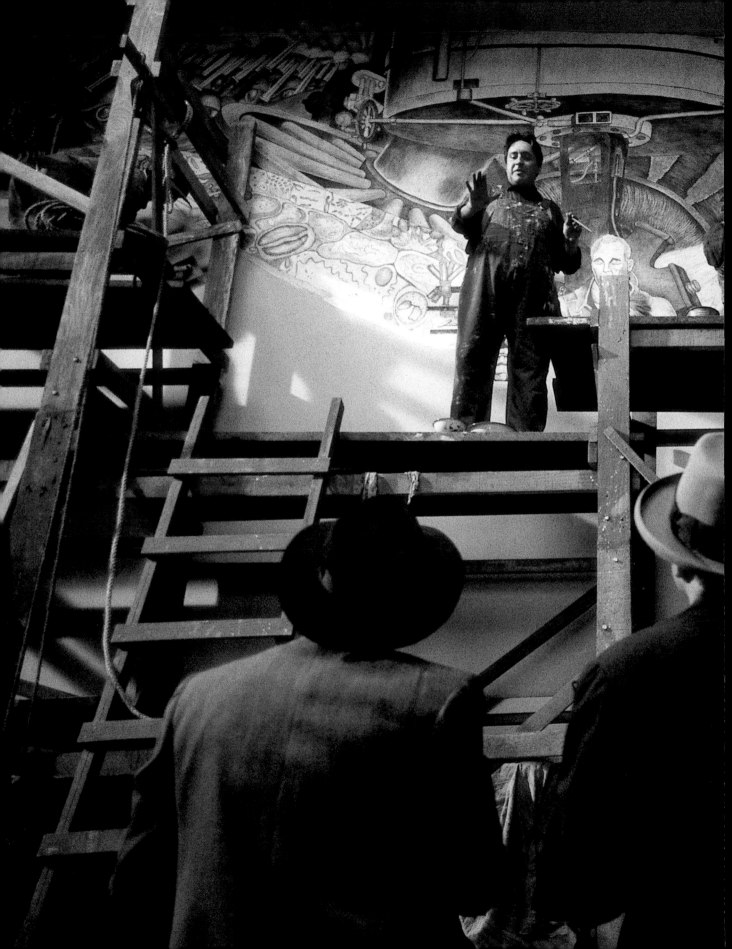

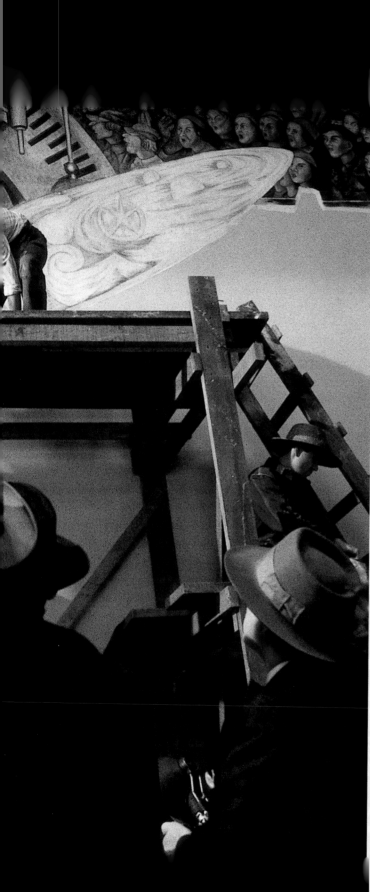

Re-creating Rockefeller Center

Diego Rivera was completely committed to his political and personal beliefs about life. He was hired by Nelson Rockefeller to paint this mural for the lobby of Rockefeller Center. There was no way of censoring Diego Rivera. He did what he thought the wall needed. He painted all his beliefs in communism and socialism and the people he most admired, which was not popular at the time, and completely stopped the whole project.

In recreating Rockefeller Center, we had to get the feeling of the space itself. We wanted to see Rivera with all the scaffolding, all of the action going on underneath him. So we redesigned the wall, but the mural itself is true to the original. After the Rockefeller Center mural was torn down, Rivera had an opportunity to repaint it in Mexico City's Palace of Fine Arts. The new mural had some variations from the original. We took photographs of the original— there are only a few photos available—and tried to merge the two versions.

The theme of this mural is very complex and was a challenge to duplicate. I don't think there is ever a "perfect" replica of any artwork. You can almost always tell the difference between the original and the replica. What we wanted to do was to get the expression of the painting. I'm sure an expert would find mistakes in the details, but the essence of the work is there.

—BERNARDO TRUJILLO, ART DIRECTOR

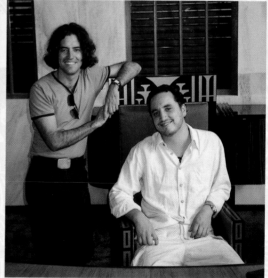

ABOVE: Production designer Felipe Fernández del Paso and art director Bernardo Trujillo (right).

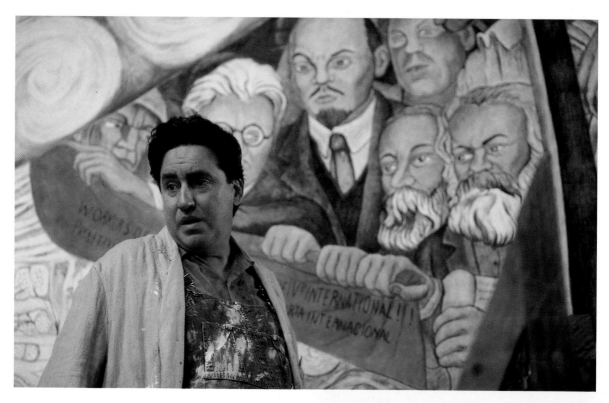

DIEGO
It's the people's wall, you bastard!

In a wide shot, we see Rockefeller walking toward us, dwarfed by the enormous mural behind him.

MATCH DISSOLVE TO:

INT. RCA BUILDING - NIGHT

The scaffold is now totally covered in tarp, completely hiding the mural. We hear the sound of jackhammers.

CLOSE-UP: at the base of the mural we see white chips of plaster and paint falling slowly through the frame as dust rising from below DISSOLVES INTO...

INT. TENEMENT APARTMENT - 13TH ST. - BATHROOM - DAY

SNOW FALLING on a miniature of the Empire State building. As the camera pulls out we are in FRIDA'S POV of her soaking in a bathtub, staring at her own feet (as in the painting, WHAT THE WATER GAVE ME). KING KONG FALLS from the top of the building

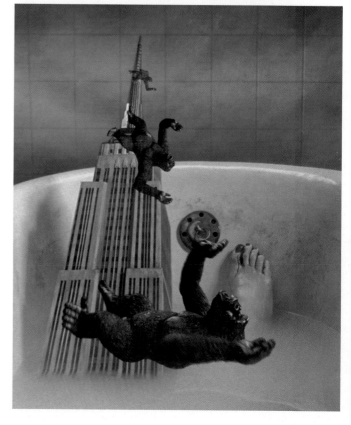

RIGHT: Montage created for the movie to visualize what Frida was thinking when she and Diego were in New York.
FAR RIGHT: What the Water Gave Me, *1938.*

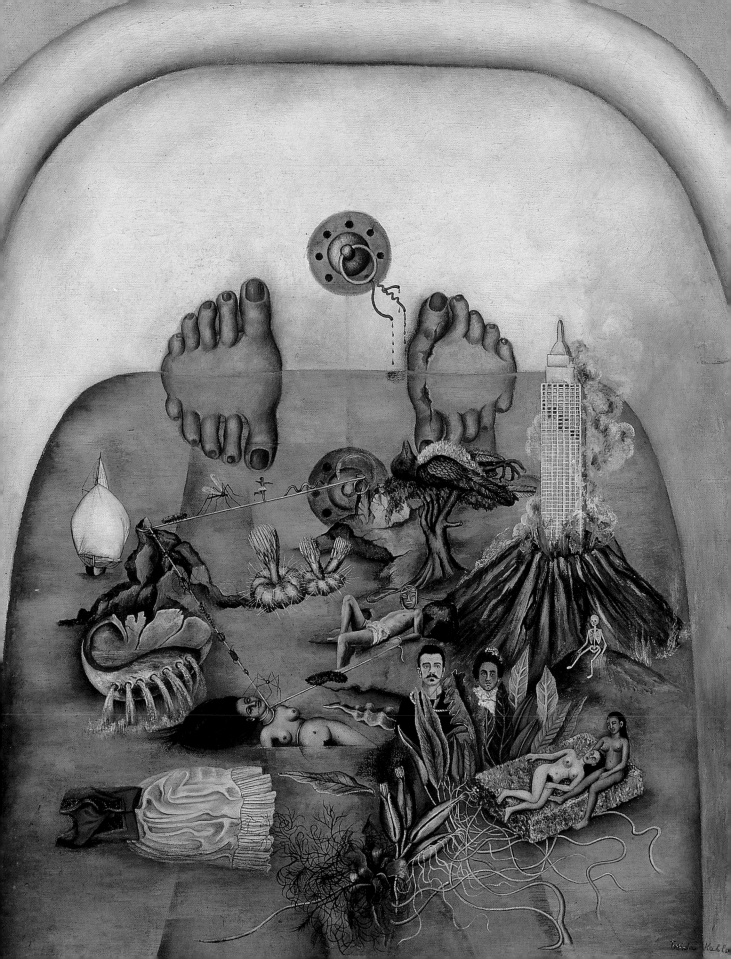

into the water (in the three stage style of the SUICIDE OF DOROTHY HALE).

THE SOUND OF THE FRONT DOOR OPENING snaps her trance...

INT. TENEMENT APARTMENT - 13TH ST. - KITCHEN - DAY

Diego is rummaging for food. He is agitated. There is an EASEL by the window with a PAINTING OF A CACTUS. FRIDA appears in the doorway in a robe, her hair down and still wet. She stares at him. He doesn't turn...

> FRIDA
> Diego, let's go home.

> DIEGO
> Frida! We have to fight these bastards! They tore down the wall, but the painting is up here! I'll do it again, and I'll use his money!

He sits and starts eating...

> FRIDA
> What money? We don't even have enough to get to Chicago.

> DIEGO
> We're not going to Chicago. *(beat)* They cancelled the commission.

She is silent, knowing this must have destroyed him.

> FRIDA
> It's time to go home.

> DIEGO
> What, with my tail between my legs...?

> FRIDA
> We don't belong here. I'm tired of these people, and I'm tired of who you are around them!

He leaps up, still holding his dinner knife, and grabs his CACTUS PAINTING...

> DIEGO
> You see that! You want to go back to that?!

> FRIDA
> Yes! I want to go back to that!

Furious, he stabs the painting with the knife, slashes it to shreds, throws it down and storms out the door.

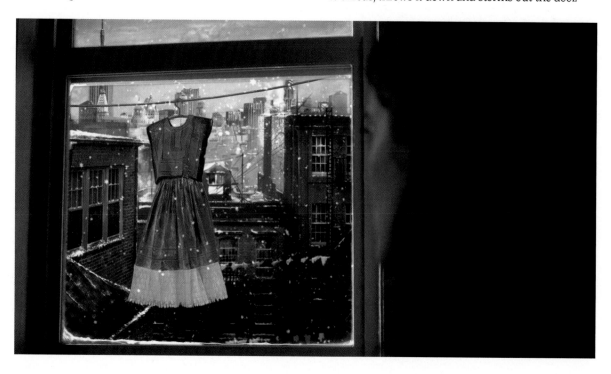

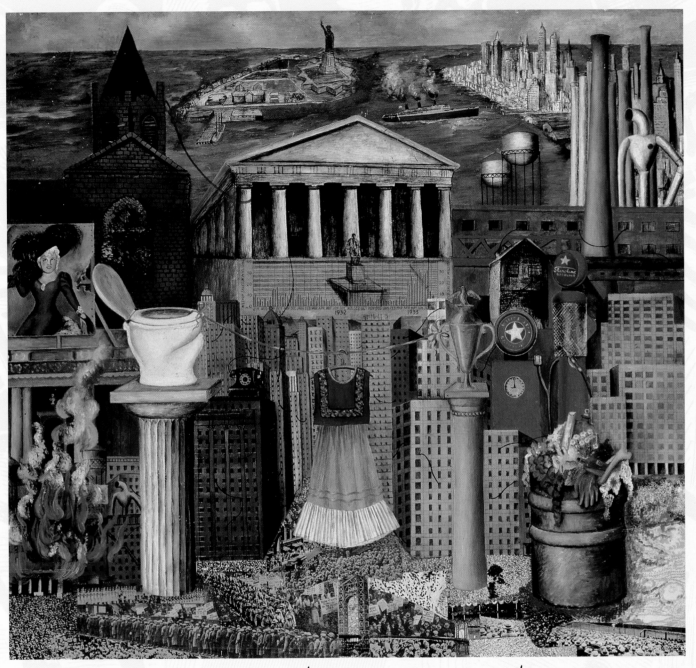

I'd like to paint you but there are no colors, because there are
so many, in my confusion, the tangible form of my great love.

—FRIDA KAHLO

LEFT: Montage created for the movie inspired by My Dress Hangs
There *(above), a painting Frida created in New York, 1933.*

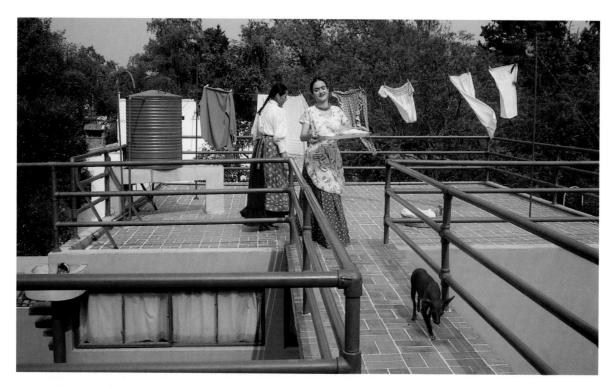

FRIDA turns and stares out the window... On a clothes-line her TEHUANA DRESS hangs, colorful against the grey backdrop of the city and snow.

I/E. TENEMENT APARTMENT - 13TH ST. - KITCHEN - DAY

The image freezes, evoking MY DRESS HANGS THERE, and then slowly melts into...

EXT. SAN ANGEL HOUSE - DAY

...a DRESS on a line up on a roof in the warm Mexican sun. Pulling back, FRIDA emerges up some stairs carrying a tray of food, walking gingerly on her bad foot...

WIDE: THE SAN ANGEL HOUSE... Two separate houses joined together by a bridge between the roofs. Frida walks across this bridge carrying the tray. She is followed by one of her little chihuahuas.

SCREEN READS: San Angel, Mexico City, four months later

INT. DIEGO'S STUDIO - SAN ANGEL HOUSE - DAY

Diego's studio is a chaos but without clear signs of pro-ductivity... No finished paintings... DIEGO sits on the floor reading the paper. He looks pale.

Frida comes down into the open passageway that looks down onto Diego's high-ceilinged studio space. The dog runs past her yapping... DIEGO looks up from his paper...

> **DIEGO**
> I'm working!

> **FRIDA**
> *(ignoring his mood)*
> I can see that. I've brought you some lunch. The doctor says you should eat more for once.

She enters the studio and puts the food on the floor. He glances at it, looks at her, then past her...

> **DIEGO**
> Puta madre!

THE LITTLE DOG is pissing on a stack of unfinished sketches leaning against the wall. DIEGO LEAPS UP, grabs a machete and runs after the dog.

> **FRIDA**
> Diego! Diego! All right! That's enough! Diego! Stop!

ABOVE AND RIGHT: These scenes were filmed in the San Angel home of Diego and Frida, which is now a museum.

Cornering it, he grabs it by the scruff of the neck and prepares to strike...

DIEGO'S POV: the little dog stares at him quivering.

Diego laughs and cuddles it...

DIEGO
Lord Xolotl, Prince of Darkness. You're the best art critic there is! *(aimed at Frida)* Only you see what shit this country has made of me.

FRIDA
(looking at the mess)
Diego, you need help.

He looks up at her with the expression of a lost dog.

EXT. SIDEWALK ALONG THE SIDE OF SAN ANGEL HOUSE - DAY

Frida, Cristina and children are walking home with groceries and entering the gates to the house.

ISOLDA
Frida, why do you and Diego have separate houses?

FRIDA
Because we are two different people, but our love makes us into one. That's why we have the bridge.

ISOLDA
So you mean the bridge is your love?

FRIDA
Yes. That's a good way to put it.

ISOLDA
Then why is it such a small bridge?

Frida and Cristina laugh.

EXT. COUTYARD - SAN ANGEL HOUSE - DAY

Frida, Cristina and kids are shucking corn.

FRIDA
He's not working, he's sick, he's depressed. He says the people in this country are like mules, they're so stupid. And he blames it all on me for making him come back.

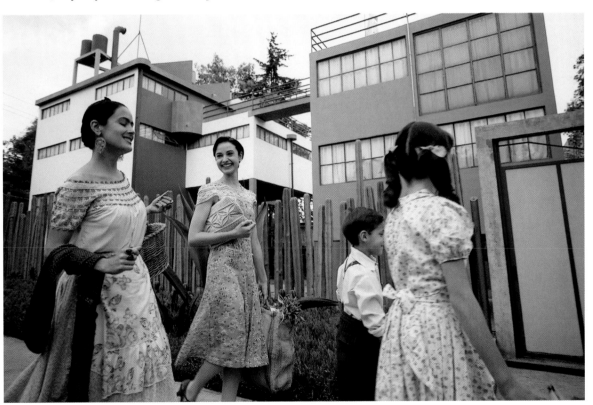

San Angel

The Riveras' curious relationship of independence and interdependence was symbolized by the two houses in which they lived, and by the bridge that linked the dwellings to each other. Both houses belonged to Diego. But when Frida was angry at him, she could lock the door on her end of the bridge, forcing him to go downstairs, cross the yard, and knock on her front door. There, as often as not, he would be told by a servant that his wife refused to receive him. Huffing and puffing, Rivera would climb his stairs, cross the bridge again, and through Frida's closed door, plead for forgiveness. . . .

[The house was] a mecca for the international intelligentsia. Writers, painters, photographers, musicians, actors, refugees, political activists, and people with money to spend on art all found their way to the pink and blue houses on the corner of Palmas and Altavista. John Dos Passos and Waldo Frank were among the foreign visitors who sought out the Riveras. Among their fellow countrymen, they could count as friends such people as President Lázaro Cárdenas, the photographer Manuel Alvarez Bravo, and the beautiful film star Dolores del Rio. Although Rivera's fame made some of Mexico's other celebrities jealous, most of them delight in their memories of Diego and Frida, who, in her Tehuana finery, presided over the heterogeneous but generally bohemian milieu.

—HAYDEN HERRERA, *FRIDA: A BIOGRAPHY OF FRIDA KAHLO*

Shooting in San Angel

For seventeen years, I had been going to the Diego Rivera Museum. This museum was his studio at the end of his life and the place where Diego and Frida lived together. One house was Frida's and the other was Diego's; the two houses were connected by a bridge, but the bridge is now closed because it's very fragile. Many other parts of the museum are also closed to the public.

For so many years, I would visit this place and try to imagine what was behind the closed doors. When we were shooting in San Angel, however, there were no closed doors or barriers.

I got chills when we first entered the house and I was dressed like Frida. There was Diego and their little dog. The dog we used was a descendant of one of Frida's dogs. It was such an amazing experience to be in that space and recreate history.

I so revered the house that I was terrified someone would break something. I became much more neurotic than the guards. I would say to them, "Look, you're getting distracted by the filming. You have to make sure nobody comes this way." I was completely protective of the place.

—SALMA HAYEK

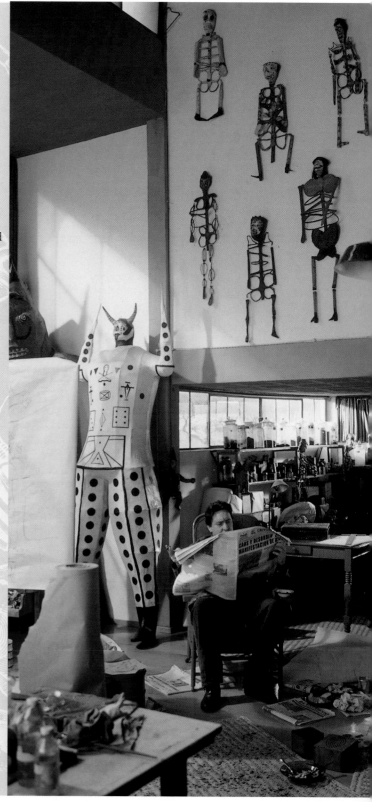

CRISTINA

That's ridiculous. Still, you're lucky to have him. I feel so desperate every day. Sometimes I even think of going back.

FRIDA

Well, you're not. What about a job? You could help me out organizing Diego's studio.

INT. DIEGO'S STUDIO - SAN ANGEL HOUSE - DAY

Frida and Cristina walk into the room. Cristina looks at the mess, overwhelmed.

CRISTINA

Where do I start?

DIEGO

Don't touch anything.

FRIDA

Diego.

Frida grabs Diego by the arm, pulling him to the door. She shoos him out and turns to her sister.

FRIDA (Cont'd)

Don't worry. He's a pussycat.

EXT. ARTESANIAS MARKET - NIGHT

Frida browses with Antonio and Isolda, festive, stopping to laugh and talk with shop owners. She is limping badly. They pause at a stall displaying enormous papier-mâché skeletons and Judases. Fireworks and toritos are wildly shooting off in the streets.

EXT. ROOF - SAN ANGEL HOUSE - NIGHT

Frida, Isolda and Antonio emerge out onto the roof of Frida's house... They carry a huge Judas figure and bags of toys, their faces are painted into devilish masks. Laughing and talking...

WIDE: We see them creep across the bridge, Frida shushing them...

INT. DIEGO'S STUDIO - SAN ANGEL HOUSE - NIGHT

Frida opens the door, entering the passageway that runs above Diego's studio. The children are on her heels. Frida puts her finger to her lips, motioning for

them to stay quiet. The three of them tiptoe toward the rail... Frida leans over...

FRIDA'S POV — Diego and Cristina are having sex on the floor, Cristina is on top of Diego, her back to Frida. There is an unfinished nude sketch of Cristina nearby.

Diego looks up and sees her and reacts... Cristina turns sharply and gasps...

CRISTINA

Oh my god...

Frida turns, blocking the children...

FRIDA

Go downstairs and play. Now. Now!

They go. Frida throws the Judas over the railing and charges down the stairs into the studio. Cristina, grabbing her clothes, dashes past Frida out the door, sobbing and Diego scrambles to pull his overalls up...

Frida charges at him, a scream erupting from her.

FRIDA (Cont'd)

She's my goddam sister. You're an animal. DIEGO DE PUNTA.

DIEGO
Frida, Fri...

FRIDA
GET OUT! GET OUT!

As Diego retreats around the studio, Frida HURLS anything she can lift at him, shattering Mexican pottery, anything...

He flees out the door and she falls to her knees sobbing.

INT. FRIDA'S STUDIO - SAN ANGEL HOUSE - NIGHT

Frida sits frozen, staring out the window. A KNOCK at the door on the ground floor.

EXT. BRIDGE BETWEEN SAN ANGEL HOUSES - NIGHT

Diego charges over the bridge toward Frida's studio. He pounds on the door...

DIEGO
Frida! Frida!!

He is met with silence.

DIEGO *(Cont'd)*
I'm a beast yes, I, I, I'm an idiot but it, it meant nothing Frida, nothing. Frida, talk to me!!

He leans against the door, listening. Suddenly...

Frida is standing there looking at him, ice cold.

FRIDA
There have been two big accidents in my life, Diego. The trolley, and you. You are by far the worst.

INT. APARTMENT BUILDING - DAY

Two men walk up the stairs of the old building carrying a bed.

INT. FRIDA'S NEW APARTMENT - DAY

WIDE: the lonely tableau of an empty apartment.

Frida leans against a bare wall near the window looking out while her SPIDER MONKEY jumps around her feet. The bed has been shoved in the corner and TWO WORKMEN put two cardboard boxes in the middle of the floor then leave.

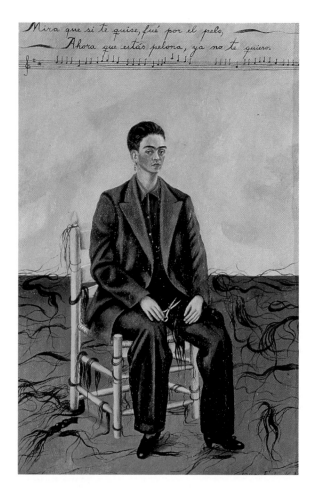

TIGHTER on Frida against the bare wall, the monkey jumps into her arms and screeches as the...

MUSIC BEGINS: LA PALOMA NEGRA and we ....

CUT TO:

INT. FRIDA'S NEW APARTMENT - DAY

LATER—the apartment is set up with only bare essentials...

FRIDA, in an oversized man's suit, sits on a chair in the middle of the room facing her easel, which has a mirror resting on it. She stares at herself in the mirror, takes a long pull off a bottle of whiskey and then lifts a pair of scissors and begins to CUT HER HAIR OFF. The scene ends in a 3-D painting of SELF-PORTRAIT WITH CROPPED HAIR.

THE SONG CONTINUES OVER:

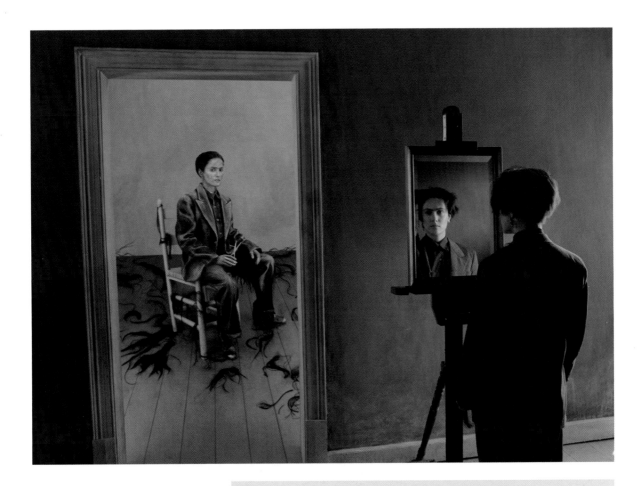

If I loved you, it was for your hair. Now that you are bald, I don't love you anymore.

—Translation of the words to a popular song quoted on top of *Self-Portrait with Cropped Hair*

Above left : Self-Portrait with Cropped Hair, *1940.*

Inside Frida's mind

We've tried to get into Frida's mind, and extract some of the things she would have thought of or seen and later painted. So sometimes in the middle of a scene, the camera movements change, and we will go inside Frida's mind. We will see suggestions of why she painted certain things, how her pain and her surroundings affected her painting.

We have created something like 3-D paintings or paintings that come to life. For example, in one scene, Frida goes completely mad because Diego has betrayed her. She moves into a lousy apartment, and is drunk all the time. She realizes her life is a mess, so she cuts her hair off as a sign of despair and wanting to change. As she's cutting her hair, she sees herself in one of her most famous paintings, *Self-Portrait with Cropped Hair.* On the painting she wrote the lyrics to this song that roughly says, "if I ever loved you it was because of your hair, but now that you are bald I don't love you anymore."

So we recreated the painting in 3-D with Salma cutting off her hair and then appearing live in this painting. We built and designed a forced perspective set with a slanted floor. Then we designed the chair she's sitting on (also with a forced perspective), and we hand-painted and airbrushed her clothing. The scene was then shot with a motion control device, and the effect is completely magical.

—Felipe Fernández del Paso, Production Designer

INT. FRIDA'S APARTMENT - NIGHT

The lurid spinnings of a party. Seen haphazardly, a disjointed and drunken camera... Colored lights, the sound muted under the wildness of the song:

Young unfamiliar faces, Frida drinking hard and recklessly in a way that does not seem light or fun. A YOUNG MAN whispers in her ear.

Frida sits in the window sill with her bottle looking at the people laughing and drinking in the candlelit room. Then she glances out to the night street and sees...

EXT. STREET IN FRONT OF FRIDA'S APT. - NIGHT

CRISTINA'S CAR stopped across the street. Cristina looks up from the driver's seat to the window, her face a mask of regret. Isolda and Antonia are in the car.

INT. FRIDA'S APARTMENT - NIGHT

FRIDA, looks down at her, maybe a flicker of sadness, but then she reaches up, pulls the cord and drops the blinds. She turns to the party...

FRIDA
Get Out. Out... OUT! GO!

THE SONG ENDS

INT. FRIDA'S APARTMENT - DAY

Frida sits, hungover. Lupe has cooked, and they are talking...

FRIDA
It's a limp up three flights of stairs, I can't afford any furniture and it's cold at night; but at least I know who's fucking who in my own house.

I drink to drown my sorrows but the damn things have learned to swim.

—FRIDA KAHLO

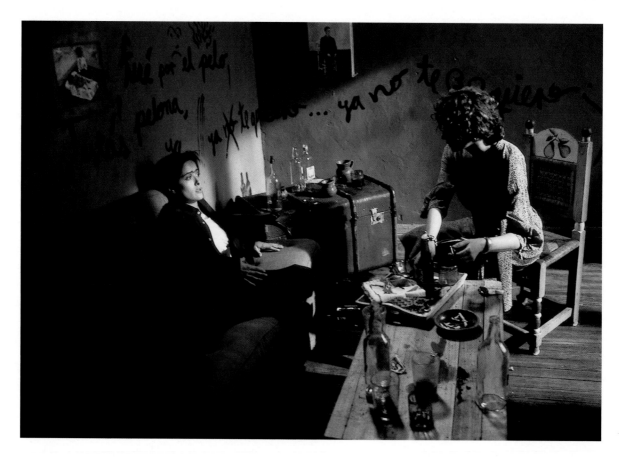

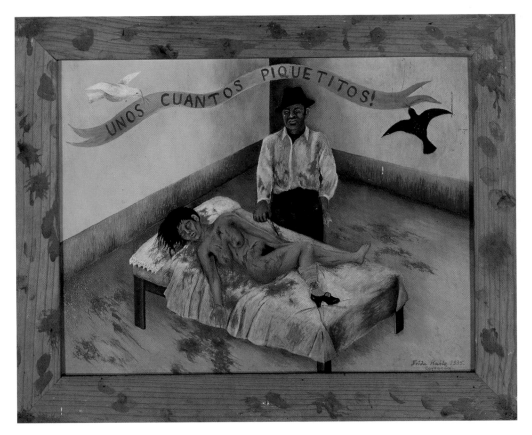

LUPE
Diego's not giving you any money?

FRIDA
I'd rather be poor.

Frida's eyes glitter, fierce.

FRIDA *(Cont'd)*
She was my sister. Not some model. My own sister.

Frida looks away.

LUPE
To hell with him.

FRIDA
To hell with him.

ABOVE: A Few Small Nips, *1935, shown hanging behind Salma Hayek (above left). Kahlo based this painting on a newspaper story about a man who stabbed his wife 22 times and told the judge, "It was just a few small nips."*

LUPE
Find some work, pay your own bills for a while...

FRIDA
I'll sell some paintings...

LUPE
Not enough to cover your bar bill. Oh, don't get me wrong, I love your paintings. I'm just not sure you should count on them for a living... They're tough, you know. I mean look at this, what the hell is this...?

She points at the painting A FEW SMALL NIPS.

FRIDA
It was in the damn papers. A man stabbed his wife 22 times and when the judge asked him why he did it, he said, "But it was just a few small nips."

Frida takes a swig of tequila. Lupe raises an eyebrow.

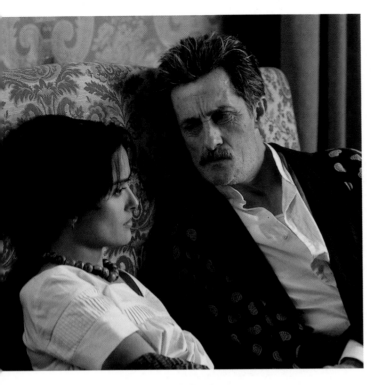

EXT. BLUE HOUSE - DAY

Birds roost in the eaves of the house. Age has dilapidated the place.

INT. BLUE HOUSE - PARLOR - DAY

Dust hangs in the air. Guillermo sits on a couch with some of his old photographs, lost in thought. Frida knocks on the door that is half open.

> GUILLERMO (O.S.)
> Who's that?

> FRIDA
> The ghost of Frida Kahlo.

> GUILLERMO
> I remember her.

Frida comes and sits beside him. He is tired and pale but in good humor.

> FRIDA
> How are you?

> GUILLERMO
> Lonely. Only you ghosts come to visit these days. So how is your Diego?

> FRIDA
> I don't know why I called him that. He was never mine, never will be. But he's fine—painting, I guess.

> GUILLERMO
> And you? Are you also painting?

> FRIDA
> Yes, and I want you to pose for me. You don't even have to leave the house.

> GUILLERMO
> I want to leave the house.

> FRIDA
> All right then. We'll go somewhere different every day.

> GUILLERMO
> That sounds good. You've painted everyone else in the family.

> FRIDA
> Yes, a long time ago. Remind me what I wanted then.

> GUILLERMO
> You wanted to be your own person.

They sit together.

EXT. CEMETARY - NIGHT

DAY OF THE DEAD: The cemetary is filled with people celebrating; candles, candied and baked skeletons covering the graves, singing and story telling.

Frida is at her mother's grave, staring at one of Guillermo's photos of her. Diego approaches from behind. He looks ill, thin and pale.

> DIEGO
> Frida.

She doesn't look up.

> FRIDA
> She never liked you, you know? She told me you would only bring me troubles.

He nods and remains silent for a beat.

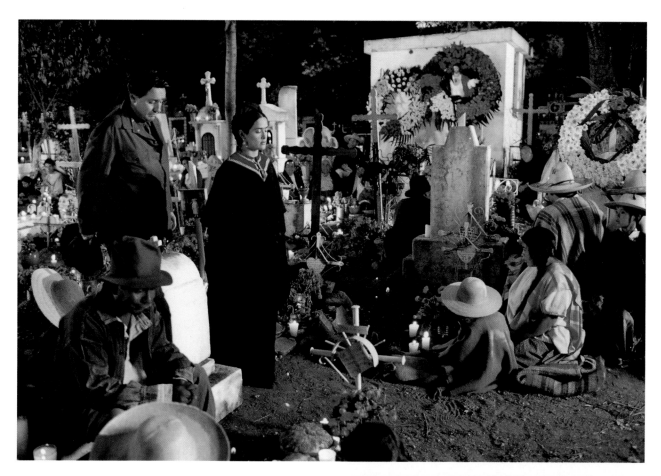

DIEGO
There is something I must discuss with you... A favor I need to ask of you...

FRIDA
You've got a lot of nerve to come here asking me to do you favors!

She turns to leave.

DIEGO
No. It's not for me—it's Trotsky.

This gets her attention. She stops and turns to look at him.

DIEGO *(Cont'd)*
The Norwegians have expelled him. No other country will take him. I have appealed to President Cárdenas myself. They have granted him asylum here in Mexico.

Frida is impressed.

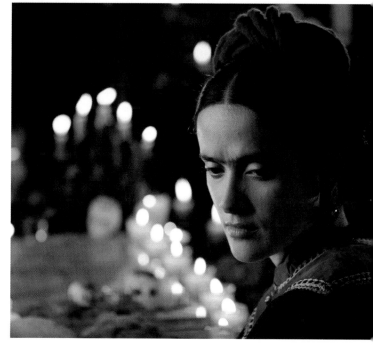

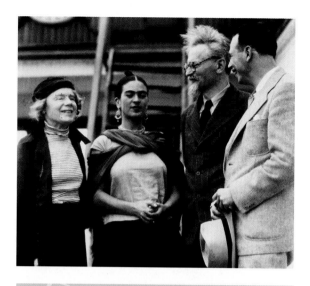

DIEGO *(Cont'd)*
I want you to welcome him with me. Let him live in your father's house. I know it's a lot to ask, but this is a difficult transition for them. And you, Frida, you bring life and warmth to any place. Anyway Trotsky is a very great man in enormous danger, and we have the opportunity to help him.

She takes this in and then nods...

FRIDA
Yes. All right.

They move off together.

EXT. BLUE HOUSE - STREET - DAY

A machine gun is being hoisted to an emplacement on the roof. Workmen swarm over the Blue House, transforming it into a secure home for the great exile...

EXT. BLUE HOUSE/COURTYARD - DAY

FRIDA directs the workers who are moving furniture to make space. GUILLERMO and AURORA emerge with his suitcases.

GUILLERMO
Such a commotion! I don't understand such commotion for a philosopher!

FRIDA
A very great man, Papa. It's an important service we're doing.

GUILLERMO
I should meet him. If you admire him, I want to advise him not to get involved in politics... Politics are ruinous!

FRIDA
Good advice, Papa. I'm sure he'll agree.

They move him out through the gate.

EXT. BLUE HOUSE - STREET - NIGHT

Armed sentries man their guard posts—on the roof, at the gate, at the front door.

At the front gate, Diego waits, nervous, pacing.

Headlights turn onto the lane. And then we see a slow procession of three cars guarded by heavily armed men.

The cars pull up in front of the house. The armed men move, taking up their positions. Then the door to the middle car opens. FRIDA climbs out and turns to help NATALIA TROTSKY (50s), worn and tired beyond her years.

Then LEON TROTSKY (50s) steps out. Piercing eyes, handsome older face, he carries himself with a military bearing—like a hero.

EXT. BLUE HOUSE - COURTYARD - NIGHT

Frida leads them to the house. A beat and then Diego clasps Trotsky's hands warmly.

DIEGO
I regret it was not possible for me to meet your boat.

TROTSKY
Natalia and I, we are deeply indebted to you for your generosity in these difficult times. And your charming wife, she's made the last leg of our trip such a delight.

Diego is almost overcome with emotion.

DIEGO
We are profoundly honored to have you and your wife in our home.

FRIDA
Diego, they're starving. Let's feed them!

Everyone laughs, and they usher the Trotskys in. Diego and Frida move in behind them, and he looks at her with his eyes wet with gratitude and happiness...

TROTSKY
Ya oostalna, eta prokraznaya, Natalia.

NATALIA
Da.

DIEGO
Thank you.

She doesn't smile, but as they turn to follow, she pats his back.

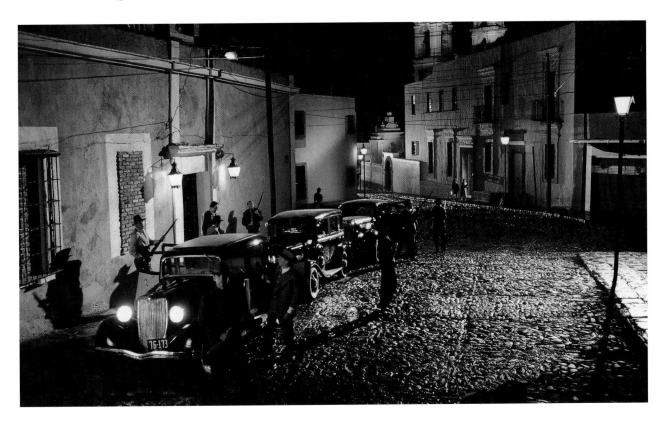

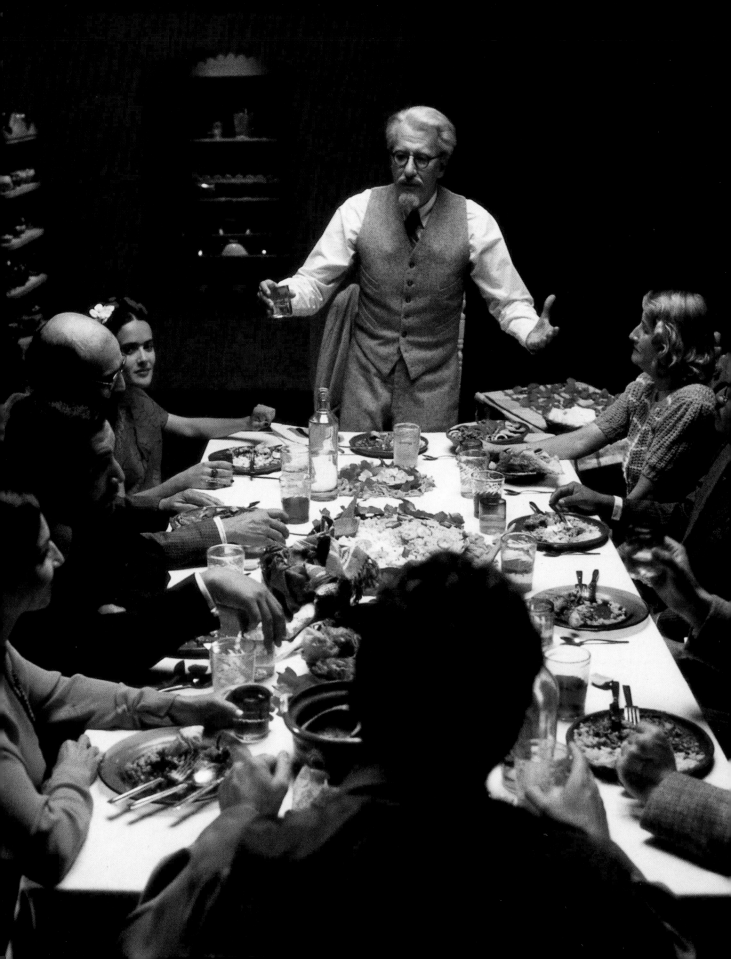

INT. DINING ROOM - BLUE HOUSE - NIGHT

Dinner: Diego, Frida, Natalia and assorted others, including ANDRE BRETON and his companion and a young AMERICAN GUARD, sit around a Mexican feast at a large table listening as Trotsky holds court...

DIEGO
No, it's true, it's true. I could not believe it, these people are idiots. They scream about Hitler's aggression an, an, and then sing Stalin's praises. Aren't they the same creature?!

TROTSKY
Yes, but not exactly. Of course they are both monsters, but Hitler at least is a madman with a vision.

DIEGO
Vision? He's insane.

TROTSKY
Of course he's insane, but he has the ability to mobilize the people's minds... whereas Stalin, he's... he's so dull. There is the brutality, but when you get right down to it, Stalin is nothing but a bureaucrat. And that is what is smothering our revolution. They are the same but only in that the insanity of power has overruled them and between them they will consume the continent.

FRIDA
Madness...

A somber silence hangs over the table... except in Trotsky.

TROTSKY
Yes! But a challenge. Look at us. Mexican, Russian, French, in this wonderful new Planet Rivera! I tell you this, my friends: in the experience of my lifetime, the failure and the pain have certainly outstripped the triumphs... but this has not only not destroyed my faith, my faith in reason, in truth, in human solidarity, but on the contrary, it has made it indestructible. I see the hope of the world in you and from my heart, I thank you.

FRIDA
Nostradovia!

Trotsky and Rivera

By December 19, 1936, when Leon and Natalia Trotsky boarded the oil tanker *Ruth* in Oslo, bound for Mexico, Trotsky had spent nine long years in exile....

So it was that on November 21, Rivera, who had joined the Mexican section of the (Trotskyite) International Communist League in September, received an urgent cable from Anita Brenner in New York saying that it was a matter of life or death to know immediately whether the Mexican government would grant Trotsky asylum. The political bureau of the Mexican section of the league met at once. Rivera and Octavio Fernández, a leader of the Mexican Trotskyite group, were secretly dispatched to see President Cárdenas, who was at the moment in the north of Mexico overseeing his land distribution program at La Laguna. When they arrived at Torreón, Rivera presented the petition for Trotsky's asylum in his own name, and Cárdenas granted it, provided that Trotsky would pledge not to interfere in the internal affairs of Mexico.

The *Ruth* arrived in the harbor of Tampico on the morning of January 9, 1937.

Bad or not, Trotsky did not let up the pace of his political activity. He went to work immediately, and on January 25, two weeks after his arrival, *Time* magazine could print: "At latest reports, Host Diego Rivera had had to return to a hospital with a kidney ailment; Mrs. Trotsky had gone to bed with what seemed to be a recurrence of her malaria; Guest Trotsky respectfully watched and waited on by dark-eyed young Hostess Rivera, had resumed dictation to his secretaries of his monumental *Biography of Lenin* begun nearly two years ago."

—HAYDEN HERRERA, *FRIDA: A BIOGRAPHY OF FRIDA KAHLO*

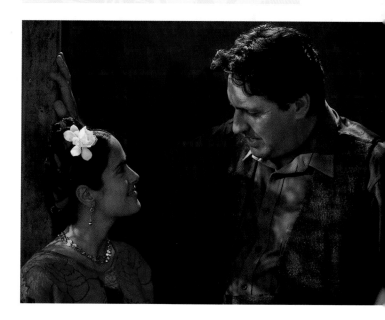

I never knew I was a surrealist until André Breton came to Mexico and told me I was one. I myself don't know what I am.

—FRIDA KAHLO

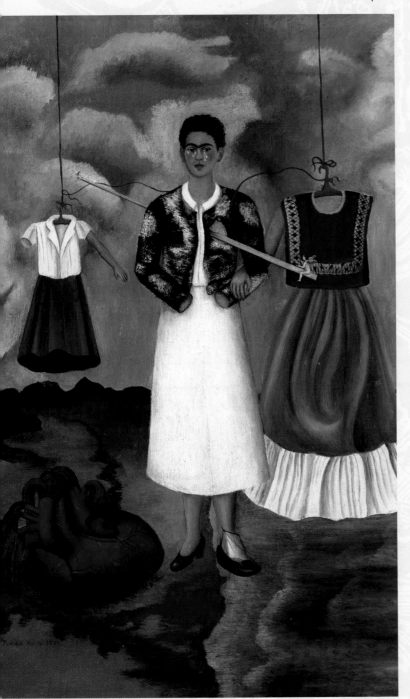

André Breton

When André Breton went to Mexico in 1938, he was charmed by Frida and by her work. "My surprise and joy," he wrote, "was unbounded when I discovered, on my arrival in Mexico, that her work has blossomed forth, in her latest paintings, into pure surreality, despite the fact that it had been conceived without any prior knowledge whatsoever of the ideas motivating the activities of my friends and myself." Breton's welcoming her into the ranks of Surrealism advanced Frida's career. Soon she was invited to have a show in New York's Surrealist-oriented Julien Levy Gallery. Of her exhibition, *Time* magazine noted that the "flutter of the week in Manhattan was caused by the first exhibition of paintings by famed muralist Diego Rivera's German-Mexican wife, Frida Kahlo." In the work *Time* discerned "the playfully bloody fancy of an unsentimental child." *Art News* praised Frida's "remarkable craftsmanship" and her "openness." The show was, it said, "definitely a beautiful achievement."

—HAYDEN HERRERA, *FRIDA KAHLO: THE PAINTINGS*

Some critics have tried to classify me as a Surrealist; but I do not consider myself to be a Surrealist... Really I do not know whether my paintings are Surrealist or not, but I do know that they are the frankest expression of myself... I detest Surrealism. To me it seems to be a decadent manifestation of bourgeois art. A deviation from the true art that the people hope for from the artist... I wish to be worthy, with my painting, of the people to whom I belong and to the ideas that strengthen me... I want my work to be a contribution to the struggle of the people for peace and liberty.

—FRIDA KAHLO

LEFT: Memory, *1937. ABOVE: André Breton. RIGHT:* The Suicide of Dorothy Hale, *1939, was commissioned by Claire Booth Luce as a gift for the deceased woman's mother. The banner on the bottom of the painting originally included the legend, "painted at the request of Claire Booth Luce, for the mother of Dorothy." Luce was so shocked when she received the painting from Mexico that she considered destroying it. Instead, she had her name painted out of the banner.*

122

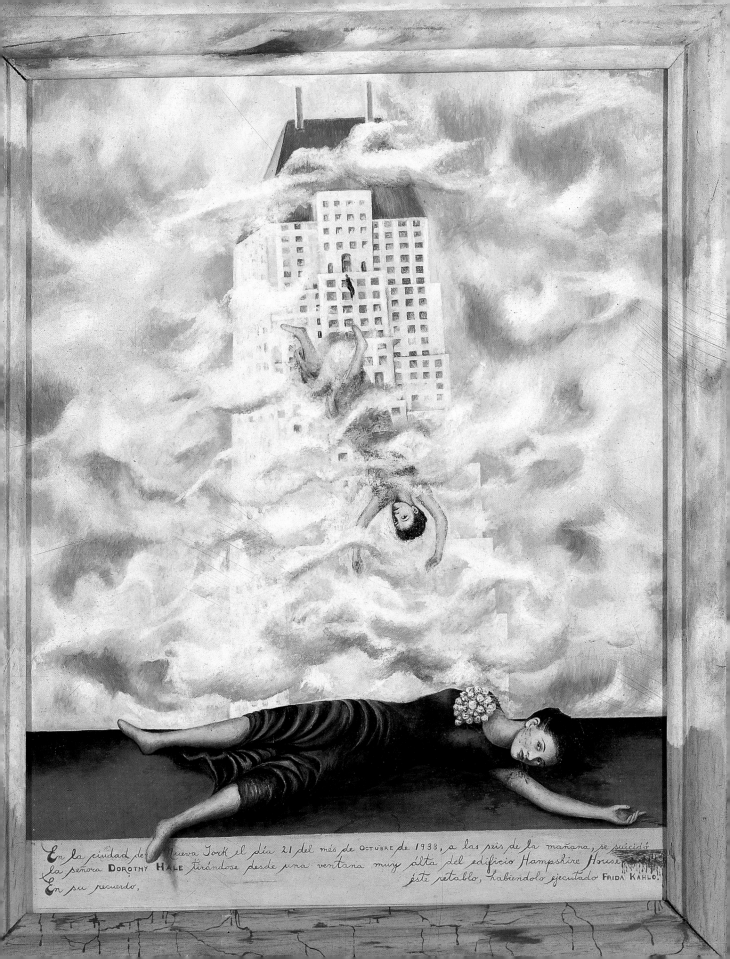

En la ciudad de Nueva York el día 21 del mes de OCTUBRE de 1938, a las seis de la mañana, se suicidó la señora DOROTHY HALE tirándose desde una ventana muy alta del edificio Hampshire House, éste retablo, habiéndolo ejecutado FRIDA KAHLO. En su recuerdo.

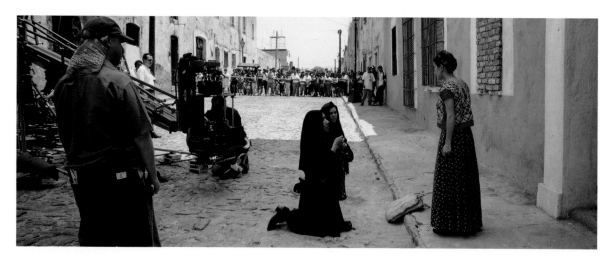

EVERYONE
Nostradovia, Salud!

They drink.

EXT. BLUE HOUSE - VERANDAH - NIGHT

Diego and Frida confer outside her bedroom door. Diego is electrified... almost in love.

DIEGO
Imagine living your life like that, with a price on your head and staying so calm.

FRIDA
Yes.

They stare at each other and he moves to kiss her. She stops him cold.

FRIDA *(Cont'd)*
Goodnight Diego.

She goes in the room and shuts the door in his face.

INT. BLUE HOUSE - FRIDA'S STUDIO - DAY

CLOSE-UPS: A series of Frida's paintings from this period—MEMORY, FULANG CHANG AND I, REMEMBRANCE OF AN OPEN WOUND, WHAT THE WATER GAVE ME, GIRL WITH A DEATH MASK, THE SUICIDE OF DOROTHY HALE, MY BIRTH, MY DRESS HANGS THERE.

INT. BLUE HOUSE - FRIDA'S STUDIO - DAY

WIDER: Breton and Trotsky stand in the slanting light of the studio room staring at the canvases, riveted.

Frida sits on a chair in the corner, smoking, nonchalant.

EXT. BLUE HOUSE - COURTYARD - DAY

Diego sits reading in the shade. Frida emerges from the house out into the courtyard, followed closely by Trotsky and Breton, who is extremely excited.

FRIDA
(dismissive)
Oh, stop it André, I hate flattery.

BRETON
I don't care, it's wonderful, wonderful work...
(to Diego)
You've seen all this I take it?

DIEGO
Of course. I tell her all the time. Julien Levy took a couple of her paintings to New York and sold both of them and she sold another four to that actor... the gangster...

FRIDA
Edward G. Robinson.

DIEGO
For two hundred dollars a piece!

FRIDA
He was robbed, we haven't been able to fool anyone else. My little paintings can't mean anything to anyone but me.

GUARD (O.S.)
STOP!! GET DOWN!

Their heads all turn as the guards up on the wall over the street react violently to something out on the street..

SHOTGUNS RACKED—a guard leaps down and dives toward Trotsky pulling him down behind the tree and shouting...

Breton and Diego scramble for cover, but Frida turns to see what's going on.

The guards have their weapons trained on TWO ELDERLY WOMEN crouching by the front gate, chanting in Spanish and sprinkling something on the ground.

GUARD (Cont'd)
They put a bag by the door! Get back!

GUARD ON THE ROOF
GET BACK!

GUARD
They put a bag by the door, get down, get down...

DIEGO
Inside! Everybody inside! Frida, what are you doing?

Frida yanks the gun out of the crouching guard's hands. She marches into the middle of the yard, points the gun straight at the women and calls out...

FRIDA
I give you five seconds to get out of here. One... two...

She FIRES, and the bullet strikes the archway just over their heads. The elderly women shriek and scurry away. Frida turns and hands the gun back to the guard as Natalia emerges, panicked, out the door. Everyone stares at her. She shrugs...

FRIDA (Cont'd)
It's all right, it's all right. Sorry about that. It's my mother's sisters.

TROTSKY
What do you mean?

FRIDA
They were leaving icons and sprinkling holy water. They think this house is cursed and that you are the anti-Christ.

She laughs, and Trotsky laughs with her.

EXT. MEXICAN COUNTRYSIDE - DAY
MUSIC SWELLS as we see a small line of three cars heading into the broad, colorful vista of the rural countryside...

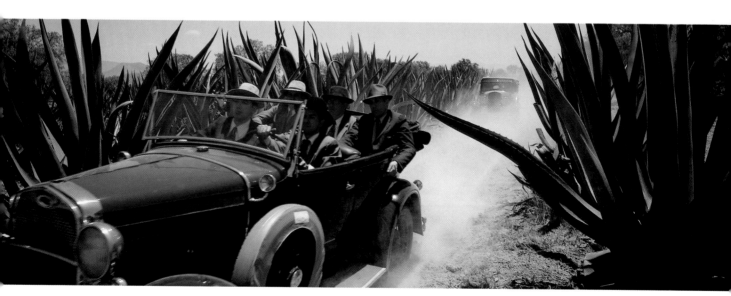

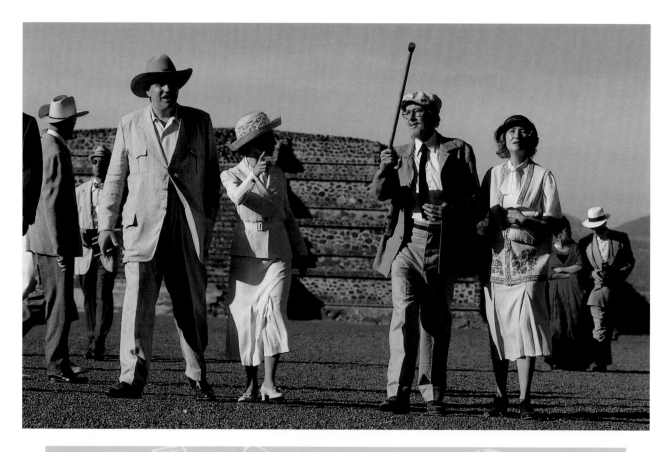

This Sacred Place

The scenes where Frida and Diego take the Trotsky party on an outing were filmed in the ancient city of Teotihuacán, not far from Mexico City. Obtaining permission to shoot in this sacred place was extremely difficult. Salma Hayek had to ask special permission from government officials as the place has rarely, if ever, been shot for a movie.

The name, Teotihuacán, means "the place where men become gods." Once the center of a vast empire with a population of 250,000 people, Teotihuacán stretches over six square miles and includes two gigantic pyramids. The Pyramid of the Sun (210 feet high) and the Pyramid of the Moon (138 feet high) were built long before the Aztecs entered the Valley of Mexico. The Aztecs attributed them to the giants who once inhabited the earth, especially after the discovery of elephant fossil bones, which they thought to be those of humans. According to legend, Teotihuacán was the burial place of kings and noblemen, but no graves have ever been found near the two immense pyramids.

To this day no one knows who built the pyramids. By A.D. 600 the city was already declining, and by A.D. 900 it appears to have been abandoned. It left no written history, no songs or legends by which it might be remembered. We do not know what happened, and we cannot guess.

Even though a great civilization vanished from here, it did not wholly perish. The influence of Teotihuacán culture was far-reaching, extending over the Valley of Mexico, over Oaxaca in the south, and Mayan Yucatan in the southeast. Nearly seven hundred miles to the southeast, in the highlands of Guatemala, are tombs and temples which are clearly derived from Teotihuacán.

—ADAPTED FROM *MEXICO CITY*, BY ROBERT PAYNE

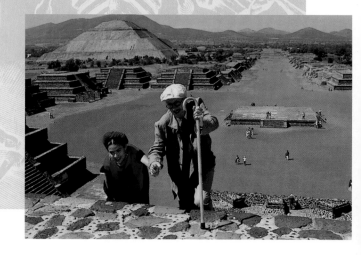

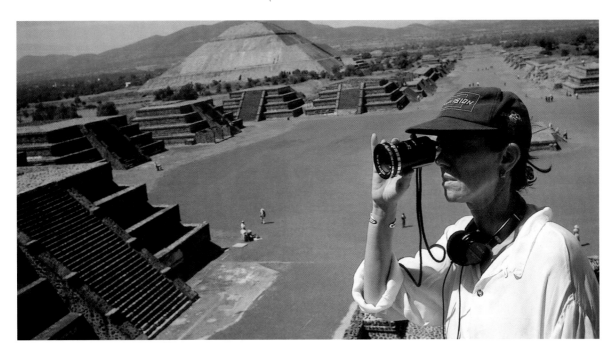

EXT. TEOTIHUACAN RUINS - DAY

The Trotskys, the Riveras, Breton and his friend walk a path near the Avenue of the Dead. In the distance are the pyramids of the sun and the moon. The bodyguards shadow the group.

Diego, Trotsky and Breton's friend talk. Breton is bending Frida's ear as they stroll with Natalia.

> **BRETON**
> I want you to think about this exhibition. You could be part of the Mexican exhibition in Paris.

> **FRIDA**
> What I really want is a show in my own country.

> **BRETON**
> Which they'll give you once you become famous somewhere else. Your paintings should be seen.

She stops, looks at him for a beat and softens.

> **FRIDA**
> All right. I'll think about it.

EXT. BASE OF THE PYRAMIDS - LATER

Joining the others they arrive at the base of the pyramid of the moon. Trotsky takes off his jacket and hands it to a bodyguard.

Shooting at the Pryamids

After much negotiating over permissions and strict limitations on the shoot for the pyramids, we finally had one day in which to cover an enormous amount of material. It's an overwhelming place, and the challenge was to try and capture its majesty while telling the story. We used the Pyramid of the Moon for our main scene between Trotsky and Frida. It was a harrowing and exhausting experience under the hot sun to climb and find camera locations on those outrageously steep steps. We were also asked not to use tripods, so the camera department had an extra challenge. It is always moving to shoot in the actual location where the historical event took place. And the notion of "sacrifice," which dominates this part of the tale had extra significance by the setting of the Aztec temples.

—JULIE TAYMOR, DIRECTOR

> **TROTSKY**
> So? Who is coming up with me?

> **DIEGO**
> It's harder than you think.

> **TROTSKY**
> Ah, everything is harder than we think.

> **FRIDA**
> I'll go.

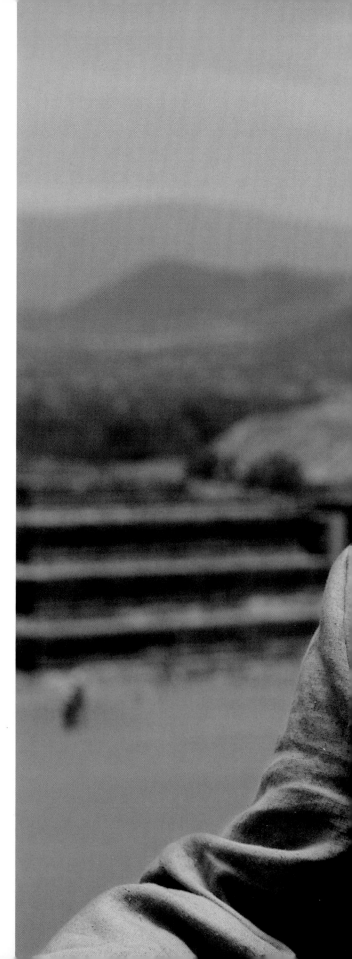

DIEGO
(concerned)
Are you sure?

FRIDA
If an old man can do it, why not a cripple?

Trotsky laughs.

NATALIA
Astorochna?

TROTSKY
Horosho.

As they begin a bodyguard follows.

TROTSKY *(Cont'd)*
No, no, no, no. It's O.K. I don't think assassins are waiting at the top.

The guard stops reluctantly. Frida and Trotsky climb alone. As they climb, Trotsky seems to have limitless energy. He helps Frida who moves slowly.

AT THE TOP OF THE PYRAMID - LATER

Alone at the top, they take in the view. Frida is limping badly and has to sit down, the climb has taken a toll... He sits next to her.

TROTSKY
Frida, how were you hurt?

FRIDA
I couldn't even tell you anymore. I've been cut into, re-broken, re-set so many times... I'm like a jigsaw puzzle.

He listens, moved. He did not guess the full extent of it.

FRIDA *(Cont'd)*
And all the operations have done more damage than the accident for all I know... Everything hurts, but the leg, the leg is the worst. But I'm all right. At the end of the day, we can endure much more than we think we can.

TROTSKY
That's what I loved about your paintings. That

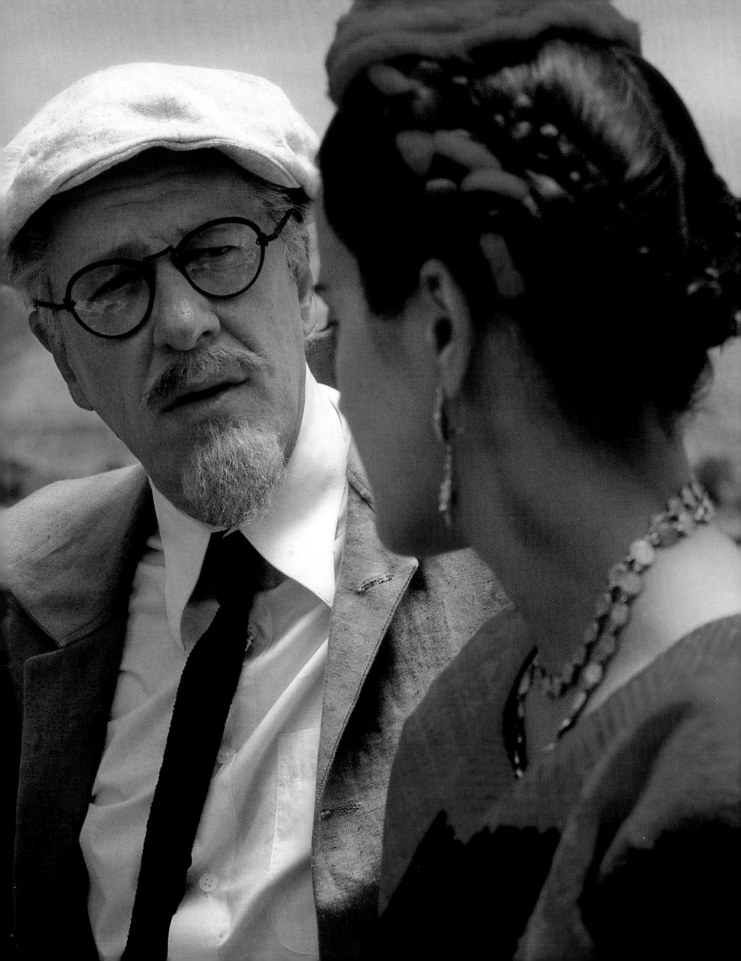

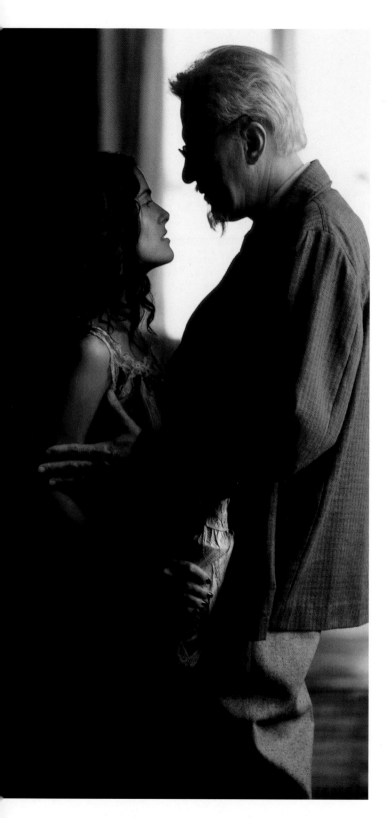

they carry that message...
(looks directly at her)
You said that nobody would care about them,
but I think you're wrong. Because your paintings
express what everyone feels—that they are alone, in
pain.

FRIDA

Maybe.
(pause)
Leon, tell me about your children.

She breaks off, and he looks at her.

TROTSKY

My children. We knew the girls had been murdered
and one of the boys. We thought the other was still
alive in the prison, but that letter came. He was executed, too. They are all gone. I have condemned my
family. As I am condemned.

FRIDA

You mustn't say that...

TROTSKY

(almost light)
But it's true. Stalin has more power than any tsar. I
am alone with few friends and no resources against
the world's biggest killing machine... So what can I
do but keep on working... living.
(he takes a breath)
You cannot imagine what a joy it is for me to be
here, to see all this... It is the first time I've felt like a
real person in years...

EXT. FRIDA'S APARTMENT BUILDING - STREET - DAY

A car pulls up to the house. A bodyguard opens the
back door and Trotsky steps out of the car and quickly
walks to the door of the building. The guards glance at
each other, concerned...

INT. FRIDA'S APARTMENT - DAY

The door opens and it's Frida, smiling. Trotsky enters
in a rush, slams the door and grabs her, kissing her
with abandon.

INT. FRIDA'S APARTMENT - BEDROOM - DAY

Trotsky and Frida make love.

INT. FRIDA'S APARTMENT - DAY

Trotsky and Frida are in bed.

TROTSKY
How long do I get to be here with you?

FRIDA
Well, you know who is never late for dinner. So I guess about another hour...

TROTSKY
And after that?

FRIDA
I don't know. What do you want a Five-Year Plan?

INT. BLUE HOUSE - STUDY - DAY

Trotsky sits at his desk, dictating his *History of the Russian Revolution* into the Dictaphone from his notes.

TROTSKY
In his book *State and Revolution*, Lenin purged from the genuine teaching of Karl Marx all the spurious ingredients introduced by the social democracy.

Frida enters with the tray of tea and sandwiches. She sets it in front of him, but not wanting to interrupt, she turns to go. He grabs her skirt and pulls her back toward him. Smiling, but glancing toward the open door, she allows him to pull her into a kiss.

TROTSKY *(Cont'd)*
John, I am picking it up from social democracy.

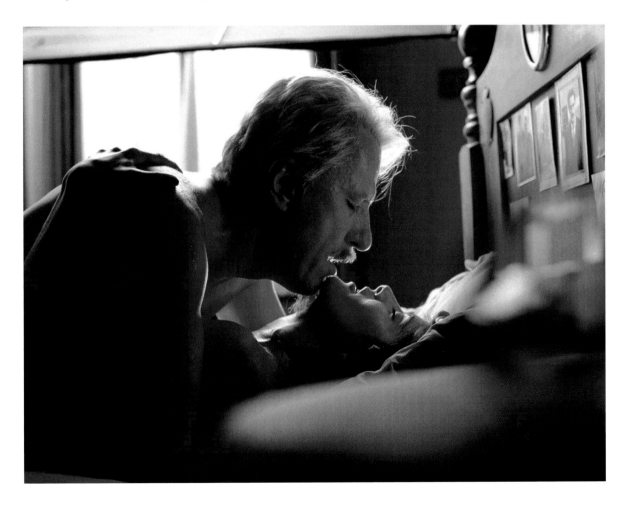

EXT. BLUE HOUSE - COURTYARD - DAY

Pull back to reveal Trotsky finishing the note inside the book. He sits out in the courtyard with Natalia, Breton and Diego.

Frida comes through on her way out to do the shopping. Trotsky folds the note and slips it into the book, unaware that NATALIA has observed this, quizzically...

TROTSKY
Frida, this is the book I mentioned. Tell me what you think.

FRIDA
Thank you.

She smiles, despite herself, as he hands it to her with a wink.

NATALIA: she realizes and looks down, shattered.

FRIDA (O.S.)
I'll be back in an hour.

INT. BLUE HOUSE - KITCHEN/DINING ROOM - LATER

Frida comes in with food from the market and sets it down. The house is quiet. Then as she sorts the food, she stops...

VOICES ARGUING, in Russian, coming from down the hall, muted but unmistakable—Trotsky and Natalia are in a heated discussion.

As Frida listens, a door slams and the only sound is NATALIA CRYING. Trotsky moves away from the room, down the verandah. Frida looks on, disturbed.

EXT. BLUE HOUSE - COURTYARD/STREET - DAY

The Trotskys and their entourage are moving out. Diego and Frida are there to say goodbye. Trotsky is reassuring Diego.

TROTSKY
No, no. It's better this way. We'll stop disrupting your lives. We're not going far, just around the corner.

DIEGO
I wish you would reconsider, if only for security.

TROTSKY
We'll be more than safe. Trust me.
(embraces Diego)

NATALIA
(to Frida)
Dosveydanya.

TROTSKY
Many thanks, my friend. We'll see you soon.

DIEGO
(going after her)
Natalia.

Trotsky embraces Frida and kisses her twice then gets in the car.

The cars rumble off.

Frida is fighting to keep her emotions in check. Diego stands there, still concerned and confused.

DIEGO (Cont'd)
It makes no sense... It was for his own well-being...

FRIDA
He's not thinking of his well-being; he's thinking of hers.

DIEGO
What are you talking about?

Her emotions and long pent-up resentment burst out...

FRIDA
I'm talking about somebody willing to sacrifice a little of their own pleasure rather than go on hurting the woman who loves him!

She stares at him, pointedly, then storms down the street.

Diego stares after her, and then he realizes...

Diego chases after her...

DIEGO
Have you lost your mind!?

FRIDA
Go to hell, Diego!

DIEGO
Do you know what the consequences of this could be?!

FRIDA
He's not scared, why should you be?

DIEGO
Oh, dear God! Of all people... Why?

Frida looks at him.

FRIDA
Because we wanted to.

DIEGO
You've broken my heart, Frida.

FRIDA
It hurts, doesn't it? But why? It was just a fuck, like a handshake!

DIEGO
No. I told you who I was when you married me!

FRIDA
Yes, you did, and I married you anyway. And you promised to be loyal. You've been my comrade, my fellow artist, my best friend. But you've never been my husband. I can't do this anymore, Diego.

She turns and walks away from him.

DIEGO
Friducha...

FRIDA
I can't.

I am DISINTEGRATION. . . .

—FRIDA KAHLO

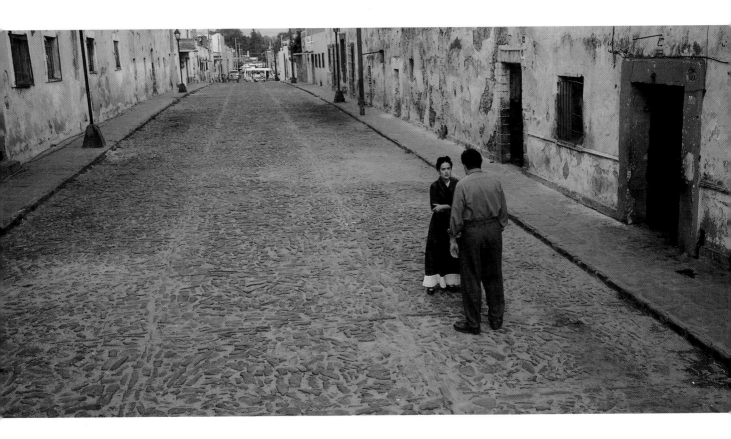

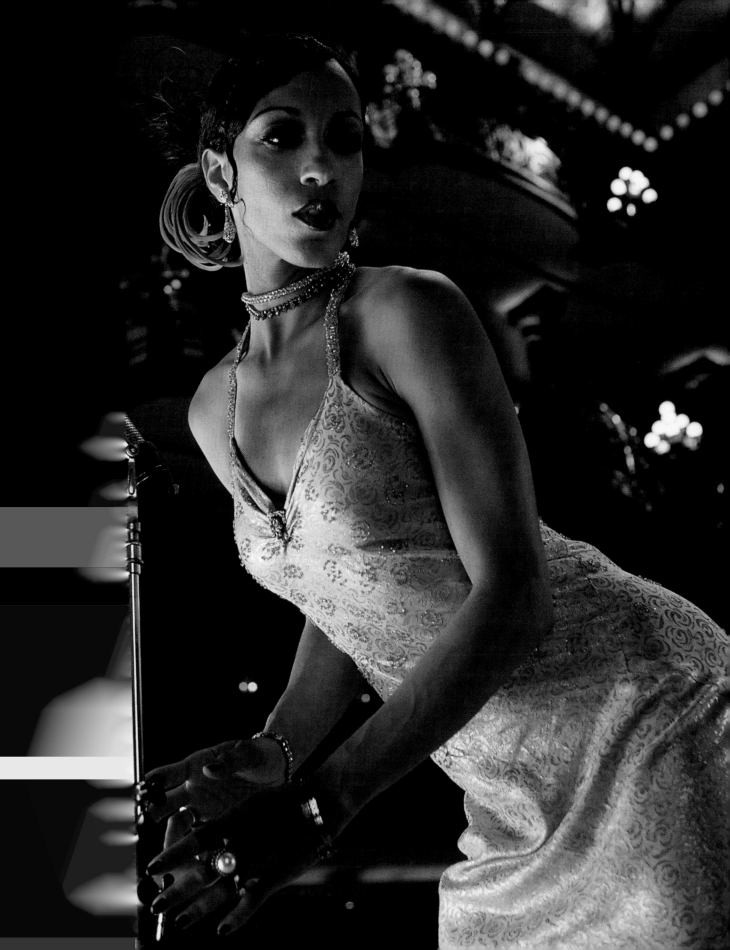

EXT. PARIS STREET - DAY

A SNAPSHOT OF PARIS featuring the Eiffel Tower... IT TURNS AWAY, replaced by A SHOT OF NOTRE DAME... That turns away, replaced by BOATS ON THE SEINE and we PULL BACK to find...

...FRIDA TURNING A POSTCARD RACK selecting postcards...

MONTAGE BEGINS:

EXT. PARIS CAFE - DAY

Frida sits in a sidewalk cafe, drinking wine and writing a letter.

> **FRIDA (V.O.)**
> Dear Diego, How are you, panzon? Why didn't you tell me Paris was such a nightmare?

INT. PARISIAN NIGHT CLUB - NIGHT

A "Josephine Baker" sings a sexy jazz tune to the dancing crowd. Frida, at a table laden with rich food, downs a glass of champagne in the company of two or three handsome and well-dressed men, who clearly are smitten with her.

> **FRIDA** (V.O. *Cont'd*)
> The French are the most pretentious bores in the world. I'd rather sit on the floor of a market in Toluca selling tortillas than have to listen to the prattling of the artistic "bitches" of Paris.

INT. PARIS ELEVATOR - NIGHT

Frida stands behind a beautiful young woman in a crowded elevator. Her breath on the nape of the woman causes the woman to stir.

The elevator doors open, everyone exits.

Frida and the woman remain in the elevator, kissing.

INT. PARIS BEDROOM - NIGHT

Frida in bed with a woman.

INT. PHOTOGRAPHER'S STUDIO - PARIS - DAY

A handsome photographer (à la Nick Muray) is posing Frida. He makes her laugh, and she smiles at him...

INT. PARIS GALLERY - NIGHT

A packed room, FLASH BULBS. The cognoscenti and society crowd sipping wine and gabbing. FRIDA amidst it all...

> **FRIDA** (V.O. *Cont'd*)
> There really hasn't been as much interest in the exhibition as Breton promised.

We see Breton introduce her to a man who quite clearly is Pablo Picasso.

> **BRETON**
> Frida Kalho, Pablo Picasso.

> **FRIDA**
> Mexican artists are nothing but an exotic curiosity here. All in all, it's been lonely, and I crave news from home.

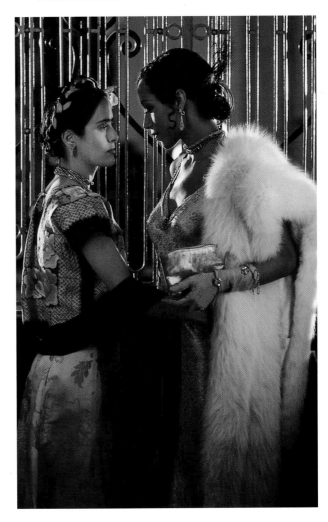

135

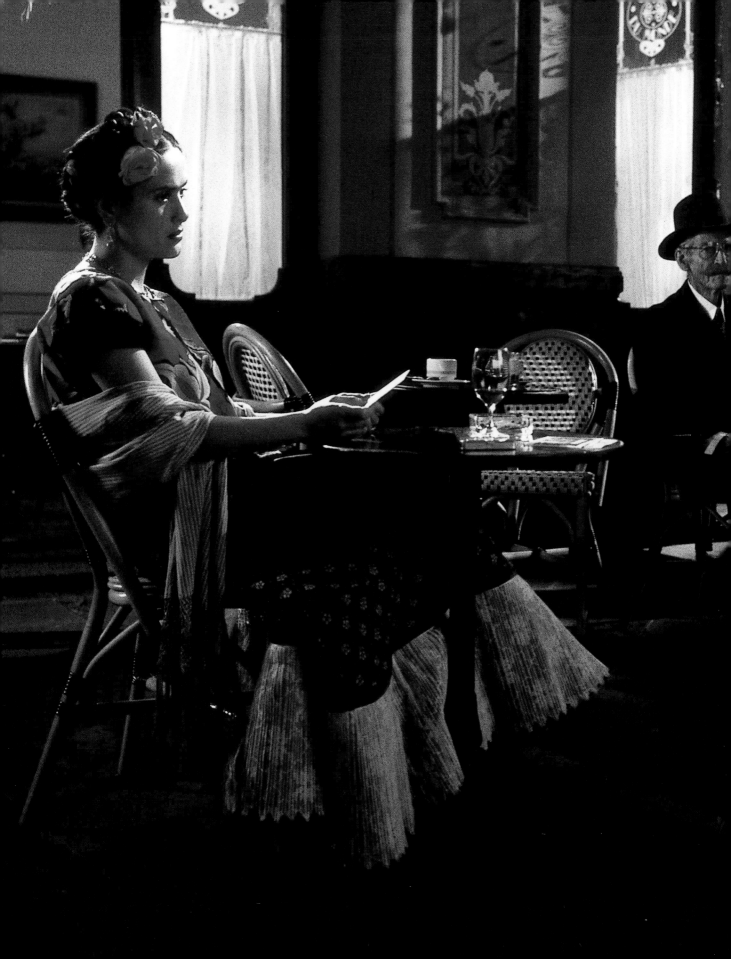

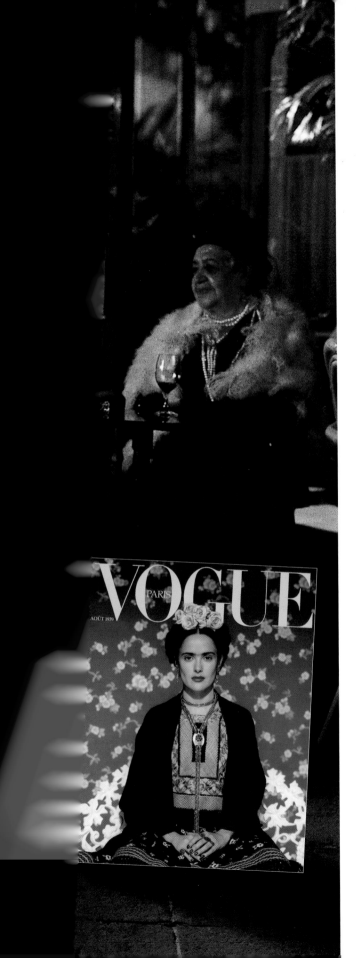

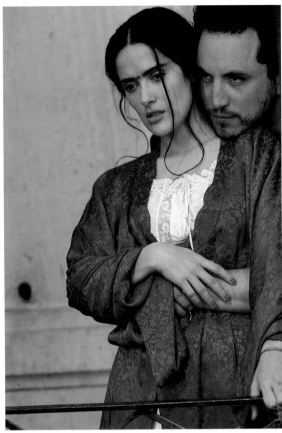

EXT. TERRACE OF PARIS APARTMENT - EARLY MORNING

Frida leans over terrace railing. The photographer's arms slip around her body. She melts into him, but her gaze is far away.

EXT. CAFE/PARIS - DUSK

Frida stops and rereads some of the letter. We see her face clearly for the first time. It's full of longing. She begins writing again.

> **FRIDA** (V.O. *Cont'd*)
> Diego: this letter is a lie: Paris has been good to me, but without you it means nothing.

INT. DIEGO'S STUDIO - SAN ANGEL HOUSE - SUNSET

ON A COPY OF VOGUE MAGAZINE—Frida's beringed hands grace the cover.

Diego sits in his robe, staring down at the magazine. Paulette Goddard comes up from behind, and leans over his shoulder to see.

137

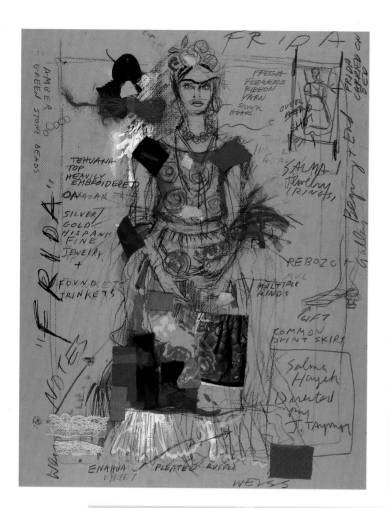

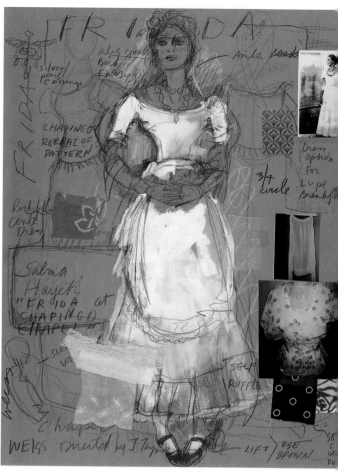

"This is who we are"

People get dressed for many, many different reasons: to disguise themselves, to copy other people, to show their social stature or to draw attention to themselves. Some people walk down the street, and you can tell what year was the best in their life because their hair and clothes got frozen in that time. Few people get dressed just to keep warm. But the key to costume design is to get past the clothes. The clothes should not fight what the camera is capable of catching—that little moment, that glimpse into a person and who they really are.

In *Frida*, I am answerable to an existing story. I couldn't possibly compete with how Frida Kahlo dressed. When she walked down the street, she exuded an aura. It didn't demand, "Look at me"; rather, it said, "This is who I am," and that is a major difference.

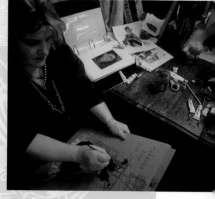

Most of us tend to copy people who we see in fashion magazines, the media, or people we admire. Frida reached inside herself and looked for who she was. Much of her work is biographical and her life can be traced through the visual diary of her paintings. Certainly, she's a non-traditionalist, wearing her grandmother's traditional Oaxacan dresses, but, at some points, she moves into a more radical mode of masculine dress; for example, during her separation from Diego. Being accepted was not the reason Frida Kahlo got dressed in the morning. She was a woman of presence and self-confidence. She was connected to her art.

When Frida and Diego Rivera walked down the street holding hands, everything about them said, "This is who we are, and you will continue to look until you embrace us."

—Julie Weiss, costume designer

Above: Two of the many sketches done by costume designer Julie Weiss. Right: Julie Weiss, costume designer. Photo by Seth Joel.

138

In the beginning, I only hinted at the idea of divorce, but when the hints brought no response, I made the suggestion openly. Frida, who had by now recovered her health, responded calmly that she would prefer to endure anything rather than lose me completely.

The situation between us grew worse and worse. One evening, entirely on impulse, I telephoned her to plead for her consent to a divorce, and in my anxiety, fabricated a stupid and vulgar pretext. I dreaded a long, heart-wrenching discussion so much that I impulsively seized on the quickest way to my end.

It worked. Frida declared that she too wanted an immediate divorce. My "victory" quickly changed to gall in my heart. We had been married for 13 [actually 10] years. We still loved each other. I simply wanted to be free to carry on with any woman who caught my fancy. Yet Frida did not object to my infidelity as such. What she could not understand was my choosing women who were either unworthy of me or inferior to her. She took it as a personal humiliation to be abandoned for sluts. To let her draw any line, however, was this not to circumscribe my freedom? Or was I simply the depraved victim of my own appetites? And wasn't it merely a consoling lie to think that a divorce would put an end to Frida's suffering? Wouldn't Frida suffer even more?

During the two years we lived apart, Frida turned out some of her best work, sublimating her anguish in her painting.

—DIEGO RIVERA, *MY ART, MY LIFE*

FRIDA (V.O. *Cont'd*)
All the rage of our 12 years together passes through me and I am left knowing that I love you more than my own skin and though you may not love me as much, you do love me a little — don't you?

EXT. CAFE/PARIS - DUSK

Frida writing...

FRIDA (V.O. CONT'D)
If this is not true, I'll always be hopeful that it could be. I adore you. Frida.

Over the last lines, Frida folds the letter, seals it in an envelope, marks it with the print of her kiss and circles that.

END MONTAGE.

INT. TROTSKY'S BEDROOM - NIGHT

A CRY OF ALARM awakes the sleeping couple. Hearing shouts and running feet, Trotsky shoves Natalia to the floor off the far side of the bed just as...

Machine gun fire rips through the room, deafening, tearing plaster out of the wall and shredding the bed until....

SILENCE. Trotsky and Natalia slowly raise their heads, unharmed.

EXT. SAN ANGEL HOUSE - DAY

We see Frida moving toward Diego's door. She knocks.

TIGHT ON: the door opens and Diego stands there. He smiles and they embrace.

EXT. MARKET - NIGHT

Diego and Frida sit at a table in the nearly deserted market.

DIEGO
...There are rumors going around that I wanted him killed. We fought lately it's true, but... They may try to arrest me again.

FRIDA
Talk to the President.

DIEGO
No. No, I'm going to California...

FRIDA *(surprised)*
California...?

DIEGO
Yes... and Frida... *(a deep breath)*
I want us to divorce.

She is stunned. She cannot hide the hurt.

The Divorce

To Nickolas Muray, Frida Kahlo wrote on October 13, 1939: "Two weeks ago we began the divorce. I have no words to tell you how much I been suffering and knowing how much I love Diego you must understand that this troubles will never end in my life, but after the last fight I had with him (by phone) because it is almost a month that I don't see him, I understood that for him it is much better to leave me... Now I feel so rotten and lonely that it seems to me that nobody in the world has suffer the way I do, but of course it will be different I hope in a few months."

—HAYDEN HERRERA, *FRIDA KAHLO: THE PAINTINGS*

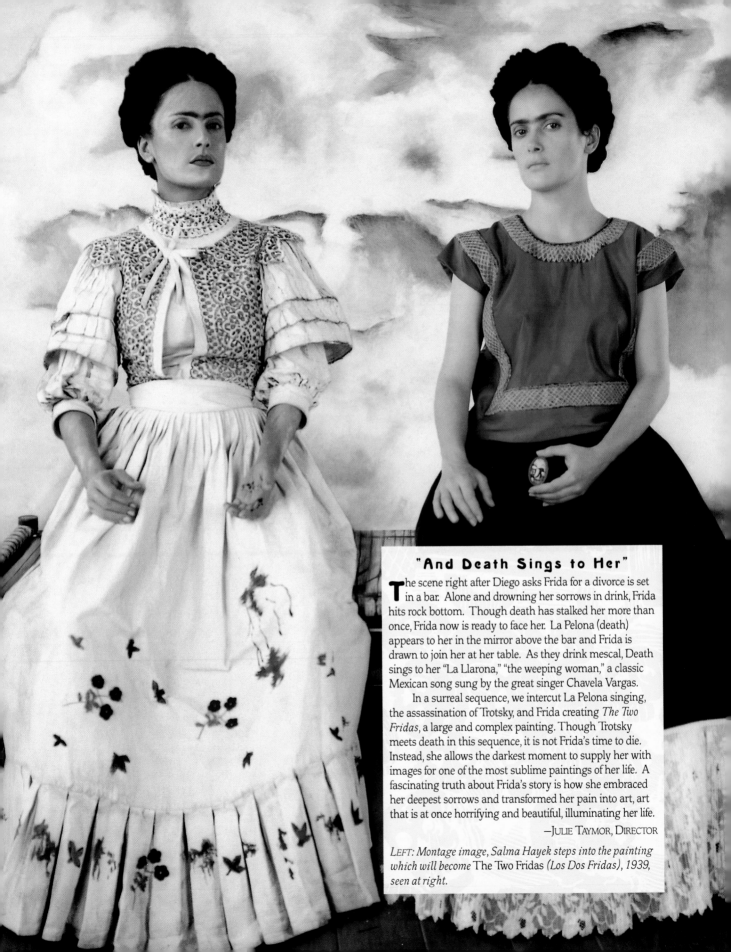

"And Death Sings to Her"

The scene right after Diego asks Frida for a divorce is set in a bar. Alone and drowning her sorrows in drink, Frida hits rock bottom. Though death has stalked her more than once, Frida now is ready to face her. La Pelona (death) appears to her in the mirror above the bar and Frida is drawn to join her at her table. As they drink mescal, Death sings to her "La Llorona," "the weeping woman," a classic Mexican song sung by the great singer Chavela Vargas.

In a surreal sequence, we intercut La Pelona singing, the assassination of Trotsky, and Frida creating *The Two Fridas*, a large and complex painting. Though Trotsky meets death in this sequence, it is not Frida's time to die. Instead, she allows the darkest moment to supply her with images for one of the most sublime paintings of her life. A fascinating truth about Frida's story is how she embraced her deepest sorrows and transformed her pain into art, art that is at once horrifying and beautiful, illuminating her life.

—JULIE TAYMOR, DIRECTOR

LEFT: Montage image, Salma Hayek steps into the painting which will become The Two Fridas (Los Dos Fridas), *1939, seen at right.*

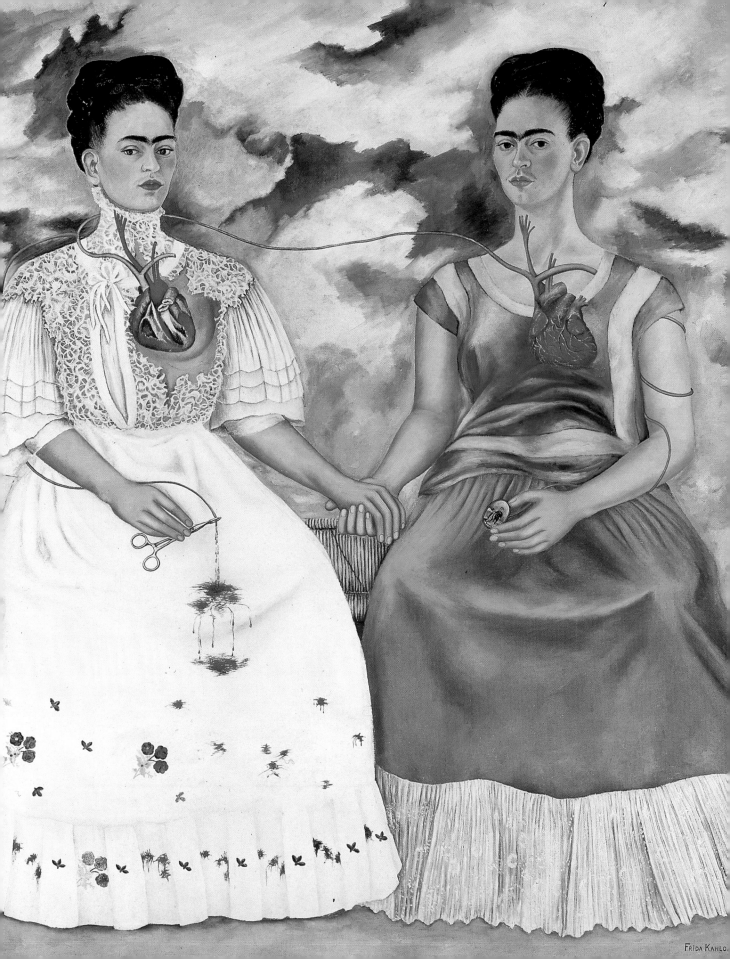

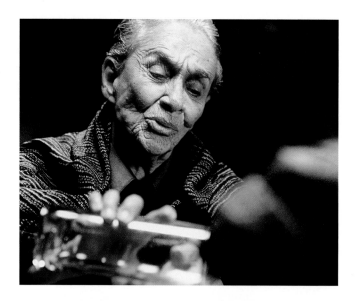

Chavela Vargas

Chavela Vargas is an icon, a living myth. She is in her eighties now, and she's been singing forever. She has the most amazing voice that combines soul and sorrow. Chavela and Frida were very good friends; she sang for Frida. She told me they were also lovers once.

In this movie, Chavela sings to me as Frida, and that was an unforgettable experience. She sang to me with her whole heart. It was very touching. After, she told me it was very moving for her, too, because she felt like she got one last chance to sing to Frida and that this would probably be her last performance.

We are very honored by her presence in the film.

—SALMA HAYEK, ACTOR AND PRODUCER

FRIDA
For who, that American actress? Jesus, Diego.

DIEGO
No, Frida... no. It will be better this way, we have both done better as friends.

FRIDA
I haven't.

DIEGO
You have. You're doing very well on your own. I'm proud of you. You don't need—

FRIDA
Enough, if you want to go, just go.

INT. CANTINA - NIGHT

AN UNEARTHLY SONG BEGINS: LA LLORONA.

Frida sits at the bar, drinking mezcal, facing her reflection in a cracked mirror over the bar. She looks up and in the mirror behind her she sees...

LA PELONA, a DEATH SKELETON, seated at a corner table, the SONG pouring from its mouth. Frida turns away from the mirror to find only the back of a bent figure... She goes to the table and, instead of the skeleton, is an OLD WOMAN who offers Frida a seat. As the song continues, the two clink glass like old comrades and drink...

TIGHT ON: the old woman's MOUTH, as she swallows the WORM.

THE SONG CONTINUES over crosscutting between close details of FRIDA merging into the 3-D painting of THE TWO FRIDAS and RAMON MERCADER, the assassin, moving to TROTSKY with a cup of tea:

FRIDA walks down a silent street.

Mercader's HAND pours a cup of tea.

FRIDA's HAND turns a doorknob.

Mercader's HAND stirs the cup of tea.

FRIDA'S HAND clutches a small portrait of DIEGO.

TROTSKY'S HAND writing with a quill pen.

Mercader's feet walk down a hall.

BLOOD drips from a vein onto the white dress in patterns of flowers.

INK blots on the paper.

A DOOR OPENS. A DOOR OPENS.

THE BLUE FRIDA moves to the WHITE FRIDA.

Out of the dark behind TROTSKY, THE TORSO OF Mercader emerges, a TOWEL over his arm carrying the TRAY OF TEA.

THE BLUE FRIDA clamps the vein of the WHITE FRIDA, stopping the blood flow.

We do not see his face as Mercader sets the tray down. TROTSKY nods...

THE BLUE FRIDA sits beside the WHITE FRIDA, CLASPING HER HAND.

Behind TROTSKY writing, we see THE ICE PICK EMERGE FROM THE TOWEL. AS IT IS RAISED

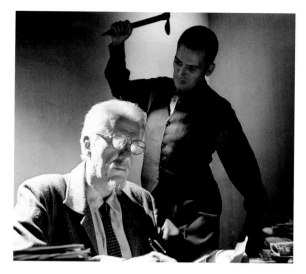

WE SEE NOW THE FACE OF THE ASSASSIN and, just for a second, the death mask, ghostly over the face.

TROTSKY SENSES, slowly raises his head, and as the song climaxes....

THE ICE PICK plunges down. Death has come for Trotsky, not Frida...

BLACK.

INT. FRIDA'S STUDIO/BLUE HOUSE - MORNING

Frida sits regarding her finished painting of THE TWO FRIDAS. An ashtray filled with cigarette butts and an empty bottle of gin by her side. She has clearly been up all night.

ANGRY KNOCKS on the door startle her.

INT. POLICE STATION - DAY

A GLARING LIGHT BULB blinds Frida. Pale and exhausted, she's being interrogated by a cold, unrelenting FEDERAL POLICEMAN.

    DETECTIVE
Listen to me, I don't particularly care for Mr. Trotsky. But we can't go around having political refugees murdered in our country, now can we?
(beat)
Once more, where is your husband?

    FRIDA
I don't have a husband.

INT. JAIL CELL - DAY

Frida huddles in agony on the bare, dirty cot. The door to the cell creaks open. Someone enters.

    CRISTINA (O.S.)
Frida? Oh my god.

Frida, with great effort and difficulty, turns over to see her sister standing over her. Cristina gasps, shocked at Frida's condition.

A long beat as the two women look at one another. A full range of emotions crosses Frida's face. Then everything between them starts to melt away. Holding back tears, Frida tries to smile.

    FRIDA
Cristi.

Cristina bends down to hold Frida.

    CRISTINA
I'm so sorry.

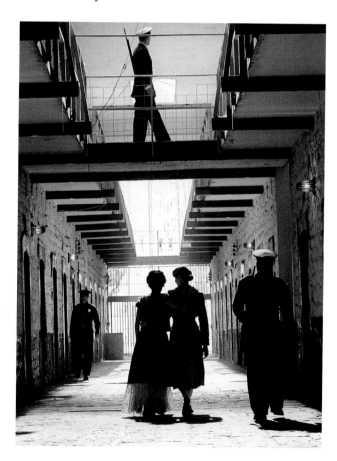

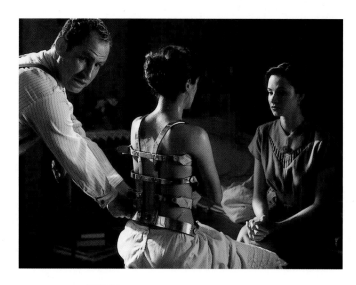

FRIDA
It was not your fault. It was mine.

I should have never put you in a room with him.

INT. JAIL HALLWAY - LATER
FRIDA and CRISTINA walk towards the exit, holding tight to each other.

FRIDA
What did you do to get me out of here?

CRISTINA
Diego. He went crazy when he heard. He called President Cárdenas immediately.

FRIDA
Diego.

INT. BLUE HOUSE - BEDROOM - DAY
TIGHT ON: a steel and leather corset, binding flesh. Frida sits, gasping each time DR. FARILL tightens the bands on her naked back.

DR FARILL
Not much more...

Cristina holds Frida's hand. He finishes and sits back, glancing down. He bends and examines her toes as Cristina helps her dress... The toes of one foot are black.

RIGHT: The Broken Column, *1944. INSET: The painting was shot as a 3-D image for the film.*

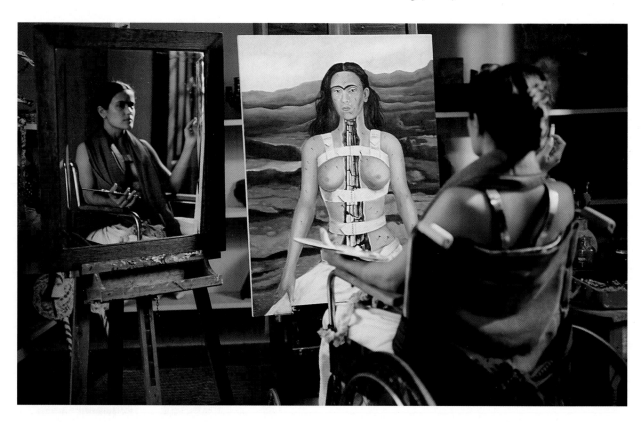

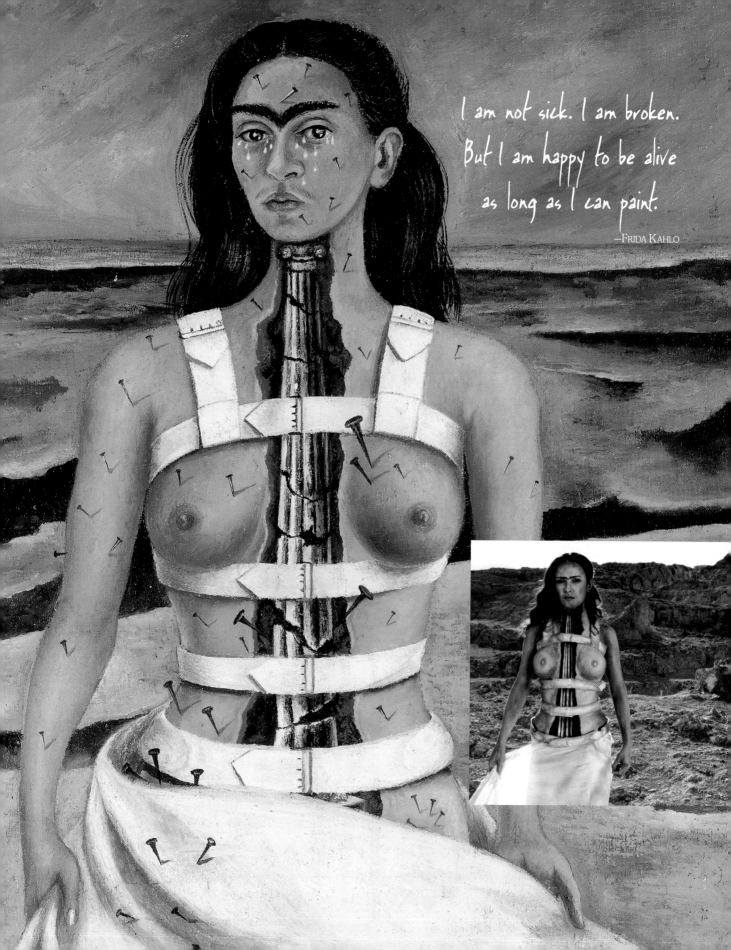

I am not sick. I am broken. But I am happy to be alive as long as I can paint.

—FRIDA KAHLO

DOCTOR FARILL
How long has your foot been like this?

FRIDA
Who knows? Let's take it one disaster at a time. Just patch me up, so I can paint please.

DOCTOR FARILL
These are gangrened. They'll have to come off. You're lucky it hasn't spread to your leg.

Frida looks at Cristina who kisses her tenderly. Then...

EXT. VOLCANIC LANDSCAPE - DUSK

A tiny figure stands in the center of a plain of dark ravines—Frida—in the steel corset with a split in her torso like an earthquake fissure.

A 3-D recreation of THE BROKEN COLUMN; the nails enter the body to match the painting, and then a real hand enters the frame, painting real tears onto the eyes... We pull back to...

INT. BLUE HOUSE - FRIDA'S STUDIO - DAY

Frida, adding the detail to the canvas, tied to her wheelchair with a red sash, a cigarette in her lips.

EXT. BLUE HOUSE - COURTYARD - DAY

Frida with a bandaged foot, sits in a wheelchair, in the garden, writing in her diary as Antonio and Isolda play. Behind them in the glare of the sun, the shape of a man emerges... DIEGO... thin, his face older. Frida stares at him, her hand shaking in her lap. He stops a few feet from her.

FRIDA
You've lost weight.

DIEGO
You've lost your toes.

FRIDA
Is that why you're here? To offer your condolences?

DIEGO
I'm here to see how you are. How do you feel?

FRIDA
Tired of answering that question. Otherwise, like

shit. How are you?

DIEGO
I'm... I'm here to ask you to marry me.

FRIDA
I don't need rescuing, Diego.

DIEGO
I do.

Frida thinks about it.

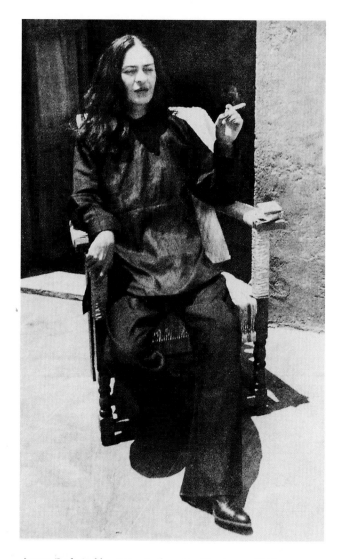

ABOVE: *Frida Kahlo, sitting in the patio of her house, 1947.*

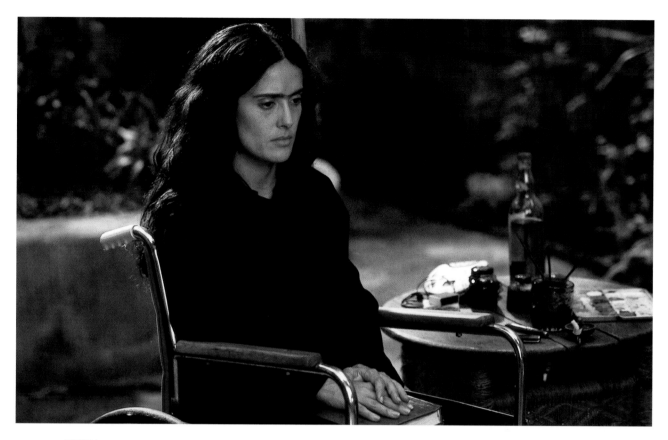

FRIDA
I've lost the toes of one foot. My back is useless. I have an infection of the kidneys. I smoke, I drink, I curse and I can't have children. I have no money and a stack of hospital bills. Should I keep going?

DIEGO
It's practically a letter of recommendation. Frida, Frida, I miss us.

He reaches out a hand and turns her face to his. She's starting to cry. She tries to brush him away.

FRIDA
They say you should never believe a limping dog or the tears of a woman.

DIEGO
They're wrong.

Frida smiles through her tears. Diego takes her face in his hands, kissing her.

EXT. CANALS OF XOCHIMILCO - MEXICO CITY - DAY

On a FLAT BOAT WITH A FLOWERED COVERED CANOPY, Frida and Diego float slowly through the canal, pushed along by a man with a pole... In other boats, boys and girls pelt each others with roses and marigolds in a festival ritual.

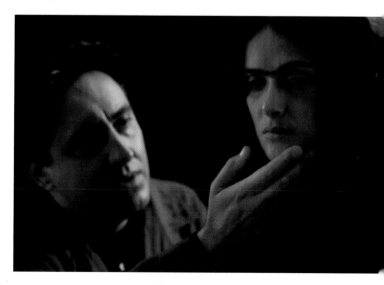

Sacred Monsters

Years after Frida and Diego died, friends remembered them as "sacred monsters." Their escapades and eccentricities were beyond the petty censorings of ordinary morality; not simply condoned, they were treasured and mythologized. As for being "monsters," the Riveras could harbor Trotsky, paint paeans to Stalin, build pagan temples, wave pistols, boast of eating human flesh, and carry on in their marriage with the vast imperiousness of Olympian deities. By the 1940s, Diego, of course, was an ancient myth. Frida, on the other hand, was new to mythic stature, and during this decade their myths meshed.

After the remarriage, while the bond between Frida and Diego deepened, so did their mutual autonomy. Even when they lived together, Diego's absences were frequent and long. Both had love affairs: his were open, hers (with men) she continued to keep secret because of his wild jealousy. Not surprisingly, their life was full of violent battles followed by bitter separations and tender reconciliations.

—HAYDEN HERRERA, *FRIDA: A BIOGRAPHY OF FRIDA KAHLO*

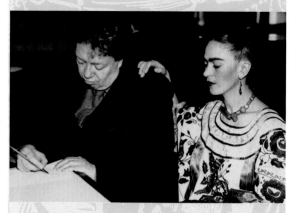

"I love Diego more than ever," Frida told her journalist friend Bambi not long before her death, "and I hope to be of use to him in something and to keep on painting with all alegría and I hope nothing will ever happen to Diego, because the day that he dies I am going with him no matter what. They'll bury us both. I have already said "don't count on me after Diego goes." I am not going to live without Diego, nor can I. For me he is my child, my son, my mother, my father, my lover, my husband, my everything."

—HAYDEN HERRERA, *FRIDA: A BIOGRAPHY OF FRIDA KAHLO*

ABOVE: Diego and Frida apply for a marriage license in San Francisco, December 1940. This was their second marriage after a divorce that lasted 13 months.

Frida throws flowers at Diego, one by one. Tenderly, he tosses them back at her but Diego and Frida are not playful—there's a serious intensity to this.

A floating marimba and a trio moves by them, spilling soft music into the air.

Music continues over following images:

EXT. BLUE HOUSE - COURTYARD - DAY

The Blue House and its courtyard—old and run down
FADE INTO:

EXT. BLUE HOUSE - COURTYARD - DAY

A RENOVATED EDEN: Fresh bright blue paint, alive with animals of all kinds: monkeys, parrots, dogs, cats, a small deer.

INT. BLUE HOUSE - DINING ROOM - DAY

THE DINING TABLE—The family at a leisurely breakfast. Frida feeds the animals from her plate. There is a peacefulness...

INT. BLUE HOUSE - FRIDA'S BEDROOM - DAY

FRIDA'S BEDROOM—In silence, we see Frida screaming and writhing in agony in her plaster cast, literally crazed with pain.

> FRIDA
> Cristina!!

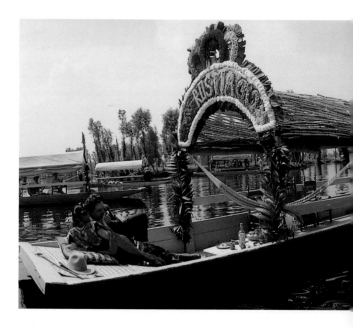

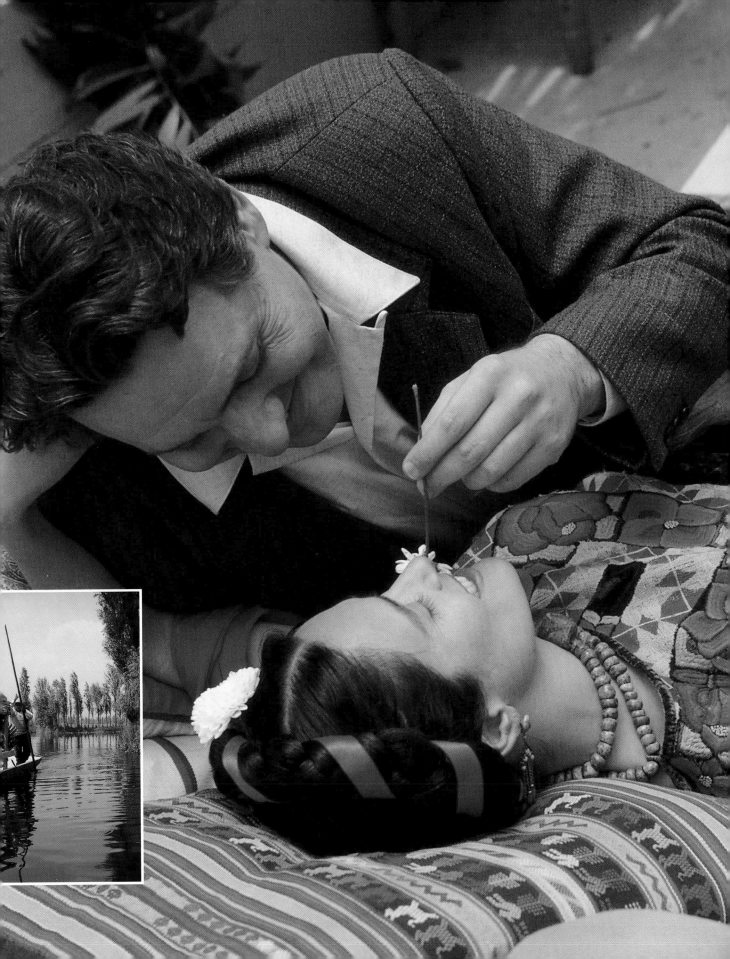

Cristina rushes in, Frida pleads and Cristina injects her with morphine putting her immediately unconscious...

EXT. BLUE HOUSE - VERANDAH - DAY

PARLOR—A picture of Guillermo in her hands, Frida weeps sitting on the couch with Diego. His arm goes around her...

INT. BLUE HOUSE - DINING ROOM - DAY

BREAKFAST TABLE—In a fury, she hurls a glass at Diego's head, just missing him, and in silence we see them shout at each other before he storms out...

INT. BLUE HOUSE - FRIDA'S STUDIO - DAY

FRIDA'S STUDIO—In warm light, Frida hangs in one of her horrifying contraptions, painting while she waits for the plaster corset to dry. We see glimpses of much of her remarkable, visionary work from this period.

INT. HOSPITAL ROOM - DAY

HOSPITAL ROOM—Lying in a new body cast, autographed and covered with decals and mirrors, Frida laughs hard as Diego dances and clowns for her in a jaguar mask and costume. Her right foot is in balloon receiving oxygen.

JUMP CUT TO:

A small tent is over her leg with string puppets attached. She's giving a puppet show for Diego and Cristina, Dr. Farill, Aurora and her children.

JUMP CUT TO:

Frida sits alone in her hospital bed.

THE MUSIC ENDS

INT. FRIDA'S BEDROOM - NIGHT

From above we look down at Frida on the bed and Diego sitting in a chair next to her.

FRIDA'S RIGHT LEG IS GONE

ANGLE ON: Diego. Thinking she's asleep, he lifts her diary off of her chest and looks at it.

> **DIEGO**
> Feet, what do I need you for if I have wings to fly?

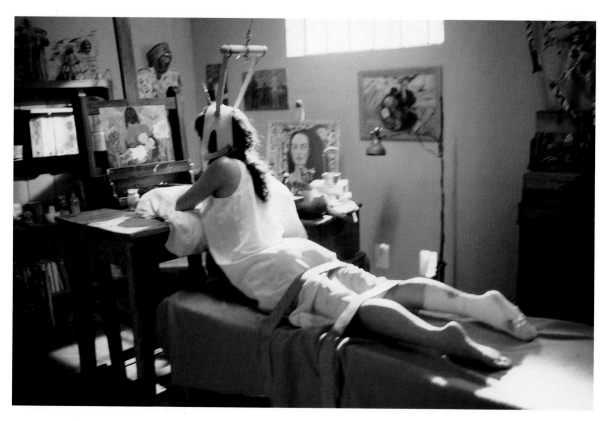

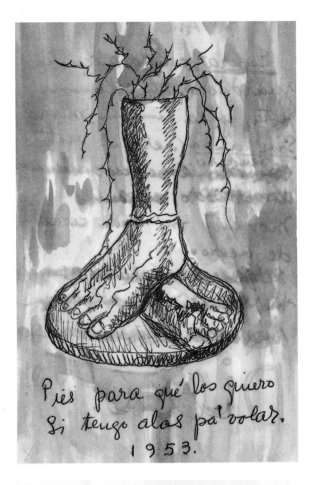

Pies para qué los quiero
Si tengo alas pa' volar.
1 9 5 3.

They amputated my
leg 6 months ago
It seemed to me
centuries of torture and
at times I nearly went
crazy. I still feel like
committing suicide
Diego prevents me from
doing it in the vain
belief that maybe he will
need me. He had told me
so and I believe him. But
I have never suffered so
much in my life.
I'll wait a while.
—FRIDA KAHLO, DIARY
ENTRY, 11 FEBRUARY 1954

ABOVE: Page from Frida Kahlo's diary where the script reads:
"Feet, what do I want them for if I have wings to fly?" In the
movie, Diego reads this page out loud at Frida's bedside.

DIEGO'S POV: Frida's sketch of "Feet, what do I want them for if I have wings to fly?"

He stares at it, moved and starts at the sound of her voice.

> **FRIDA**
> I want you to burn this Judas of a body. I don't want to be buried. I've spent enough time lying down. Burn it!

> **DIEGO**
> Frida...

> **FRIDA**
> I don't think I'm Frida anymore. I think all the Frida in me has disappeared. And look at what's left.

Diego climbs into bed. He strokes her hair.

> **FRIDA** *(Cont'd)*
> Why do you stay?

Diego's voice is tender.

> **DIEGO**
> You stupid girl.

INT. BLUE HOUSE - HALLWAY -DUSK

Dr. Farill comes down the hall. He can hear sounds of loud voices... a fight.

> **DIEGO (O.S.)**
> Are you crazy?

> **FRIDA**
> I'm going.

> **DIEGO**
> I forbid it!

> **FRIDA** (O.S.)
> Stop it, Diego. You can't force me to stay.

> **DIEGO** (O.S.)
> Oh, yes I can.

> **FRIDA** (O.S.)
> Give it to me!

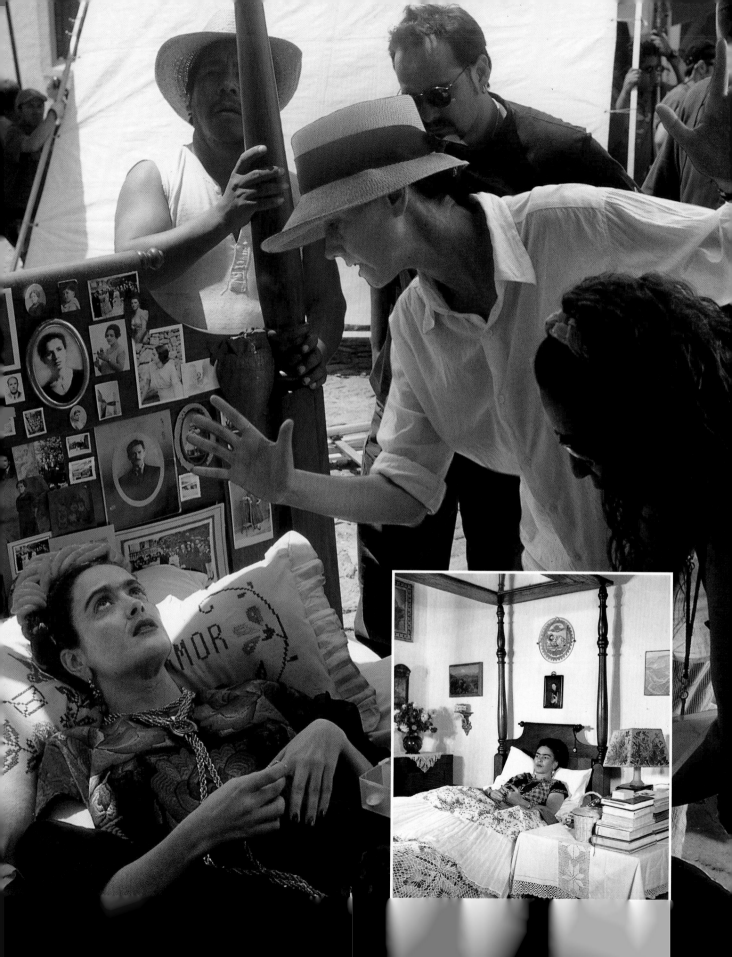

The Music

In *Frida*, the approach I took scoring the music is that of melodic intimacy (scoring with melodies or tunes as opposed to motific fragments). To achieve additional intimacy, I chose a small ensemble of acoustic instruments: the small Mexican guitar (*Vihuela*), standard classical guitar, Mexican bass guitar (*guitarron*), accordion, Mexican harp, marimba, and glass armonica (a Benjamin Franklin invention). I found that the guitars provided the full range of lyricism and percussion I needed.

Mexican music cannot be generalized, it varies greatly from one region to the next, but in its folkloric music there is a certain harmonic fingerprint—the use of consecutive thirds and a proud avoidance of over-complex harmonies. I found that if I adhered to this essential harmonic signature, and stayed very honest with my melodies, the movie invited me in. The few times I tried to reach for more complex harmony and structure, the movie kicked me out with pointy Mexican boots. These ideas remain on my studio floor under a pile of empty Corona bottles.

—ELLIOT GOLDENTHAL, COMPOSER

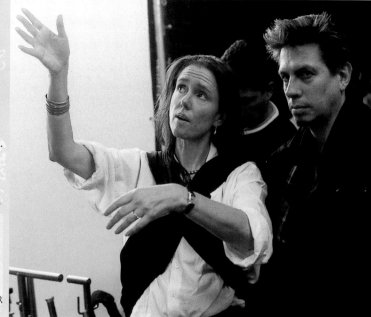

INT. BLUE HOUSE - FRIDA'S BEDROOM - EVENING

Frida is propped up in bed, raging at Diego. She looks very unwell. Diego's keeping her prosthetic leg from her.

DIEGO
No! Frida, no, we've been through this all before!

FRIDA
I'm going, damn it! Give me back my fucking leg.

The doctor enters.

FRIDA (Cont'd)
Doctor, please help me.

DR. FARILL
What's going on here?

DIEGO
I told her she had to stay in bed. She demanded we call you.

FRIDA
I'm going to my exhibition.

LEFT: Recreating the bed for the opening and closing scenes in the film. INSET: Frida in her famous bed. Above, a mirror is attached to the canopy. ABOVE: Julie Taymor and composer Elliot Goldenthal.

DR. FARILL
Frida.

FRIDA
(near tears)
I've waited for a show in my own country my whole life. I'm not going to miss it.

Frida coughs violently.

DOCTOR
If the bronchitis gets worse, it will turn into pneumonia. Frida, under no circumstances are you to leave this bed.

Diego, trying to be cheerful, kisses her forehead.

DIEGO
I'll bring you back all the gossip. I promise.

Blinking back tears of frustration, Frida grips Diego for a moment. Then she releases him and watches as he pulls the doctor out of the room, concerned.

Frida lies quiet a moment. Then she turns to the door, calls.

FRIDA
Cristina!

153

Frida's Exhibition, 1953

In the spring of 1953, Lola Alvarez Bravo decided to organize an exhibition of Frida's paintings in her Galería Arte Contemporaneo at Amberes 12, in the city's fashionable Pink Zone. "They had just performed a bone transplant, and unfortunately, the bone was diseased and they had to remove it again," she recalled. "I realized that Frida's death was quite near. I think that honors should be given to people while they are still alive to enjoy them, not when they are dead." She proposed the idea to Diego. He was enthusiastic, and together they told Frida. "It was a very joyful announcement for her, and her health actually improved for a few days while she was planning and thinking about it. The doctors thought that she could not get any worse and that this might give her a boost."

The show was to be Frida Kahlo's first one-person exhibition in her native land, and to Frida, devastated by illness, it was a triumph.

Certainly it is true that Frida's presence turned the opening into a display of personal sentiment and emotion, rather than an artistic celebration. But if Frida had to perform to conceal her pain, this was the kind of performance that she loved—colorful, surprising, intensely human, and a little morbid, very like her theatrical self-presentation in her art.

Frida was amazed at the success of her exhibition. So was her gallery. Lola Alvarez Bravo recalls that "we received calls from Paris, London, and from several places in the U.S.A. asking us for details about Frida's exhibition... we were surprised that anyone outside Mexico should have heard of it." The gallery had to extend the show for a month because of popular demand, and the press loved it, extolling Frida's heroic presence at the opening as much as it admired her work....

In his autobiography, Diego remembered Frida's exhibition with pride and pleasure. "For me, the most thrilling event of 1953 was Frida's one-man show in Mexico City during the month of April. Anyone who attended it could not but marvel at her great talent. Even I was impressed when I saw all her work together." But he also recalled that at her opening, Frida hardly spoke: "I thought afterwards that she must have realized she was bidding goodbye to life."

—HAYDEN HERRERA, *FRIDA: A BIOGRAPHY OF FRIDA KAHLO*

INT. TRUCK - NIGHT

We are back where we started: on Frida's bed in the back of a truck. ON FRIDA—staring up. In the large MIRROR on the underside of the canopy's bed, Frida's reflection stares back at her. The woman in the mirror and the woman on the bed share a conspiratorial smile.

INT. GALERIA DE ARTE CONTEMPORANEO MEXICO CITY - NIGHT

A sea of people including many children. The walls are a panorama of Frida's life. A beautiful violent mix of color and images. A phenomenal collection of her work.

Diego stands before THE TWO FRIDAS. He addresses the crowd.

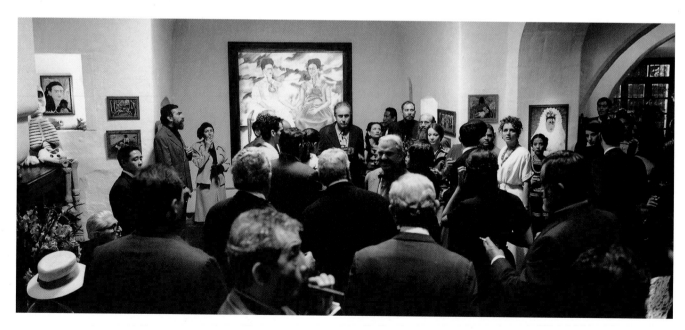

DIEGO
There was this skinny kid with these eyebrows, shouting up at me: "Diego, I want to show you my paintings." But, of course, she made me come down to look. I did and I've never stopped looking. But I want to speak about Frida not as her husband but as an artist... an admirer. Her work is acid and tender, hard as steel and fine as a butterfly's wing, lovable as a smile and cruel as the bitterness of life... I don't believe that ever before has a woman put such agonized poetry on canvas...

The room is utterly silent for a moment. Then:

FRIDA (O.S.)
Shut up, panzon! Who died?

Frida reclines on her canopied bed as it is carried into the gallery by the workmen.

FRIDA *(Cont'd)*
Where's the music?

Diego comes over to embrace Frida. People push to get closer. A Mariachi band starts to play La Llorona as the crowd joins in. Frida talks to Dr. Farill:

FRIDA *(Cont'd)*
You see, Doctorito, I followed your orders. I didn't leave my bed.

Everyone around her laughs. Lupe hands Frida a drink.

FRIDA
Aye, doctor, if you let me have this tequila, I promise not to drink at my funeral.

"Frida Kahlo and Mexican Art," by Diego Rivera

In the middle of the panorama of all the finest Mexican art produced over the last twenty years, like a diamond in the very center of a great jewel, clear and hard, precious and sharp, shines the painting of Frida Kahlo Calderón. . . . .

Frida is the only example in the history of art of a woman who tears open her womb and her heart to recount the biological truth of what she feels inside them.

—EXCERPT FROM AN ESSAY BY DIEGO RIVERA, ORIGINALLY PUBLISHED IN *BOLETÍN DEL SEMINARIO DE CULTURA MEXICANA*, OCTOBER 1943.

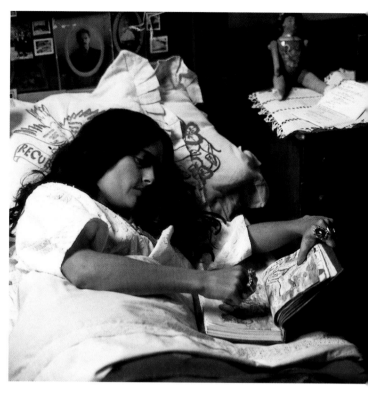

DOCTOR FARILL
It's a deal.

DIEGO
To Frida!

Everyone drinks. They all sing, Frida the loudest of all.

INT. BLUE HOUSE - FRIDA'S BEDROOM - NIGHT
An empty syringe is on the night table. Frida lies in bed working on a painting. She glows with fever.

Diego appears at the door.

DIEGO
Are you all right?

FRIDA
Lie down with me.

He comes and carefully moves her over. Spooning, they rest, cramped together, in silence. Frida digs her hand under the covers and pulls out a small gift-wrapped box. He looks at her then opens it—an antique gold ring.

FRIDA *(Cont'd)*
Twenty-five years together, my Dieguito.

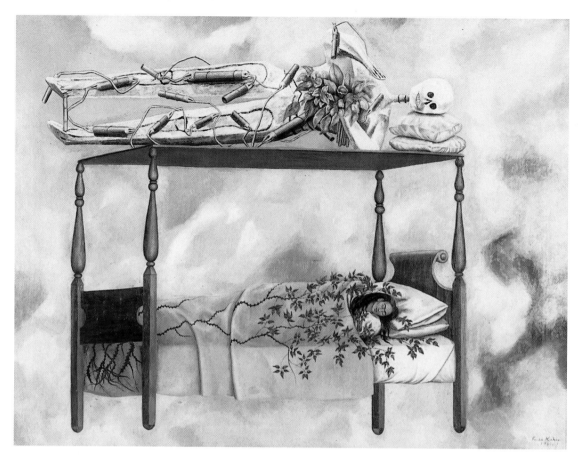

DIEGO
Frida.

FRIDA
Happy Silver.

DIEGO
It's not for two more weeks.

FRIDA
Seventeen days.

A long quiet beat. Diego buries himself into the back of Frida, holding her tight.

FADE TO BLACK

AN END CARD READS:

"I hope the exit is joyful. And I hope never to return."
—Frida

THE DREAM (3-D painting)—A sky of painted clouds. From the bottom of the frame, Frida appears in her four-poster, floating bed with the giant Judas skeleton laying on top of the canopy. The fireworks on the skeleton are ignited, setting the rest of the bed on fire in a joyous celebration. Frida looks up into the mirror above her, smiling, as the flames surround her face...

FADE OUT.

The Dream

The description of Frida's cremation haunted me as I began work on the film. It hadn't made its way into any version of the screenplay I had read and, no doubt, would have met with much resistance from the producers if it played out in a realistic manner; too gruesome for film reality. Yet I felt that her end needed the fire of her spirit and with that in mind I fastened upon her painting of *The Dream*. The image of the floating bed begins and ends the film. The reclining Judas skeleton hovering on the canopy of her bed, with its yet to be used fireworks, begged to be ignited. She would absolutely have a celebratory and joyful exit. And with that last little smile, at the end of a hand-painted animation sequence, we the filmmakers took liberty in creating a final image of Frida painted in the flames of her dream.

—JULIE TAYMOR, DIRECTOR

ABOVE: The Dream, 1940.

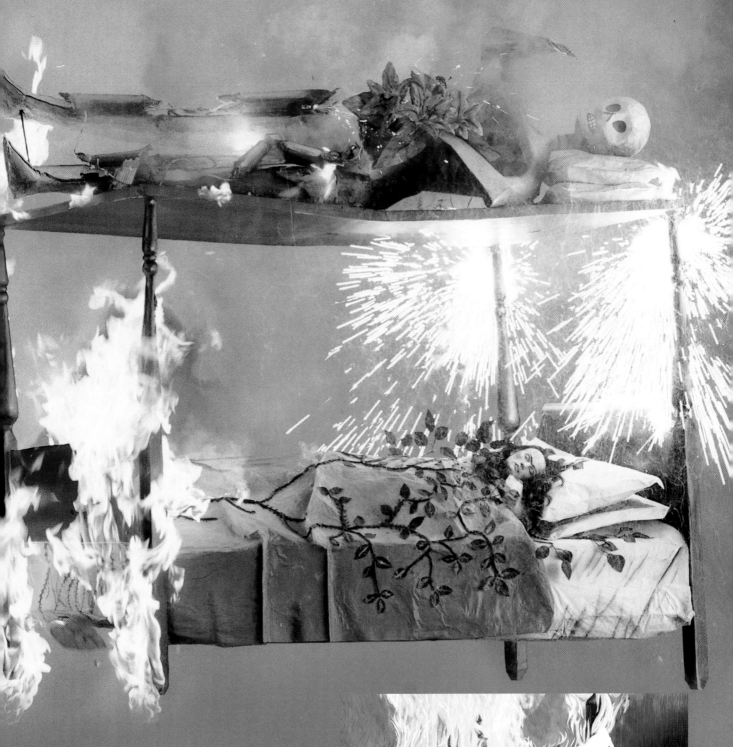

I hope the exit is joyful. And I hope never to return.

—FRIDA KAHLO'S LAST DIARY ENTRY

The Funeral

If Surrealism ever fit Frida, it applied to her funeral. Despite the rain hundreds of people crowded inside and outside the building where the cremation took place. Frida's coffin was open, showing red carnations around her head and a rebozo over her shoulders. After friends read speeches and poems and shared memories about her, Frida was taken out of the coffin by Diego and the family and placed onto a rolling cart, which would take her into the oven. Diego kissed Frida on the forehead, and everyone sang the song Frida had long ago whistled to Diego, the Communist "Internationale."

As the oven door opened, Frida's body moved slowly toward the fire as her friends sang songs of farewell. Stopping only when they felt the overwhelming heat of the fire, people cried and tried to take the rings off her fingers, just to keep something that belonged to her. As the cart hit the most intense heat, Frida's body suddenly sat up with blazing hair surrounding her face, looking, according to one witness, as though she were smiling in the center of a huge sunflower. She had left the world with a stunning image no one would ever forget.

—MALKA DRUCKER, *FRIDA KAHLO*

Frida: Myth and Cult Figure

In death Frida, too, is full of life. In recent years, she became first a myth and then a cult figure. In Mexico Frida is recognized as the country's greatest woman artist, and, in the opinion of many, Mexico's greatest artist. In 1984 the Mexican government decreed Frida Kahlo's work to be national patrimony, because it has "an unquestioned aesthetic value and has reached unanimous recognition within the national artistic community." For women everywhere, and especially for women artists, Frida is an example of persevering strength. She painted against great odds: she worked in a macho culture and in the heyday of muralism, when a woman making small, highly personal easel paintings did not win much respect. She was not discouraged by the enormous fame and ferocious artistic drive of her husband—she neither competed with nor deferred to him. And she kept on painting in spite of pain. To Mexican-Americans Frida is a political heroine; she demonstrated her love for la raza in her life and in her painting. To people who are ill, indeed to anyone oppressed by almost any sorrow, she offers hope. Her paintings are so powerful that people who look at them feel that Frida speaks directly and specifically to them. And for all her anguish, Frida Kahlo's final gift is the preeminence of joy. During the last terrible months she found the strength to write in her journal:

> I have achieved a lot.
> I will be able to walk
> I will be able to paint
> I love Diego more
> than I love myself.
> My will is great
> My will remains.

—HAYDEN HERRERA, *FRIDA KAHLO: THE PAINTINGS*

MIRAMAX FILMS PRESENTS IN ASSOCIATION WITH MARGARET ROSE PERENCHIO

A VENTANA ROSA PRODUCTION IN ASSOCIATION WITH LIONS GATE FILMS

A FILM BY JULIE TAYMOR

SALMA HAYEK as Frida Kahlo

ALFRED MOLINA as Diego Rivera

and GEOFFREY RUSH as Leon Trotsky

Frida

VALERIA GOLINO as Lupe Marín

MIA MAESTRO as Cristina Kahlo

ROGER REES as Guillermo Kahlo

CO-PRODUCED BY ANN RUARK

COSTUME DESIGNER JULIE WEISS

EDITED BY FRANÇOISE BONNOT, A.C.E.

PRODUCTION DESIGNER FELIPE FERNANDEZ

DIRECTOR OF PHOTOGRAPHY RODRIGO PRIETO

MUSIC BY ELLIOT GOLDENTHAL

EXECUTIVE PRODUCERS MARK AMIN, BRIAN GIBSON

EXECUTIVE PRODUCERS MARK GILL, JILL SOBEL MESSICK, AMY SLOTNICK

BASED ON THE BOOK BY HAYDEN HERRERA

SCREENPLAY BY CLANCY SIGAL AND DIANE LAKE AND GREGORY NAVA & ANNA THOMAS

PRODUCED BY JAY POLSTEIN, LIZZ SPEED, NANCY HARDIN, LINDSAY FLICKINGER, ROBERTO SNEIDER

PRODUCED BY SARAH GREEN, SALMA HAYEK

DIRECTED BY JULIE TAYMOR

About the Contributors

Director **JULIE TAYMOR** made her feature film directorial debut in 1999 with *Titus*, starring Anthony Hopkins and Jessica Lange. Based on Shakespeare's play *Titus Andronicus*, her adapted screenplay is published in an illustrated book by Newmarket Press.

Fool's Fire, Taymor's first film, which she both adapted and directed, is based on Edgar Allan Poe's short story "Hop-Frog." Produced by American Playhouse, it premiered at the Sundance Film Festival and aired on PBS in March 1992.

Taymor has received numerous awards for *The Lion King*, including Tonys for best direction of a musical and for her original costume designs. Taymor directed Carlo Gozzi's *The Green Bird* on Broadway in 2000, and her original visual music-theater work *Juan Darién: A Carnival Mass*, presented at the Lincoln Center in 1996, received five Tony nominations, including best director.

In September 1995, Taymor directed Wagner's *The Flying Dutchman* for the Los Angeles Music Center in a co-production with the Houston Grand Opera. She directed Strauss' *Salome* for the Kirov Opera in Russia, Germany and Israel, under the baton of Valery Gergiev. In June 1993, she directed Mozart's *The Magic Flute* for the Maggio Musicale in Florence, Zubin Mehta conducting.

Taymor's first opera direction was Stravinsky's *Oedipus Rex* for the Saito Kinen Orchestra in Japan, Sejji Ozawa conducting in 1992. Her film of the opera premiered at the Sundance Film Festival and won the Jury Award at the Montreal Festival of Films on Art.

Taymor's stage production of Shakespeare's *Titus Andronicus* was produced off-Broadway by Theatre for a New Audience in 1994. Other directing credits include *The Tempest*, *The Taming of the Shrew*, *The Transposed Heads* and *Liberty's Taken*.

In 1991, Taymor received a MacArthur "Genius" Fellowship. She has also received a Guggenheim Fellowship, two Obie Awards, the first annual Dorothy B. Chandler Award in Theater, and the 1990 Brandeis Creative Arts Award. A major retrospective of twenty-five years of Taymor's work opened in the fall of 1999 at the Wexner Center for the Arts in Ohio and toured the National Museum of Women in the Arts in Washington, D.C. and the Field Museum in Chicago.

About her decision to direct *Frida*, Taymor recalls: "I signed on to do this film based on the wonderful draft of the script by Rodrigo Garcia, and enormous credit must go to Edward Norton for his revisions, which made it all possible."

SALMA HAYEK has proven herself as a prolific producer and actress in both film and television. Most recently she completed work on Robert Rodriguez's *Once Upon a Time in Mexico*, the sequel to her star-making turn in *Desperado*, opposite Antonio Banderas. She is currently directing the film *The Maldonado Miracle*.

Hayek also starred in and produced the film *In the Time of the Butterflies* for Showtime. Hayek's company Ventanarosa also co-produced *No One Writes to the Colonel*, based on the novel by Nobel Prize winner Gabriel Garcia Marquez. Other film credits include *Dogma*, *Timecode*, *Wild Wild West*, *Fools Rush In*, *54*, and *From Dusk Till Dawn*.

Biographer/historian **HAYDEN HERRERA** has lectured widely, curated several exhibitions of art, taught Latin American art at New York University and has been awarded a Guggenheim Fellowship. She is the author of numerous articles and reviews for such publications as *Art in America*, *Art Forum*, *Connoisseur*, and *The New York Times*, among others. Her books include *Frida: A Biography of Frida Kahlo*, *Frida Kahlo: The Paintings*, *Mary Frank* and *Matisse: A Portrait*. She lives in New York City.

Photographer **PETER SOREL**, born in Hungary, has worked on close to 130 films with such directors as Robert Altman, Milos Forman, Steven Spielberg, Francis Ford Coppola, Warren Beatty, Kenneth Branagh, Ang Lee, David Lynch, Costa-Gavras, Tim Burton, Julie Taymor, David Fincher, Curtis Hanson and Paul Thomas Anderson. In 1995 Sorel and four colleagues formed the Society of Motion Picture Still Photographers (SMPSP), where he currently serves as vice president. He was given a lifetime achievement award by the Society of Operating Cameramen, and was decorated by the Hungarian Republic in 1996. Throughout his career, Sorel has used Kodak films, and on the still photography of *Frida*, Sorel used medium- and high-speed Portra emulsions from Eastman Kodak.

Publisher's Note

The publisher Esther Margolis wishes to thank the following for their special contributions to the creation of this book:

At Miramax Films: Mark Gill, Jason Cassidy, Robert A. Seidenberg, Eric Roth, Lori Sale, Heather Johnson, Alexis Hilton, Chris Brescia, Katy Zuker and Lisa Sandler. Also, Bob Allen, Ivan Bess, Mara Buxbaum, Jules Cazedessus, Michael Fisher, Lauda Flores, Elliot Goldenthal, Kathleen Green and Audrey Joncker at Kodak, Sarah Green, Anne Jump, Annie Leibovitz, Gabriel Navarrete Alcaraz, Jeff Robinson, Dan Schrecker at Amoeba Proteus, Hugh Van Dusen at HarperCollins, Julie Weiss, and at Newmarket Press, Frank DeMaio, Keith Hollaman, Shannon Berning, Kelli Taylor, Chris Cousino, Harry Burton and Heidi Sachner. And most of all, our project editor Linda Sunshine and designer Timothy Shaner, and, of course, the contributors Julie Taymor, Salma Hayek, Hayden Herrera and Peter Sorel.

Soundtrack on: